The Social Dimensions of AIDS

The Social Dimensions of AIDS: Method and Theory

Edited by

Douglas A. Feldman, Ph.D.
and Thomas M. Johnson, Ph.D.

PRAEGER

New York
Westport, Connecticut
London

Library of Congress Cataloging-in-Publication Data

The Social dimensions of AIDS.

"Praeger special studies.   Praeger scientific."
Includes bibliographies and index.
1. AIDS (Disease) — Social aspects.   I. Feldman,
Douglas A.   II. Johnson, Thomas M. (Thomas Malcolm),
1947-   . [DNLM: 1. Acquired Immunodeficiency Syndrome —
psychology.   2. Social Behavior. WD 303 S6776]
RC607.A26S63   1986   362.1'9697'92   86-9491
ISBN 0-275-92110-7 (alk. paper)

Library of Congress Catalog Card Number: 86-9491
ISBN: 0-275-92110-7

First published in 1986

Praeger Publishers, 521 Fifth Avenue, New York, NY 10175
A division of Greenwood Press, Inc.

Printed in the United States of America

The paper used in this book complies with the Permanent
Paper Standard issued by the National Information Standards
Organization (Z39.48-1984).

10 9 8 7 6 5 4 3 2 1

Preface

With so many excellent publications already on the market, why yet another AIDS book? This volume is actually quite different, since it is the first concerned primarily with the psychosocial and cultural dimensions of AIDS and the methodological dilemmas of conducting this kind of AIDS research. Fifteen original chapters, never before published, are presented by AIDS researchers from highly diverse backgrounds, including anthropology, sociology, psychology, social psychology, psychiatry, social work, public health and nursing. The underlying premise of the book is that an interdisciplinary approach to AIDS, which would include research specialists in the social and behavioral sciences, as well as researchers in the biomedical science, is essential for a comprehensive understanding of this tragic epidemic.

This book is not a collection of papers from a symposium. In November 1983, it became clear to us that a volume was needed to pull together the emerging ideas and beginning AIDS-related research projects of social and behavioral scientists. Actually, many of the research projects detailed in this volume were still underway or just beginning when we first started our search for quality papers and research. We are very pleased that the development of this volume has promoted and hastened important sociomedical research on AIDS. It is our hope that this work will spur other social and behavioral scientists to begin new AIDS research projects.

One of our initial doubts of producing a book on AIDS was that new information comes along so quickly, that by the time the book would be available, much of the data would need to be revised. For that reason, we have put the major emphasis of this volume on theoretical and conceptual issues in AIDS research. These theoretical and conceptual concerns are applicable to understanding the epidemiological, psychological, cultural and sociological variable in the emergence of any major epidemic.

We wish to thank Ms. Yolanda Rivera for her excellent typing skills, Ms. Diane Bolognone for her assistance with the index, Mr. George Zimmar and Ms. Dawn Barber of Praeger for their assistance and the late Ms. Sally Libin for her encouragement.

Douglas A. Feldman, Ph.D.
Thomas M. Johnson, Ph.D.
November, 1985

Contents

The Social Dimensions of AIDS

Introduction

Douglas A. Feldman and Thomas M. Johnson

With the advent of penicillin and antibiotics in the past few decades, developed nations have come to expect an increased mean life expectancy and an absence of uncontrollable plagues. For venereologists, the increase in the incidence of sexually transmissible diseases since the early 1960s contradicted the overall pattern of reduction in the kinds of epidemics that were common into the early part of this century. The incidence of syphilis, herpes, gonorrhea, chlamydia, hepatitis B. pelvic inflammatory disease, venereal warts, amebiasis, and giardiasis increased dramatically from the early 1960s to the early 1980s. Although acquired immune deficiency syndrome (AIDS) may appear to be anachronistic in an age in which modern medicine and hygienic practices have eliminated the devastating epidemics of previous centuries, to the astute venereologist AIDS is an almost inevitable consequence of the increase of sexually transmissible diseases.

AIDS, first noticed in a few homosexual (gay) men in New York City and California in mid-1981 (*MMWR* 1981a, 1981b), has grown to 14,393 Centers for Disease Control (CDC)-defined, reported cases in the United States by October 28, 1985 (CDC 1985b). 72.2% of all cases still occur in homosexual and bisexual men. Other high-risk patient groups include intravenous (IV) drug users (16.9%), hemophiliacs (0.8%), individuals who have had heterosexual contact with a person with AIDS or at risk for AIDS (1.0%), recipients of blood transfusions (1.8%), and children of a parent with AIDS or at increased risk for AIDS (1.1%). Individuals with AIDS, but with no known risk factors, excluding Haitians (2.5%), represent 3.7% of the total number of cases. The official death toll on October 28, 1985 stood at 7,418, or 52% of the total number of AIDS cases (CDC 1985b).

1

AIDS is a severely stigmatizing, lethal disease that puts at risk the health and survival of individuals in highly stigmatized populations (Kowalewski 1985). The fear of being revealed as an AIDS patient has contributed significantly to the underreporting of AIDS cases, and Caiazza (1985) estimates that there are 50% more cases than are reported (or a total of about 21,600 cases in October, 1985). Although the number of AIDS cases no longer nearly doubles every six months as it had until the first half of 1983, the number of cases in each six-month interval continues to climb dramatically. If the number of reported AIDS cases should continue to rise at the twelve-month rate of increase for 1984 of 131% (CDC 1985b), then the number of reported cases would increase tenfold to an estimated 50,000 cases in the United States at the end of 1987 and an estimated 115,000 cases by the end of 1988.

The demographic characteristics of people with AIDS in the United States have remained fairly stable (CDC 1985b). About half (47.0%) of all patients are in their thirties, with about as many in their twenties (21.0%) as in their forties (20.8%). Most (92.9%) are male. Blacks (25.2%) and Hispanics (14.3%) have a disproportionately higher rate of AIDS cases per population than do whites (59.3%).

The disease was first recognized in New York City, San Francisco, and Los Angeles, and these three cities continue to report over half of all AIDS cases in the U.S. (32.5%, 11.1%, and 8.4%, respectively). In spite of the continuing concentration of AIDS cases in these cities, the disease has rapidly spread into every state, Puerto Rico, and the District of Columbia. In the six-month interval from October 15, 1984 (CDC 1984) to April 15, 1985 (CDC 1985a), the rate of increase in the 19 states, commonwealths, or districts with 60 or more reported AIDS cases varied from a low of 31% in Florida to a high of 125% in Puerto Rico.

AIDS has become a worldwide phenomenon: it has been confirmed in North America (CDC 1985b; LeBlanc et al. 1983), Western Europe (*MMWR* 1985a), the Caribbean (Gorbea et al. 1985; Pape et al. 1985), Central Africa (Bayley 1984; Mann et al. 1985; Van de Perre et al. 1984), Australia (Gold, McGinness, and Vodicka 1985), and—to a lesser extent—in other areas (AIDS Center News 1984; Anderson et al. 1983; Wignall et al. 1985).

AIDS is defined by immunosuppression in previously healthy individuals, with an invasive, potentially lethal form of Kaposi's sarcoma, Burkitt-like lymphoma (Biggar et al. 1985; Chaganti et al, 1983), *Pneumocystis carinii* pneumonia, and other opportunistic infections including cryptosporidiosis, strongyloidosis, toxoplasmosis, candidiasis, cryptococcosis, mycobacteriosis, cytomegalovirus, herpes simplex virus, and progressive multifocal leukoencephalopathy (Gay Men's Health Crisis 1984). Symptoms include severe weight loss, profound fatigue, purplish or brownish lesions, persistent coughing, continual diarrhea, and high fever.

AIDS is often preceded by AIDS-related complex (ARC), a disorder characterized by persistent, generalized lymphadenopathy (i.e., swollen glands). Symptoms may include night sweats, profound fatigue, thrush, low-grade fever, weight loss, and (about as often as weight loss, because fatigue usually leads to inactivity) weight gain (*MMWR* 1982). Although ARC is not a notifiable (to the CDC) disease, an estimated ten ARC cases exist for every reported AIDS case (Abrams et al. 1985). Thus, by October 1985, an estimated 140,000 ARC cases could be found in the United States. In one longitudinal study (Mathur-Wagh et al. 1984), eight of forty-two (19%) people with ARC developed AIDS. The other thirty-four patients have remained stable or have improved. Abrams et al. (1985), however, have determined that the best predictor of AIDS among ARC patients is lymphadenopathy with thrush. Over half of all ARC patients in their sample with those two symptoms developed AIDS.

The economic impact of AIDS in the United States has been especially severe. A. Hardy et al. (1985) calculate the direct costs of hospitalization, outpatient costs, and insurance administration for 7,100 reported AIDS cases through November 1984 at $955 million. With nearly 100,000 years of potential life lost, the indirect costs of lost productivity through premaure death or disability total an additional minimum of $650 million.

But much more costly than these economic considerations are the sociocultural and psychological effects of this insidious epidemic on at-risk groups and individuals. The social and psychological stress, as well as the physical distress, have been enormous. For gay men, the fear of not knowing whether or not sex several years ago with a lover or partner will cause their untimely, painful death is difficult to live with. Every new sexual contact could be deadly. Every bout with a cold or flu could be a precursor to ARC. Every blemish could be a Kaposi's sarcoma lesion.

Curran (1985) estimates that one million people in the U.S., mostly gay men, are infected with lymphadenopathy-associated virus/human T-cell lymphotropic virus-type III (LAV/HTLV-III), which is believed to be the primary causal factor in AIDS transmission. The prevailing mood in the New York City gay community has become somber, at times bleak, occasionally morbid. There is a heightened feeling of being in the midst of a battlefield, as gay men read the obituaries, visit dying friends in hospitals, and experience personal anxiety and ambivalence when meeting someone new whom they are interested in. William M. Hoffman's Broadway play *As Is* captures the despair and poignancy of two friends and former lovers who discover that one of them has ARC, which progresses to AIDS. Larry Kramer's play *The Normal Heart*, although more political, captures the anguish of this monstrous epidemic.

Perhaps the most horrifying recent discovery is that the mean latency time from exposure to AIDS to diagnosis may be considerably longer than previously thought. Curran et al. (1984), in a study of transfusion-associated people with AIDS, determine that the observed mean is 26.6 months. However, Lawrence et al. (1985) indicate that relying only upon actual cases in a growing epidemic may result in substantial underestimation. They calculate an estimated mean latency time of nearly five years, with an upper limit of 77 months (i.e., about six-and-one-half years). The idea that one can contract a lethal disease from a "one-night stand" is chilling. The possibility that the AIDS epidemic has only barely begun is equally frightening.

The gay male community is, of course, not the only adversely affected population. Publicity about the occurrence of AIDS among Haitian-Americans has caused employment and housing discrimination againt them in the United States and a precipitous decline in tourism to Haiti. Hemophiliacs, transfusion patients, and IV-drug users remain fearful of AIDS. Children with AIDS have been abandoned by their parents and kept out of school. Hospital personnel who suffer needle-stick injuries with needles used for patients with AIDS undergo considerable stress.

Yet, in spite of this depressing situation, individuals and groups have risen above this adversity to volunteer their time, money, and labor in a wide variety of self-help organizations across the nation and internationally. The Gay Men's Health Crisis in New York, for example, had a 1984 operating budget of $800,000, 70% of which was raised through private donations within the gay community. The organization served 540 persons with AIDS or ARC and 200 family members or lovers in 1984 (Mark Chataway, personal communication. 1985).

With a vaccine and a cure both probably years away, little reason for much optimism can be found. But several new immunorestorative treatments, drugs, and a preventative gel are very promising. These include IMREG-1 (Gottlieb et al. 1985), Nonoxynol-9 (Fain 1985), Fansidar (D. Hardy et al. 1985; Wong et al. 1984). Ribavirin (McCormick et al. 1984), VePesid (etoposide) (*Oncology Times* 1985), weekly dosages of ICRF-159 (Volberding et al. 1985), suramin, inosine pranobex, phosphonoformate (*Lancet* 1984), and—perhaps most promising of all—isoprinosine (Blaun 1985).

From the very beginning of the AIDS crisis, research has been dominated by the biomedical community. After television and the other media "discovered" AIDS in May 1983, biomedical research and funding grew at a phenomenal rate. By April 1985, an AIDS conference in Atlanta, sponsored by the CDC and the World Health Organization, had over 3,000 participants, mostly physicians, attending from fifty countries (*MMWR* 1985b).

Research activity by social and behavioral scientists has been substantially less noticeable; fewer researchers and significantly fewer dollars are available to them. Indeed, only recently has there been a grudging acceptance on the part of some biomedical researchers that AIDS cannot fully be understood solely from a biomedical perspective; understanding requires additional input from social and behavioral scientists.

This volume introduces the reader to the pioneering sociocultural and psychosocial research on AIDS conducted by anthropologists, sociologists, psychologists, social psychologists, and others. There are three major areas in which social and behavioral scientific inquiry on AIDS is urgently needed.

1. Social Epidemiology: discovering the etiology, prevalence, cross-cultural variations in occurrence, and transmissibility of AIDS.
2. Basic Sociocultural and Psychosocial Research: documenting and understanding the dynamics of social and cultural change within affected high-risk populations and within the larger societal context in response to AIDS; and probing and delineating the psychological factors affecting individuals with AIDS or ARC or at risk for AIDS and ARC.
3. Intervention: developing and implementing programs for counseling people with AIDS or ARC; health promotion and education for high-risk individuals; and evaluating AIDS health-care delivery.

The 15 original papers in this volume have been grouped into six topics: AIDS social research strategies, social epidemiology, lifestyles and behavioral change, AIDS and the media, health beliefs and behavior, and the impact of AIDS on health care delivery. There has been very little published in the literature on AIDS social research methods. Siegel and Bauman ("Methodological Issues in AIDS-Related Research") discuss the major methodological problems of conducting AIDS social and behavioral research. AIDS research presents unique difficulties that require specialized research strategies. Zich and Temoshok ("Applied Methodology: A Primer of Pitfalls and Opportunities in AIDS Research"), in a question-and-answer format, show the reader how they have applied these research strategies within the University of California at San Francisco's Biopsychosocial AIDS Research Project, and AIDS sociobehavioral research organization.

Flam and Stein ("Behavior, Infection, and Immune Response: An Epidemiologic Approach") review the epidemiologic evidence for the transmissibility of AIDS. Although the dominant view today (November 1985) is that AIDS is caused primarily by LAV/HTLV-III or AIDS-associated retrovirus (ARV) (Kaminsky et al. 1985), there is growing widespread agreement that cofactors need to be present before the retrovirus can produce AIDS or ARC symptoms in an individual. Possible cofactors include cytomegalovirus (Drew et al. 1981), recreational nitrite drug use (Haverkos et al. 1985; Marmor et al. 1982), African Swine Fever Virus (Ortleb 1984), or acompanying immunosuppression through amebic and parasitic diseases (common in gay men, Haitians, and Central Africans), stress, or other lifestyle influences.

Alternate theories for the causality of AIDS range from the ludicrous notion that it is nothing more than mass hysteria (Schmidt 1984), to the fanciful view popular within the gay community in 1982 and 1983 that AIDS is an intentional Central Intelligence Agency plot to attack gays, Haitian-Americans, and IV-drug users (Kus 1984), to the questionable evidence from Belle Glade, Florida, that mosquitoes may be contributing to the spread of the virus from one individual to another (Whiteside et al. 1985).

The evidence clearly indicates that LAV/HTLV-III is not transmitted by casual social contact even within households (Fischl et al. 1985; Thomas et al. 1985). It is transmitted through heterosexual and homosexual intercourse, by needle-sharing by IV-drug users, by transfusion of contaminated blood and blood products, by infected mothers to their babies, and probably by repeated use of needles and other unsterile instruments used for piercing skin or mucous membranes (*MMWR* 1985).

The evidence is strong for a central African origin of AIDS (Bayley 1984; Bygbjerg 1983; Fettner 1985; *Lancet* 1973; Mann et al. 1985; Vandepitte et al. 1983; Wery-Paskoff et al. 1970). But Moore and Le Baron ("The Case for a Haitian Origin of the AIDS Epidemic") present equally convincing evidence for a Haitian origin of AIDS, which will undoubtedly intrigue the reader. Darrow, Gorman, and Glick ("The Social Origins of AIDS: Social Change, Sexual Behavior, and Disease Trends") demonstrate the ways in which the growth of the gay community and of international travel in the late 1970s and early 1980s permitted AIDS to spread rapidly throughout the United States and the world.

Relatively ignored in AIDS research has been the IV-drug user (Helquist 1985). Ginsburg et al. (1985) found that the awareness of AIDS mortality and morbidity rates among IV-drug users is higher in those communities in which AIDS is more common. Des Jarlais, Friedman, and Strug ("AIDS and Needle Sharing within the IV-Drug-Use Subculture") describe the lifestyle of IV-drug users and the ways in which AIDS may have a major impact upon their subculture.

The lifestyle of gay men has already been severely affected. Significant reductions in the mean frequency of sexual activity, the number of sexual partners, and the kinds of sexual behaviors engaged in have been documented in Chicago (Ostrow et al. 1985), Denver (Judson 1983; Judson and LeMaster 1985), Detroit (Joseph et al. 1985), San Francisco (McKusick et al. 1985), and Madison, Wisconsin (Golubjatnikov et al. 1983). In this volume Kotarba and Lang ("Gay Lifestyle Change and AIDS: Preventive Health Care") describe and analyze the pattern of behavioral change within the gay community of Houston and observe variations in the direction of such change. Feldman ("AIDS Health Promotion and Clinically Applied Anthropology") discusses behavioral change in the New York City gay community and utilizes a model originally developed during the anticigarette-smoking campaign of the 1960s in order to generate a health-promotion program for AIDS prevention.

Though some popular magazines were occasionally having articles about AIDS in 1982 and early 1983, most of the mass media (especially television, radio, and newspapers) did not "discover" AIDS until May 1983, two years after it was first reported in the medical literature. This discovery appears to have been prompted by a circus sponsored by the Gay Men's Health Crisis that sold out Madison Square Garden in New York City and by a candlelight march held by gay men and women lobbying for increased federal funding for AIDS research. Although the mass media involvement succeeded in releasing tens of millions of previously unavailable federal dollars for AIDS research, much of the reporting was sensationalistic, promoting widespread fear and even panic among the public.

Many undertakers refuse to go near deceased people with AIDS. Correction officers demand to wear masks and gloves when going near prisoners with AIDS. Some dentists (D'Eramo 1984), some physicians (see, e.g., Plumeri 1984), and other health-clinic and hospital personnel refuse to treat or handle people with AIDS. Albert ("Illness and Deviance: The Response of the Press to the AIDS") analyzes the role the print media has had on public attitudes toward AIDS. Baker ("The Portrayal of AIDS in the Media: An Analysis of Articles in the *New York Times*") conducts a content analysis of articles concerning AIDS in one major newspaper.

Public attitudes toward AIDS are shaped not only by the media, but also by previously held health beliefs. These beliefs and attitudes affect both social behavior and public policy. Even within the gay community no consensus of opinion can be found regarding several AIDS-related social issues. In San Francisco, gay bathhouses were ordered closed (Baker 1984; Crews 1984) and warning labels were put on nitrite drugs (DeStefano 1984), whereas in New York, Los Angeles, and San Diego the gay communities at that time rallied to keep their bathhouses open (Enlow 1984; Stadler 1985). There has also been considerable debate over the issue of whether gay men should take the HTLV-III test (Caiazza 1984; France 1985). Many are concerned that because the names of those individuals with positive test results would be reported to the Food and Drug Administration, this information could be used detrimentally by other federal agencies and perhaps even by private employers and insurance companies. Indeed, this fear may not be too absurd when one considers that Edward Brandt, the former Assistant Secretary of Health, said that "such extreme measures as a quarantine and mass firings of gays and other high-risk individuals from schools and hospitals has been seriously discussed within administration councils" (Talbot and Bush 1985:36).

Very little, if anything, had been published regarding health belief systems and health behavior in relation to AIDS. Casper ("AIDS: A

Psychosocial Perspective") discusses concepts of disease, physician/patient interaction, labeling theory, the sick role, and other psychosocial factors affecting Haitians and gay men. Bolognone and Johnson ("Explanatory Models for AIDS") utilize empirical data from their study of gay men and heterosexuals in Dallas to better understand the differing lay and professional explanatory models for AIDS and the implications of these models for AIDS public health affects. Callero, Baker, Carpenter, and Magarigal ("Fear of AIDS and Its Effects on the Nation's Blood Supply") examine the impact that the unfounded fear of contracting AIDS by donating blood may have upon the supply of blood in the United States.

The social and behavioral sciences have a potentially crucial role to play in understanding and assisting people with AIDS within various health-care settings. Geis and Fuller ("Hospice Staff Response to Fear of AIDS") describe some of the reactions to AIDS patients by caregivers at four Midwestern hospices. Lessor and Jurich ("Ideology and Politics in the Control of Contagion: The Social Organization of AIDS Care") discuss the social dynamics of health care in an AIDS ward at a large hospital.

There may be some understandable reluctance on the part of many social and behavioral scientists to become involved in AIDS research. However, the work is interesting and the need is urgent. Hopefully, this volume will encourage others to make the commitment and become so involved.

REFERENCES

Abrams, Donald I., T. P. Mess, and P. Volberding. 1985. Lymphadenopathy: Update of a Forty Month Prospective Study. Unpublished paper presented at International Conference on AIDS, Atlanta.

AIDS Center News. 1984. World Hemophilia AIDS Center: Survey Responses as of 25 September 1984. *AIDS Center News* 1(3), November.

Anderson, R., O. Prozesky, H. Eftychis, et al. 1983. Immunological Abnormalities in South African Homosexual Men. *South African Medical Journal* 64:119–122.

Baker, Ron. 1984. San Francisco Health Director Bans Sex in Bathhouses. *New York Native*. April 23–May 6; p. 6.

Bayley, A. C. 1984. Aggressive Kaposi's Sarcoma in Zambia, 1983. *Lancet* I(8390):1318–1320.

Biggar, R. J., J. Horm, J. Lubin, J. Goedert, M. Greene, and J. Fraumeni. 1985. Cancer Trends in a Population at Risk of AIDS: 1973–82. Unpublished paper presented at International Conference on AIDS, Atlanta.

Blaun, Randi. 1985, Insurance Against AIDS? *New York Magazine*. June 3; pp. 62–65.

Bygbjerg, I. C. 1983. AIDS in a Danish Surgeon (Zaire, 1976). *Lancet* I(8330): 925.

Caiazza, Stephen S. 1984. Why You Should Not Be Tested For HTLV-III. *New York Native.* October 8–21.

_____ . 1985. Comment on the Sally Jessy Raphael TV show, February.

Centers for Disease Control (CDC). 1984. Weekly Surveillance Report. October 15.

_____ . 1985a. Weekly Surveillance Report. April 15.

_____ . 1985b. Weekly Surveillance Report. October 28.

Chaganti, R. S. K., S. Jhanwar, B. Koziner, et al. 1983. Specific Translocations Characterize Burkitt's-Like Lymphoma of Homosexual Men with the Acquired Immunodeficiency Syndrome. *Blood* 61:1265–1268.

Crews, M. 1984. End Foreseen For San Francisco Bathhouses. *New York Native.* September 24–October 7.

Curran, James W. 1985. The Epidemiology and Prevention of AIDS. Talk given at International Conference on AIDS, Atlanta.

Curran, James W., D. Lawrence, H. Jaffe, J. Kaplan, L. Zyla, M. Chamberland, R. Weinstein, K. Lui, L. Schonberger, T. Spira, W. Alexander, G. Swinger, A. Amman, S. Solomon, D. Auerbach, D. Mildvan, R. Stoneburner, J. Jason, H. Haverkos, and B. Evatt. 1984. Acquired Immunodeficiency Syndrome (AIDS) Associated with Transfusions, *New England Journal of Medicine* 310:69–75, January 12.

D'Eramo, James E. 1984. Dentists Refuse to Treat AIDS Patients and Gay Men: State Issues New Dental Guidelines. *New York Native.* January 30–February 12.

DeStefano, George. 1984. San Francisco Supervisors Curb Poppers. *New York Native.* January 2–15.

Drew, W. Lawrence, L. Mintz, R. Miner, M. Sands, and B. Ketterer. 1981. Prevalence of Cytomegalovirus Infection in Homosexual Men. *Journal of Infectious Diseases* 143:188–192.

Enlow, Roger W. 1984. Hands Off Baths. *New York Native.* June 4–17.

Fain, Nathan. 1985. Dr. Voeller's Magic Lube: Will This Gel Make Sex Safe Again? *Village Voice.* February 19, p. 50.

Fettner, Ann Guidici. 1985. Flash Point: A Safari into the Origins of AIDS. *New York Native.* April 8–21, pp. 29–35, 58.

Fischl, Margaret A., G. Dickinson, C. Scott, N. Klimas, M. Fletcher, and W. Parks. 1985. Evaluation of Household Contacts of Adult Patients with the Acquired Immunodeficiency Syndrome. Unpublished paper presented at International Conference on AIDS, Atlanta.

France, David. 1985. HTLV-III Test Licensing Postponed: Controversy Over Effects of Test Reaches New Height. *New York Native.* February 25–March 10, p. 10.

Gay Men's Health Crisis (GMHC). 1984. Health Letter/3. *GMHC.* May.

Ginsburg, Harold M., M. Rose, and S. Weiss. 1985. Educating Parenteral Drug Users about AIDS. Unpublished paper presented at International Conference on AIDS, Atlanta.

Gold, J., S. McGinness, and P. Vodicka. 1985. AIDS in Australia. Unpublished paper presented at International Conference on AIDS, Atlanta.

Golubjatnikov, R., J. Pfister, and T. Tillotson. 1983. Homosexual Promiscuity and and the Fear of AIDS. *Lancet* II:681.

Gorbea, H. F., Y. Kouri, C. Ramirez-Ronda, J. Rodriguez, E. Frankhanel, and J. Garib. 1985. Epidemiological Aspects of AIDS Cases From Puerto Rico. Unpublished paper presented at International Conference on AIDS, Atlanta.

Gottlieb, A. Arthur, J. Farmer, A. Levine, P. Gill, M. Flaum, and M. Gottlieb. 1985. Reconstitution of T-Cell Function in AIDS and ARC Patients by Use of the Endogenous, Leukocyte-Derived Immunomodulator, IMREG-1. Unpublished paper presented at International Conference on AIDS, Atlanta.

Hardy, Ann M., K. Rausch, and J. Curran. 1985. The Economic Impact of AIDS in the United States. Unpublished paper presented at International Conference on AIDS, Atlanta.

Hardy, David, P. Wolfe, M. Gottlieb, S. Knight, R. Mitsuyasu, and L. Young. 1985. Fansidar Prophylaxis for *Pneumocystis carinii* Pneumonia (PCP). Unpublished paper presented at International Conference on AIDS, Atlanta.

Haverkos, Harry W., P. Pinsky, D. Drotman, and D. Bregman. 1985. Disease Manifestation Among Homosexual Men with Acquired Immunodeficiency Syndrome (AIDS): A Possible Role of Nitrites in Kaposi's Sarcoma. Unpublished paper presented at International Conference on AIDS, Atlanta.

Helquist, Michael. 1985. I.V. Drug Users: The Neglected Risk Group. *Connection* January 17–30.

Joseph, Jill G., C. Emmons, R. Kessler, D. Ostrow, and K. O'Brien. 1985. Changes in Sexual Behavior of Gay Men: Relationship to Perceived Stress and Psychological Symptomology. Unpublished paper presented at International Conference on AIDS, Atlanta.

Judson, F. N. 1983. Fear of AIDS and Gonorrhea Rates in Homosexual Men. *Lancet* II:159–160.

Judson, F. N., and F. LeMaster. 1985. Fear of AIDS and Rates of Gonorrhea in Denver, CO. Unpublished paper presented at International Conference on AIDS, Atlanta.

Kaminsky, Lawrence S., C. Foxall, and J. Levy. 1985. Serological Evidence Linking the AIDS-Associated Retroviruses (ARV) to AIDS and Related Conditions in the United States. Unpublished paper presented at International Conference on AIDS, Atlanta.

Kowalewski, Mark R. 1985. Lepers in Our Midst: a Stigmatized Community Deals With Trouble from Within. Unpublished manuscript.

Kus, Robert J. 1984. AIDS as Planned Genocide: a Gay Ethnotheory. Unpublished manuscript.

Lancet. 1973. Kaposi's Sarcoma, *Lancet* I(798):300–301.

_____ . 1984. Blood Transfusion, Haemophilia, and AIDS. *Lancet* II:1433–1435.

Lawrence, Dale N., K. Lui, D. Bregman, T. Peterman, and W. Morgan. 1985. A Model-Based Estimate of the Average Incubation and Latency Period for Transfusion-Associated AIDS. Unpublished paper presented at International Conference on AIDS, Atlanta.

LeBlanc, R. P., M. Simard, K. Flegel, and N. Gilmore. 1983. Opportunistic Infections and Acquired Cellular Immune Deficiency Among Haitain Immigrants in Montreal. *Canadian Medical Association Journal* 129:1205–1209.

Mann, Jonathan M., R. Ruti, H. Francis, B. Kapita, T. Quinn, and J. Curran. 1985. AIDS Surveillance in a Central African City: Kinshasa, Zaire. Unpublished paper presented at International Conference on AIDS, Atlanta.

Marmor, M., A. Friedman-Kien, L. Laubenstein, et al. 1982. Risk Factors for Kaposi's Sarcoma in Homosexual Men. *Lancet* I:1083–1086.

Mathur-Wagh, U., R. Enlow, I. Spigland, et al. 1984. Longitudinal Study of Persistent Generalized Lymphadenopathy in Homosexual Men: Relation to Acquired Immunodeficiency Syndrome. *Lancet* I:1033–1038.

McCormick, Joseph B., S. Mitchell, J. Getchell, and D. Hicks. 1984. Ribavirin Suppresses Replication of Lymphadenopathy-Associated Virus in Cultures of Human Adult T Lymphocytes. *Lancet* II:1367–1369.

McKusick, Leon, T. Coates, R. Stahl, G. Saika, M. Conant, and J. Wiley. 1985. Stability and Change in Gay Sex: The Case of San Francisco. Unpublished paper presented at International Conference on AIDS, Atlanta.

Morbidity and Mortality Weekly Report (MMWR). 1981a. Pneumocystis Pneumonia—Los Angeles. *MMWR* 30:250–252, June 5.

––––––. 1981b. Kaposi's Sarcoma and Pneumocystis Pneumonia among Homosexual Men—New York City and California. *MMWR* 30:305–308, July 3.

––––––. 1982. Persistent, Generalized Lymphadenopathy among Homosexual Males. *MMWR* 31:249–252, May 21.

––––––. 1985a. Update: Acquired Immunodeficiency Syndrome—Europe. *MMWR* 32:21–22, 28–31, January 18.

––––––. 1985b. World Health Organization Workshop: Conclusion and Recommendations on Acquired Immunodeficiency Syndrome. *MMWR* 34:275–276, May 17.

Oncology Times. 1985. OT Briefs. *Oncology Times*. February, pp. 34–35.

Ortleb, Charles L. 1984. Editorial. *New York Native*. January 30–February 12, pp. 3, 11.

Ostrow, David G., C. Emmons, N. Altman, J. Joseph, J. Phair, and J. Chmiel. 1985. Sexual Behavior Change and Persistence in Homosexual Men. Unpublished paper presented at International Conference on AIDS, Atlanta.

Pape, J., B. Liautaud, F. Thomas, M. Boncy, J. Dehovitz, W. Johnson, et al. 1985. AIDS in Haiti. Unpublished paper presented at International Conference on AIDS, Atlanta.

Plumeri, P. A. 1984. The Refusal to Treat: Abandonment and AIDS. *Journal of Clinical Gastroenterology* 6:281–284.

Schmidt, Casper G. 1984. The Group-Fantasy Origins of AIDS. *Journal of Psychohistory* 12(1):37–78.

Stadler, Matthew. 1985. National News. *New York Native*. February 25–March 10, p. 7.

Talbot, David and L. Bush. 1985. At Risk. *Mother Jones Magazine*. April, pp. 28–37.

Thomas, Pauline A., K. Lubin, R. Enlow, and J. Getchell. 1985. Comparison of HTLV-III Serology, T-Cell Levels, and General Health Status of Children Whose Mothers Have AIDS with Children of Healthy Inner City Mothers in New York. Unpublished paper presented at International Conference on AIDS, Atlanta.

Van de Perre, Philippe, D. Rouvroy, P. Lepage, J. Bogaerts, P. Kestelyn, J. Kayihigi, A. Hekker, J. Butzler, and N. Clumeck. 1984. Acquired Immunodeficiency Syndrome in Rwanda. *Lancet* 2(8394):62–65.

Vandepitte, J., R. Verwilghen, and P. Zachee. 1983. AIDS and Cryptococcosis (Zaire 1977). *Lancet* 1(8330):925–926.

Volberding, Paul A., D. Abrams, L. Kaplan, M. Conant, and G. Carr. 1985. Therapy of AIDS-Related Kaposi's Sarcoma (KS) with ICRF-159. Unpublished paper presented at International Conference on AIDS, Atlanta.

Wery-Paskoff, S., K. Maertens, H. Helsen, and F. Gatti. 1970. Contribution a L'étude de la Toxoplasmose à Kinshasa. *Annales de la Société Belge de Medicine Tropicale* 50:703–710.

Whiteside, Mark E., D. Withum, D. Tavris, and C. Macleod. 1985. Outbreak of No Identifiable Risk Acquired Immunodeficiency Syndrome (AIDS) in Belle Glade, Florida. Unpublished paper presented at International Conference on AIDS, Atlanta.

Wignall, F. Stephen, W. Reeves, R. deBritton, J. Clark, C. Saxinger, Z. Salahoudin, et al. 1985. Epidemiology of HTLV-III Infections in Panamanian High Risk Populations. Unpublished paper presented at International Conference on AIDS, Atlanta.

Wong, B., J. Gold, A. Brown, et al. 1984. Central-Nervous-System Toxoplasmosis in Homosexual and Parenteral Drug Abusers. *Annals of Internal Medicine* 100:36–42.

PART I
AIDS SOCIAL RESEARCH STRATEGIES

Chapter One

Methodological Issues in AIDS-Related Research

Karolynn Siegel and Laurie J. Bauman

Social scientists face considerable challenges in designing valid research studies. A great many factors can introduce error into social science data, and few of these are under the researcher's direct control. The AIDS epidemic represents a particularly formidable challenge to the social science enterprise, for this complex and tragic phenomenon presents a great many obstacles to the conduct of social research and the collection of quality data. In this paper we will identify and discuss some of the principal methodological issues social science researchers of AIDS will confront. Based on our own experience of trying to solve some of these problems, as well as the existing body of empirical research on survey methodology, we shall try to outline alternative solutions to these problems—each inevitably representing various tradeoffs.

In the discussion that follows, our observations are primarily concerned with research in which the subjects are homosexual (gay) or bisexual people with AIDS. We are also assuming that in many of the studies likely to be undertaken of the AIDS population, comparison or "control" groups composed of people with AIDS-related complex (ARC) and/or "healthy" (i.e., asymptomatic with respect to AIDS) homosexuals will be included in the design. Therefore, some of our remarks relate to these populations as well.

SAMPLING ERROR AND REFUSAL RATE

Sampling problems are likely to occur in any study that includes people with AIDS, those at risk for AIDS, and asymptomatic homosexuals. The sources of these problems can be divided into two groups: 1) those related to the identification and selection of eligible respondents, and 2) those related to patterns of cooperation and refusal to participate.

Defining the Populations: AIDS, Prodromal Syndromes, and Homosexuals/Gays

In order to identify eligible subjects for a research study of people with AIDS, it is necessary to adopt a set of classificatory criteria of AIDS. One option—the one usually chosen in social research on patient population—is to rely on medical criteria to define eligibility. Although such an approach has the appeal of apparent objectivity and precision, not all physicians or researchers classify cases the same way. Although the Centers for Disease Control (CDC) in Atlanta have developed a case definition of AIDS, problems of classification remain. In some instances, dissatisfaction with the CDC definition has led to the development of alternative AIDS criteria (Ma and Armstrong 1984). Even when the CDC definition is accepted, sufficient clinical judgment is involved in applying the criteria such that physicians may differ in their determination of individual cases. These problems of classification mean that samples of people with AIDS who are referred to a research study from different sources will probably contain some degree of heterogeneity and interstudy comparisons may be problematic.

The discrepancies within the medical profession in classifying AIDS cases may in part be due to varying research considerations. However, because AIDS is regarded as a critical public health problem, decisions concerning whether to use more inclusive or more restrictive criteria in classifying AIDS cases could be influenced by political considerations. The greater the number of AIDS cases diagnosed, the more important the problem will be perceived to be by those allocating public funds for research, patient care, and support services. The greater the perceived seriousness of the problem and the larger the number of people affected, the more resources are likely to be directed toward this population. Generally speaking, more public funds will be allocated to researching and treating a disease if it qualifies or is perceived as an "epidemic." An awareness of these circumstances could create a motivation on the part of those involved in research and patient care to adopt more inclusive diagnostic criteria.

Ambiguity concerning the criteria for the identification of AIDS cases has other implications. From a medical point of view, cases manifesting prodromal syndromes and cases meeting the CDC's formal criteria for classification as AIDS may simply represent vaguely differentiated points on a continuum. From a social science perspective, however, the patients at different points on the continuum may occupy significantly different statuses that have profoundly different social and psychological ramifications.

What we are suggesting is that individuals' subjective senses of illness or well-being in relation to AIDS may be critical factors in defining the population. For the purposes of social science research, the social reality may be as important as the medical reality. For example, if the study objective was to assess the impact of the diagnosis of AIDS on an individual's psychological and social status, then what he had been told concerning his diagnosis would be as important as his medical status. If, for whatever reason, his physican had chosen not to use the term "AIDS" in talking with a patient, the researcher might consider eliminating that patient from the sampling frame. Such patients would not have been required to accept the self-definiton of "a person with AIDS" and with its inevitable accompanying psychological changes. In addition, because the labeling process had not occurred, the social reactions from others that usually result from being assigned such a label may not have been set in motion. Or, conversely, suppose the purpose of the study was to describe the extent and kinds of discrimination experienced by those with AIDS. In this instance, there will be some gay men who will be erroneously assumed by family, friends, or colleagues to have AIDS. Despite the fact that this perception is mistaken, these men will experience the same kinds of discrimination as will those diagnosed with the disease.

A further consideration in defining suitability for a social science study of AIDS patients is that some individuals will psychologically defend themselves against the emotional threat of a diagnosis of AIDS by denying it and not accepting the label. This denial may also be manifested by those diagnosed with AIDS-related complex (ARC). The loss from the study sample of people who deny their diagnoses may not represent a serious problem for medical research because there is no reason to believe that these people are significantly different as medical entities from those who do acknowledge the diagnoses. On the other hand, their omission in studies of the social or psychological sequelae of a diagnosis of AIDS or ARC may significantly bias the sample and therefore the generalizability of the study findings. More specifically, the absence of such cases might result in an underrepresentation of individuals with the more extreme psychological reactions to the diagnosis of the illness. One way to avoid the loss of these cases is to present the study inclusion criteria to potential subjects in more ambiguous (i.e., less threatening) terms that permit them to define themselves as eligible without having to accept the diagnosis and label as an AIDS or ARC patient.

If the study design includes a comparison or control group of "healthy" or "asymptomatic" homosexuals, similar problems of case definition emerge. "Healthy" or "asymptomatic" in this context refers to the absence of a symptom constellation that has been shown to be associated with AIDS or a prodromal condition. It is difficult, however, to draw sharp lines delineating groups. Because many of the symptoms associated with AIDS and ARC are similar to those associated with other illnesses and infections common among gay males (e.g., sexually transmitted diseases), it may be difficult to determine if the individual is asymptomatic with respect to AIDS or a pre-AIDS condition. There is also a lack of consensus among medical researchers concerning the medical criteria for diagnosing cases of ARC. Depending on how these criteria are manifested, different samples of cases could be classified as eligible or ineligible.

Social science researchers who have studied homosexuality in the past have usually relied on the subjects to identify themselves as eligible subjects (see, for example, Bell and Weinberg 1978; Bell et al 1981). But these studies document a great diversity in sexual practices among those who identify themselves as homosexual. The spectrum includes those who define themselves as exclusively homosexual at one end, to those who are predominantly heterosexual with only sporadic or insignificant homosexual behavior at the other end. Depending on the research objectives, one may want to sample only from certain segments of this continuum. Earlier research (Bell and Weinberg 1978; Kinsey et al. 1953) has also revealed that the bases by which individuals place themselves on this continuum may vary. For some it will be predicated on actual behavior, for others on their fantasies or dreams, the extent to which they feel sexually responsive to people of the same or opposite sex, or the extent to which homosexual thoughts, feelings, or actions are ego-syntonic.

Further, the researcher may decide to define an individual as homosexual or gay using criteria other than merely a pattern of sexual behavior. Indeed, some critics of research on homosexuality have charged that insufficient attention has been given to the nonsexual aspects of homosexuality. Eligibility requirements may therefore include, in addition to engaging in gay sexual practices, participating in a certain lifestyle or holding a set of values and attitudes that are associated with the subculture, In some instances even these criteria would be insufficient. For example, if the focus of the research was the impact of the AIDS epidemic on the extent and kinds of discrimination all homosexuals suffer, then defining acceptable people solely on the basis of the sexual practices they engage in would not be adequate. It would also be necessary that their sexual orientation not be concealed from the public.

In many studies of AIDS patients, the design will include comparison groups of healthy homosexuals who also represent the full spectrum of homosexual orientation. The problems of trying to sample from this population are many and have plagued earlier studies of homosexuals. Eligible people are statistically relatively rare and usually dispersed. Many have not publicly identified themselves as homosexual or openly participated in a gay lifestyle. Because an unknown proportion of the homosexual population remains hidden or "in the closet," they cannot be enumerated or sampled directly. Furthermore, the extent of the sampling bias created by this problem cannot be evaluated, because no data exist on the characteristics of the total population.

Recruitment, Cooperation, and Refusals

Most previous research of homosexuals has had to rely on recruiting techniques such as public appeals and advertisements in gay and other newspapers, approaching individuals in gay establishments, and obtaining mailing lists from homophile organizations in order to select eligible cases. Clearly, however, with the exception of public appeals in nongay media, all other sources of referrals would tend to overrepresent individuals who openly engage in a gay lifestyle and underrepresent those who actively attempt to conceal their homosexual behavior.

Few strategies exist for significantly increasing the representation of covert or "closet" homosexuals in the study sample. The principal one is to place advertisements in nongay publications and to emphasize two things in the ads: 1) the importance to the study's success of including such generally understudied members of the subculture; and 2) the promise of strict confidentiality. The perceived importance of the study's purpose will be a major determinant in whether individuals are willing to risk self-disclosure to the researchers.

Another strategy is to adopt snowball sampling, in which the researcher asks subjects who are hard to identify or locate to refer others like themselves to the study. One would try to recruit a small core of gay individuals who conceal their sexual orientation and do not participate in gay organizations or groups or frequent gay establishments. These individuals may be aware of other covert homosexuals who engage in a surreptitious lifestyle and could be asked to recruit them for the study.

Snowball sampling can also be used to obtain a community sample of all homosexuals—including those engaging in both overt and covert lifestyles. Some researchers resort to this strategy because it tends to be relatively inexpensive. Because a complete sampling frame cannot be constructed, however, they recognize the impossibility of obtaining a truly random sample. Limited resources may sometimes dictate such a sampling strategy, but snowball sampling usually yields several kinds of biases including: 1) undersampling socially isolated members of the population; 2) bias in the socioeconomic characteristics of the sample, because better-educated, higher-income individuals tend to have more extensive social networks; 3) undersampling deviant members of the group; and 4) bias due to the tendency of people to associate primarily with others with social characteristics similar to their own (Welch 1975).

Beyond the constraints on achieving a representative sample is the problem of subject cooperation. Systematic bias can be introduced into a study if refusal rates tend to be higher in certain subgroups within the research population. The reasons for participation in research studies can be grouped into three broad categories: 1) intrinsic satisfaction (enjoying acting in the expert role; pleasure in the interviewer-respondent interaction); 2) instrumental benefit (immediate concrete benefit such as information, counseling, free medical care, or monetary payments); and 3) altruism (the desire to help others or the holding of a generalized value of the importance of contributing to scientific research). Several specific factors can influence cooperation in social research on AIDS: the patient's physical condition, his previous experience with research studies, the sponsorship of the research, and the degree to which the questions are anticipated to be threatening or sensitive.

In research involving patient-subjects, variation in the physical and mental capacities of subjects to complete lengthy survey interviews is one source of bias. The more seriously ill the subject is, the less energy and ability he will have to provide adequate responses and the less complete and less accurate the data are likely to be. People with AIDS experience a number of debilitating symptoms (including persistent fatigue and periodic fevers), and there is a strong likelihood that such patients will be less able to participate in social science studies.

Another source of special concern to AIDS researchers is the problem of the small size of the population under study—a population that is often approached by two or more researchers for participation in different studies. The emergence of AIDS—a new, communicable, deadly disease—is a dramatic phenomenon. For scientific, humanitarian, and in some instances opportunistic reasons, many scientists have been drawn to researching its origins, treatment, and consequences.

There is a relatively small pool of patients to draw from and a large number of studies seeking subjects. It is in the interest of most AIDS patients to help medical researchers pursue as many leads as possible, but social research may be perceived as less important. If subjects feel that social researchers are asking them to provide redundant information or if they in any way felt "exploited" by earlier investigators, their willingness to participate in subsequent studies is likely to decline. It is, therefore, in the interests of all researchers to combine their data-gathering efforts whenever possible. It is their ethical obligation, as well, to protect research subjects from excessive respondent burden.

Participation by the same subjects in several different studies has implications beyond those of reduced cooperation rates. When subjects participate in different studies addressing related topics, responses to items in later studies may be influenced by participation in earlier studies. Preceding studies may have caused these items to take on a heightened salience (as an artifact of earlier questioning). This may contaminate the measurement of feelings or attitudes, which may change due to repeated probing and possible rethinking of the issues. In some instances, however, the later studies benefit if respondents' accuracy in reporting of events is improved through earlier stimulation of memory or insight.

The sponsorship of a research study is also likely to affect cooperation rates, because different auspices may elicit different motivations for participating. Because these varied motivations may be associated with particular personality or social characteristics, each kind of sponsorship may attract the disproportionate cooperation of certain subgroups of the population under study. For example, research carried out under the auspices of a major medical research center or institute, such as the Centers for Disease Control (CDC), is likely to secure the participation of individuals who place a high value on medical research and its potential to develop effective treatments or care. The expectation of immediate or direct personal gain from their participation may be less important to these individuals than would be contributing to the ultimate goals of saving lives in the future.

Research carried out under the auspices of the hospital at which subjects with AIDS are being treated is likely to evoke very different motivations. The subject's perception that he is dependent upon the institution for care may cause him to feel compelled to cooperate in the research endeavor. Despite the fact that the researchers are obliged, both ethically and legally, to assure the potential subject that a decision not to participate will in no manner influence the medical care he receives, a patient subject may feel that nonparticipation will have unfavorable consequences and will adversely affect the staff's attitude toward him.

This raises an important ethical issue regarding the extent to which participation under these conditions is truly voluntary. It highlights the importance of providing meaningful assurances to the patient that should he decline to participate, he can feel assured that his medical care will not be affected in any way. Such assurances will be more readily accepted if it can also be honestly represented that even the patient's decision concerning participation will not be disclosed to his physician or the medical staff involved in his care.

Medical researchers are often required as part of informed consent procedures to explain to patients that although their participation in the study may lead to benefits for others, the patients themselves will probably not benefit directly. Nevertheless, we have found patients frequently continue to hope that in some way the finding will improve their own prognosis and outcome. Hospital-sponsored research may profit from this hope of potential personal gain, because that hope creates an important incentive for cooperation. Although such hope is not necessarily undesirable (it may even help forstall an overwhelming sense of despair and hopelessness), the research should not instill false expectations of personal benefit in order to obtain a research sample.

Other positive motivations to participate can also be stimulated when the research is being conducted under the auspices of a medical center at which AIDS patients are being treated. Patients who are satisfied with the quality of their medical care often welcome the opportunity to "give something back" or in some way to "pay back" their caretakers for the help they have received. These individuals are generally quite willing to cooperate in research, even though they recognize that it may provide no direct or immediate benefit to themselves. At our cancer center (Memorial Sloan-Kettering) this is a widely observed phenomenon.

Research on AIDS carried out under the auspices of a gay organization would appeal to still other motivations. In this case, subjects might be inclined to participate because they would expect the researchers to be fair, sympathetic to their plight, and accepting of their lifestyle. Because such organizations are advocates of the interests of the gay community, subjects are more likely to assume that even though they as individuals might not profit from participating, at least some members of their community would be beneficiaries of the research.

When social research is conducted by researchers affiliated with a university, subjects' motivations for participation are less easy to discern. Research as a quest for greater knowledge or understanding may not be perceived as an end in itself sufficient to stimulate participation, especially when the study deals with sensitive topics. Additionally, individuals asked to be study subjects by university professors sometimes feel that the research primarily serves the interests of the researchers by providing the basis for books, articles, and professional presentations. Unless eligible study subjects are able to discern from their participation some benefit for themselves or others, they may not be highly motivated to take part in such research.

Finally, cooperation rates for social science studies on AIDS may be affected by the potentially threatening or embarrassing nature of the data collected, as well as by respondents' fears that their homosexuality or the diagnosis of AIDS will become public. It is particularly important, then, for researchers to assure potential respondents that they, as scientists, make no negative value judgments about the sexual practices or preferences of the subject and that the respondents' participation in, and answers to, the research will be kept strictly confidential (Kinsey et al. 1953:41). Sufficient guarantees must be offered to justify the risks to self-esteem inherent in intimate self-revelations or the loss of social status that might result if confidentiality were compromised.

RESPONSE VALIDITY: ISSUES AND TECHNIQUES

Many threats to the validity of survey data exist, and several models have been developed to systematically describe the possible factors associated with nonrandom response bias (Bradburn et al. 1981; Cahalan 1968; Summers 1969). The following discussion draws most heavily from the model posited by Cannell and Kahn (1968).

Respondents' Accessibility to Information

The accuracy of information requested of a respondent depends in part on the degree to which the information is in his possession. Memory declines as a function of time (Cannell and Kahn 1968:541) and people simply forget a great deal of behavior and factual information they may have known earlier. Memory is also a function of the salience of the information requested. Thus, important, threatening, or unusual events or actions are more easily remembered than habitual, routine behavior or insignificant occurrences. If, however, the material under study is extremely threatening or distressing, some respondents may repress events so that they genuinely cannot consciously recall the requested information. And finally, some studies may ask respondents for information they simply don't have (e.g., in instances in which a "proxy" respondent is used to report on the behavior or attitudes of others) (Cannell and Fowler 1963).

In social research on AIDS patients, key pieces of information may not be available from respondents simply because of memory loss or selective recall. For example, social and psychological research on this population will sometimes address past (prediagnosis) sexual behavior and psychological states in order to evaluate the impact of a diagnosis of AIDS (or AIDS-like symptoms) on current behavior and emotional status. However, retrospective data are subject to many kinds of bias. Simple memory lapse and remembering wrongly are particularly likely to be responses to questions that address behaviors that occurred more than three months earlier—especially if those behaviors were typical and routine rather than unusual. A more subtle kind of bias is the tendency of subjects to remember their past behavior in a way that enhances self-esteem (Cahalan 1968). Thus, retrospective questioning may result in an overreporting of sexual behavior that would be considered responsible and an underreporting of behavior that might be labeled promiscuous or that has been associated with contracting AIDS. Finally, there is the danger of forward or backward telescoping (i.e., the incorrect placement of events or behaviors in time). In forward telescoping, events that actually occurred before the time studied are included and reported; in backward telescoping, events that should be reported as part of the time studied are remembered as more distant and are omitted (Sudman and Bradburn 1982).

Respondents' Abilities to Answer

Response bias can also result from variation in subjects' abilities to answer questions. Patients' levels of functioning can range from little or no disability to severely impaired, and just as physical status can influence participation rates, so too can it influence the quality of response. Data collection sessions with people with AIDS may need to be conducted in many short episodes and be timed carefully to coincide with peaks in the respondents' energy levels.

The respondent's ability to provide valid data is also influenced by this level of cognitive functioning, his education, and by the extent to which he understands the respondent role. Questions need to be worded in precise but simple ways in order to avoid misinterpretation. Cannell and Kahn (1968:553) recommend that "choice of language should be made from the shared vocabulary of the respondent and researcher." In any study, levels of literacy and variation in language use among geographic areas, generations, and social classes must be carefully considered when wording questions.

In research on people with AIDS, an additional problem emerges concerning the choice of language—whether to use vernacular or technical terminology. Use of the vernacular in survey items is an area of disagreement among researchers. Some recommend using vernacular because doing so enhances rapport and can facilitate communication (Pomeroy 1963; Schofield 1965). Using vernacular also indicates to the respondent that the researcher possesses some understanding of his subculture. Minority group members, such as gays, may feel that "outsiders" have stereotypical, oversimplified impressions of their group. The use of expressions and terms indigenous to the subculture can convey to the respondent that the researchers have a fuller, deeper understanding of his lifestyle. Thus, the use of terms employed in everyday interaction may communicate to the respondent a level of awareness and comfort on the part of the researchers that is likely to put the respondent at ease.

The use of colloquial expressions also simulates everyday conversation, whereas standardized, formal questions can seem artificial and may inhibit responses (Sudman and Bradburn 1982). Should a decision be made to use colloquial language in data collection and if the researcher is unfamiliar with the language, a consultant from a gay organization should be asked to review the research instrument to be sure that the language is clear and that it will be comfortable for the respondents. If the vernacular is used inappropriately, great damage can be rendered to the study (Pomeroy 1963). We recommend a thorough review by more than one "insider."

There is, however, a potential problem associated with the use of everyday language. In some instances, the terms will not have a shared meaning among all members of the subculture. This can cause respondents to interpret questions differently, creating validity problems (Schofield 1965). More formal terminology, although perhaps compromising the level of rapport established, can be more precise in its meaning, which leaves less room for differing interpretations. Cannell and Kahn (1968) advocate selecting questions and terms for their precision and universal clarity.

The dilemma—respondent comfort and rapport vs. precision—has been resolved in several ways. Schofield (1965) and DeLamater (1974) used precise descriptive phrases of sexual behavior that were neither technical nor the vernacular, such as "allowed a boy to feel your breasts (over) (under) clothing," or "female oral contact with male genitals." Although such phrases can sound somewhat stiff and awkward when used to describe sexual behavior, they were usually understood. Pomeroy (1963:292), on the other hand, recommends using the most technical language that respondents can understand. Sudman and Bradburn (1982) suggest that the interviewer describe the behavior in phrases, ask the respondent to provide the word or phrase that he feels most comfortable with for that behavior, and adopt this term. Our choice has been to use precise, descriptive (and albeit awkward) phrases followed by the slang term(s) most often used in the subculture to describe the behavior. In this way, we are assured of the precision that is required for valid responses because all respondents know exactly what sexual or drug activity we are asking about. By also noting the name for the activity that the subculture uses, we hope to preserve some interview rapport and reduce skepticism about the researcher's understanding and acceptance of homosexual lifestyles. Whichever way the questions are worded, it is critical for interview rapport that the interviewer be familiar and comfortable with colloquialisms and vernacular (Cannell and Kahn 1968; Pomeroy 1963).

A final observation on adopting the terminology of the subculture: we believe that, whenever possible, social science researchers should use the term "gay" instead of "homosexual." Although "homosexual" is not necessarily perceived as pejorative by members of the subculture, gay may be preferable for two reasons: 1) it is a self-ascribed label rather than one that some gay individuals feel has been imposed on them by outsiders; and 2) it connotes a multifaceted lifestyle (implying attitudes, values, etc.) rather than focusing exclusively on a pattern of sexual behavior. If the focus of the research is limited to sexual practices, however, "homosexual" may be a more precise term to use in such circumstances.

Respondents' Motivations

The quality of survey data is perhaps most determined by the respondents' levels of motivation to provide complete and accurate information. Many factors influence the levels of motivation, including the subjects' social characteristics and personalities, their interests in the survey topic, their understanding the study's sponsorship and purpose, the interviewer's training and competence, and the potential embarrassment or threat to the subjects posed by the questions (Cannell and Fowler 1963; Cannell and Kahn 1968; Fowler 1966).

Several techniques have been developed to increase respondent motivation in order to improve the completeness and accuracy of the data obtained. Accuracy requires both working hard to provide correct and complete information (effort), and willingness to admit socially unacceptable facts or beliefs (honesty). Cannell and Kahn (1968) suggest that the researchers ask the respondent to sign a contract committing himself to provide accurate information. In at least one health study (Oskenberg et al. 1975), an experimental test of "contracting" revealed that respondents in the commitment group provided more information, more complete and potentially embarrassing information, and presented a less favorable impression of themselves.

As discussed previously in the section concerning cooperation rates, the sponsorship and purpose of the research may also have important effects upon respondent motivation. If social research is embedded in a medical study that aims to develop better preventive and curative techniques, study subjects are likely to feel a strong obligation to provide accurate and complete data. The failure to do so is seen as possibly impeding the discovery of meaningful and useful findings that could save lives or reduce suffering. Concomitantly, respondents may also be tempted to distort their answers in order to present a favorable image of themselves to health care providers. The phenomenon of providing socially desirable answers to gain the approval of the interviewer is pervasive and widely recognized (Bradburn et al. 1981; Cannel and Kahn 1968; Phillips 1971). The threat of being devalued in the eyes of the physician (or other caretakers) upon whom the patient feels very dependent creates even greater pressures to report what is perceived to be the approved behavior or attitudes. For example, since AIDS became a major public health problem, many health organizations and professional groups have advised gay men to modify their lifestyles to reduce the risk of contracting or spreading the disease. People with AIDS or ARC as well as healthy male homosexuals have been encouraged to adopt such modifications. Patients may be reluctant to acknowledge that they have maintained old patterns of behavior if they believe that their physician may become aware of their responses.

Any sponsor other than a gay organization (e.g., a college or university) may be viewed as representing the "Establishment." If respondents believe that the findings might eventually be used against the gay community, they may refuse to participate, or. if they do participate, they might be inclined to distort reports of their behavior to foster a more positive image of homosexuals and to discredit negative stereotypes of gay individuals.

Socially Acceptable Response Biases: Threatening and Sensitive Information

Bradburn et al. (1981) distinguish between two kinds of threatening questions: 1) those that address "illegal, or controversial activities or behavior that are generally not discussed without some tension" (which tend to be underreported); and 2) those that ask about socially desirable behaviors (which tend to be overreported). Generally speaking, respondents will bias their answers in an ego-enhancing or self-esteem preserving direction (Cahalan 1968), and much literature documents that response error increases with the degree to which the question is threatening (Cannell and Fowler 1963; Clark and Tifft 1966; Clark and Wallin 1964; David 1962; Ellis 1947; Knudson et al. 1967; Levinger 1966; Locander et al. 1976; Poti et al. 1962; Sudman and Bradburn 1974; Sudman et al. 1977).

Research on socially acceptable response bias has found that often the extent of error is not as large as usually feared. It also demonstrates that in general the average respondent is more honest about his present status than about his past status. Cahalan (1968:609–610) finds that unambiguous questions ("Do you own a car?") are less likely to cause respondents to stretch the truth, but if a question "permits a respondent to misremember and reconstruct his memories so he can give a response more compatible with his self-image than the actual facts would be, he may tend to rewrite history more in line with what he thinks he ought to have done than with what he actually did."

Although most sex researchers believe that sexual practices and homosexual preference are universally ego-threatening topics, this assumption should be critically examined. The 1980s have been characterized by considerable openness about sexual lifestyle and practices. The greatly increased exposure of the public through the mass media to sexual and erotic material may have considerably desensitized many people. Johnson and DeLamater (1976) believe that researchers overestimate response effects in sex research and exaggerate the threat that sex questions engender. However, most researchers believe that questions concerning sexual behavior (perhaps more than those concerning attitudes) are very likely to result in response bias (e.g., Bradburn et al. 1978; LoScuito et al. 1971; Locander et al. 1976; Pomeroy 1963). As in other investigations of sexual behavior, studies of homosexual behavior will evoke a range of respondent reactions, from highly threatened and embarrassed to minimal discomfort. Furthermore, gays generally manifest a greater acceptance and tolerance of a wider range of sexual behavior than heterosexuals do (Lumby 1976), a fact that might cause them to be more comfortable responding to questions about sexual behavior. Their greater openness about sexual matters may make disclosure of their behavior less threatening.

Studies of AIDS will often include sensitive or threatening topics, and a variety of techniques can be used to reduce the possibility of response bias. First, respondents can be asked at the beginning of the interview or questionnaire to commit themselves to provide accurate information (see "Respondents' Motivations," above). Second, one can ask the questions in ways that minimize threat and encourage admission of sensitive, embarrassing, or illegal behavior (Barton 1958). Sudman and Bradburn (1982) provide specific guidance; they suggest using open-ended instead of closed alternative questions, asking long (vs. short) questions, asking about past behavior before current practice, and asking threatening material later in the interview or questionnaire. Alternatives to direct questions are also discussed, such as randomized response (Warner 1965), card sorting, sealed envelopes and projective questions.

Identifiability, Anonymity, and Confidentiality

Regulations governing informed consent as well as professional codes of ethics require protection of research subjects' identities. This issue is particularly salient in the case of AIDS research. Healthy homosexuals, lymphadenopathy patients, and people with AIDS (not yet publicly identified) may suffer serious social consequences if their names are linked with a study of people with AIDS. The public fear, and in some cases hysteria, generated by this illness has caused many victims or suspected victims of the illness to be discriminated against and socially ostracized. For these reasons extraordinary safeguards must be instituted to protect the identities of subjects participating in AIDS-related research.

In addition to the special ethical obligations of researchers in this field, response validity and candor are likely to be significantly compromised if respondents believe that they or their responses will be identified (Selltiz et al. 1959). Reamer (1979) points out that for decades researchers have assumed that the guarantee of anonymity (i.e., that the respondent's identity is unknown to the research team) or confidentiality (i.e., that the respondent's identity is known to the research staff but will never be revealed to another party) would reduce apprehension and embarrassment, thereby increasing the respondent's willingness to answer truthfully. However, empirical data are contradictory on this point. In reviews of the literature, both Rosen (1960) and Phillips (1971) point to clear effects on response quality of varying degrees of anonymity or confidentiality provided. Considerable evidence reveals that this response bias is largely limited to instances in which the information requested is potentially ego-damaging, embarrassing, or illegal (Ash and Abramson 1952; Becker and Bakal 1970; Carey 1937; Erdos and Regier 1977; Fuller 1974; King 1970; Koson et al. 1970; Wildman 1977). Such bias, however, seems not to materialize consistently under conditions of threat. Some investigators have found little effect on response even when questions deal with sensitive issues (Benson 1941; Elinson and Haines 1950; Fisher 1946; Pearlin 1961; Singer 1978a; Singer 1978b; Stouffer 1950.)

Given the unique constellation of threats to people with AIDS should their illness become public, and to gays who conceal their lifestyles from their employers and some or all of their friends and families, strict confidentiality must unquestionably be provided. However, more important for response validity than the actual safeguards imposed is the *perception* by the respondent of that confidentiality and his trust in the research team to carry out their promise.

Assurances of anonymity can help to foster more truthful responses when a motive to misreport exists. We believe, however, that in the case of AIDS research, most respondents will accept the extreme importance of providing accurate information. Because most of the social science research in this field has important goals, such as identifying risk factors or gathering data needed to plan educational and support services, respondents are likely to be sufficiently motivated to cooperate by providing truthful and complete information. They will usually recognize that the achievement of the research objectives depends on the willingness of subjects like themselves to supply such information.

Effects of Different Methods of Data Collection

A considerable body of literature exists evaluating the relative advantages and disadvantages of interviews and questionnaires for gathering data regarding sensitive or threatening topics such as sexual behavior. In the case of AIDS research, as with most social science studies, the kinds of data needed to achieve the research objectives and the available resources (i.e., time, money, and effort) will determine the most suitable alternative.

Interviews generally permit the collection of somewhat more complex data than can be obtained by questionnaire, techniques such as filter questions and elaborate skip patterns in which only some follow-up questions may be asked and others skipped depending on the subject's response to earlier items. In the interview situation, the researcher can explain the meaning of items if necessary and can probe to clarify ambiguous replies. Interviews also tend to yield more complete information that do self-administered questionnaires. The presence of the interviewer seems to discourage refusals to provide answers to the more threatening items that might be skipped by a respondent completing a self-administered questionnaire.

Furthermore, the interview permits the establishment of rapport and the creation of a permissive atmosphere, which some researchers feel is necessary for inducing subjects to provide sensitive information. Among the disadvantages generally attributed to interviews, as compared to self-administered questionnaires, is the greater cost, reduced anonymity, and the potentially biasing effects of the interviewer's characteristics or behavior.

Self-administered questionnaires offer the advantages of being economical (an important consideration when large samples are involved), of avoiding the threats of bias introduced through interviewer attitudes or actions, and of providing anonymity. On the other hand, self-administered questionnaires are not well suited to gathering complex data, tend to yield more missing information, and generally evoke higher refusal rates.

Empirical studies of the response effects of different methods of data collection reveal some disagreement. In general, it seems that when a topic is sensitive, respondents tend to give more accurate and/or fewer socially acceptable responses on self-administered questionnaires than in interviews (Edwards 1957; Ehrmann 1959; Fuller 1974; Knudsen et al. 1967; Metzner and Mann 1952; Sorensen 1972; Wiseman 1972). Thus, when the self-administered questionnaire can be used to gather anonymous data it may be preferable to the interview because it reduces some of the usual motives to distort (e.g., to avoid an unfavorable reaction from the interviewer or to preserve self-esteem). In spite of this, some experienced researchers in sex and drug studies continue to recommend face-to-face interviews. Schofield (1966), for example, recommends the interview and claims that variation in interpretation of key items on questionnaires is a more serious source of bias than lack of anonymity. LoScuito et al. (1971), in studies on sex and pornography, used interviews to collect all but the most sensitive data and used a self-administered questionnaire during the interview for the most threatening material (a procedure also adopted by Abelson et al. 1972 and Abelson and Rappeport 1973 in drug studies). Kinsey, et al. (1953) and Pomeroy (1963) advocate interviews for gathering intimate sexual histories, because the interviewer can create an accepting atmosphere that will permit open, honest reporting.

Although the promise of anonymity can be an influential factor in an individual's willingness to report threatening or sensitive information, we believe that satisfying assurances of confidentiality can persuade a respondent to be candid in an interview. Furthermore, self-administered questionnaires are difficult to use in panel-design studies, in which earlier data provided by a subject must be linked up with subsequently collected information. Although procedures for devising respondent-generated identification numbers exist and make feasible the use of self-administered questionnaires for panel studies, these tend to be somewhat cumbersome and often difficult to employ completely successfully.

Researchers who choose the face-to-face interview to collect sensitive or threatening data from people with AIDS need to be particularly conscious of potential sources of response error, for in interview situations the sources of response bias are more numerous than with questionnaires. Nevertheless, considerable empirical research and extensive practical experience have provided a much better understanding of the possible sources of bias and of those interview procedures that can help reduce it. Of greatest concern are the behavior and characteristics of interviewers that may introduce systematic error into the data.

The sources of errors can be technical (e.g., incorrect reading of the question, inadequate probing, or inaccurate recording) or personal (e.g., opinions, expectations or attitudes about the subject or certain kinds of respondents) (Boyd and Westfall 1955). Interviewers can nonverbally and unconsciously communicate what they believe or want to hear through body language and patterns of verbal reinforcement. However, Bradburn et al. (1981) contend, based on a careful review of evidence, that "expectation effects" are usually trivial and can be avoided through careful interviewer training and by keeping the study's hypotheses confidential.

Interviewers' status characteristics have also been identified as sources of response bias. Empirical data suggest that "mismatch" of interviewers and respondents for social characteristics that are relevant to the topic of the study can result in socially desirable response patterns. For example, studies of racial attitudes have found that blacks tend to bias responses to white interviewers (Hyman et al. 1954; Lenski and Leggett 1960; Pettigrew 1964; Price and Searles 1961; Williams 1964), whereas whites tend to say that they are less racially prejudiced when they are interviewed by nonwhite rather than white interviewers (Athey et al. 1960; Bryant et al. 1966; Summers and Hammond 1966).

Similarly, surveys on sexual practices and attitudes document variations in response, depending on whether or not the interviewers and respondents are the same gender. Benney et al. (1956–1957) found that the least-inhibited communication takes place between young people of the same gender and the most-inhibited between young people of the same age and different genders. DeLamater (1974) found that the gender of the interviewer had no significant effect on reports of lifetime sexual behavior, but that male interviewers elicited fewer reports of current sexual activity from women. Schofield (1966:14) also found that teenage girls responded more openly about their sexual practices to female than to male interviewers.

The issue for AIDS researchers is whether or not to match interviewers and respondents, and, if so, on what characteristics. Because the subject concerns sensitive or threatening behavior, the importance of creating a permissive and accepting atmosphere for the interview is crucial. Because homosexuality is still stigmatized in our society (Levitt and Klassen 1974; Nyberg and Alston 1976–1977), homosexual respondents might assume that a nonhomosexual interviewer would regard them with disdain or disapproval. They may also be reluctant to openly and explicitly report that they had engaged in practices that they believed the interviewer would regard as deviant, perverse, or pathological. In addition, the tendency for interviewees to supply socially desirable responses in an effort to gain the approval of the interviewer is likely to be accentuated in situations in which the respondents feels they are devalued or stigmatized.

To mitigate these problems, one strategy is to employ a homosexual male as the interviewer. This choice has advantages and potential disadvantages associated with it, but for the purposes of many studies the former may outweigh the latter. The principal gain associated with matching the interviewer to the respondent on sexual orientation is the avoidance of false reporting due to the perception of the respondent that his lifestyle and sexual practices might be socially unacceptable to a heterosexual interviewer. Disclosing one's intimate sexual behavior can be particularly threatening if that behavior is regarded by a large proportion of the society as aberrant (Levitt and Klassen 1974; Nyberg and Alston 1976–1977) and when that behavior is implicated as a cause of one's illness—an illness that many regard as immoral. Many homosexuals believe that a significant proportion of the general public feels that people with AIDS are responsible for their own plight. Indeed, the usual compassion and tolerance afforded sick individuals have often been denied people with AIDS. As a result of these circumstances, people with AIDS and other homosexuals may be apprehensive to admit the full extent and nature of their sexual behavior. Presumably, if the interviewer is perceived as being sympathetic to the lifestyle and as nonjudgmental, it becomes easier for the subject to reveal more. Further, a homosexual interviewer is likely to feel more comfortable with the subject and to be able to convey that comfort both verbally and nonverbally. This, too, should help create a permissive atmosphere for reporting sensitive information.

The use of an interviewer matched to the subject on sexual orientation may also present certain problems. One problem is the danger of overidentification. AIDS is a life-threatening illness and an interviewer whose lifestyle is similar to those of the patients he interacts with may too closely identify with the patients and become extremely anxious. This not only creates serious psychological distress for the interviewer, but will inevitably affect his ability to behave neutrally in the interview situation.

Another potential problem of using a homosexual interviewer is that when the subject of the interview contains questions on sexual practices, rapport (which is an asset up to a point) can exceed optimal limits and turn into a subtle seductive interaction. "Talking" about explicit sexual behavior, even in the context of a formal research interview can be evocative and provocative. This is just as true in surveys of a heterosexual's practices, because the respondent might perceive an interviewer of the opposite sex as "a potential dating or sexual partner" (DeLamater 1974:33).

This danger can be reduced in several ways. The interviewer should be carefully trained to conduct himself in a way that maintains a sufficient degree of professional distance. One can use a gay mental health professional to do the interviewing, because he would be experienced with and trained in techniques for maintaining professional distance. Another strategy is to employ an older homosexual male. Because the gay subculture places a high value on youth and physical attractiveness, gay individuals over the age of about 35 are not as likely to be considered objects of sexual desire. Therefore, an older homosexual male interviewer may be less likely to evoke sexual interest in the respondent.

Interview Rapport

Rapport between interviewer and respondent has been attributed almost magical properties—i.e., it is assumed to be able to increase cooperation rates in interview studies, put respondents at ease, create a permissive atmosphere for reporting ego-threatening or sensitive data, motivate the respondent to work hard to provide accurate and complete information, reduce socially acceptable responses, and reduce suspicion about the purpose and use of the study. Nevertheless, careful examination of the phenomenon of rapport has raised serious question about its effects on response validity. Although Cannell and Kahn (1968), Dohrenwend et al. (1968), Goudy and Potter (1975), Selltiz et al. (1959), Weiss (1968–1969), and Williams (1968), all recognize a role for some interviewer-respondent rapport, their major concern is the potential bias that rapport can cause. Hyman et al. (1954) warned over thirty years ago of the dangers of "over-rapport," which could cause respondents to give answers that will maximize their status or that are designed to please the interviewer.

In other words, rapport can cause bias in which the respondent provides answers that maximize the rewards of the respondent-interviewer interaction at the expense of response validity. For example, Weiss (1968) reported that low-income welfare mothers gave more inaccurate answers on sensitive questions (e.g., child's school performance and receiving welfare) in interviews in which rapport was high than in those in which rapport was low. Williams (1968) recommended that interviewers and respondents be dissimilar in one or two key characteristics (e.g., age, sex, class, race) so that the chance of high rapport will be decreased. He also suggested than an impersonal approach rather than a friendly, warm approach will be more successful in eliciting frank responses.

The effects of rapport on interview responses are related in part to the social distance between interviewers and respondents. Matching interviewers and respondents for social status and encouraging rapport are two techniques employed by researchers to create a comfortable, permissive atmosphere, which in turn may be assumed to increase the respondent's honesty and the effort expended to provide complete data. However, if social distance between the interviewer and respondent is very low (i.e., if they share many background characteristics and values) and if rapport is also very high, then the validity of data on embarrassing, illegal, unacceptable, or unflattering behaviors are compromised.

What role should rapport have in interviews with healthy homosexuals and people with AIDS? As mentioned in the previous section, matching interviewer and respondent so that they share homosexual orientation may be a good strategy for reducing the possibility of socially desirable response bias. However, if matching for sexual preference is a strategy chosen, some social distance should also be preserved (e.g., by using an older male who does not share age status of the respondent or by using a trained professional) and high rapport should be discouraged. Some degree of rapport certainly is required in such a sensitive kind of interview in order to encourage and motivate respondents. Nevertheless, technical interviewing skills such as objectivity and neutrality, creating a permissive atmosphere for admitting socially undesirable information, and professionalism are more important for preserving validity.

CONCLUSION

Researchers need to consider many complex methodological issues in designing AIDS-related research studies. We have attempted to identify the most salient and common of these and to outline alternative solutions. Given the limitations of space we have necessarily omitted discussion of other difficult design questions that often arise. Each study presents a unique set of issues and problems and different solutions may be needed to minimize response error and maximize the usefulness of the findings.

Several critical recommendations can be made to facilitate AIDS-related research. First, a central clearinghouse should be established so that social research studies on AIDS can be catalogued. This would greatly enhance the comparability of studies and would promote the cumulation of findings if researchers could consult with each other about how they define eligible cases and measure important concepts and could solve other common methodological problems.

Extraordinary physical, social, and psychological threats confront those people with AIDS and those at high-risk. Because of the profound psychosocial consequences of this illness, the active involvement of social science researchers is crucial. The anguish and hopelessness brought about by this disease create an important ethical obligation for investigators to collaborate and share findings so that research can advance quickly. A national clearinghouse of AIDS research would facilitate these goals. In addition, research findings should be quickly disseminated to caregivers and policy makers so that practical benefits will reach AIDS patients as soon as possible.

Finally, because statistics and research data are often used for political ends, research findings should be presented with care. Precise language should be used in order to avoid misinterpretation; the research methodology and analysis should justify the conclusions drawn; sweeping generalizations should be avoided; and recommendation based on the findings should be developed in conjunction with those most affected—the patients themselves.

NOTES AND ACKNOWLEDGEMENTS

This article is based in part on research funded by the National Institute of Mental Health (R01MH39551) and by the New York State AIDS Institute (C000577).

REFERENCES

Abelson, H., R. Cohen, and D. Schrayer. 1972. Public Attitudes Toward Marihuana. In *Marihauana: A Signal of Misunderstanding*, Vol. II, Appendix, pp. 856–1010. Washington, D. C.: Government Printing Office.

Abelson, H. and M. Rappeport. 1973. Drug Experience, Attitudes and Related Behavior Among Adolescents and Adults. In *Drug Use in America: Problem in Perspective*, Vol. I, pp. 489–867. Washington, D. C.: Government Printing Office.

Ash, P. and E. Abramson. 1952. The Effect of Anonymity on Attitude Questionnaire Response. *Journal of Abnormal and Social Psychology* 47:722–723.

Athey, K. R. et al. 1960. Experiments Showing the Effect of Interviewers' Racial Background on Response to Questionnaires Concerning Racial Issues. *Journal of Applied Psychology* 44:244–246.

Barton, A. J. 1958. Asking the Embarrassing Question. *Public Opinion Quarterly* 22:67–68.

Becker, G. and D. A. Bakal. 1970. Subject Anonymity and Motivational Distortion in Self-Report Data. *Journal of Clinical Psychology* 26:207–209.

Beiber, I. 1962. *Homosexuality: A Psychoanalytic Study of Male Homosexuals.* New York: Vintage Books.

Bell, A. P. and M. S. Weinberg. 1978. *Homosexualities.* New York: Simon and Schuster.

Bell, A. P., M. S. Weinberg, and S. K. Hammersmith. 1981. *Sexual Preference.* Bloomington: Indiana University Press.

Benney, M., D. Riesman, and S. Star. 1956–1957. Age and Sex in the Interview. *American Journal of Sociology* 62:143–152.

Benson, L. E. 1941. Studies in Secret Ballot Technique. *Public Opinion Quarterly* 5:79–82.

Boyd, H. W. and Westfall, R. 1955. Interviewers as a Source of Error in Surveys. *Journal of Marketing* 19:311–324.

Bradburn, N. M. et al. 1978. Question Threat and Response Bias. *Public Opinion Quarterly* 42:221–234.

———. 1981. *Improving Interview Method and Questionnaire Design.* San Francisco: Jossey-Bass.

Bryant, E. C., I. Gardner, and M. Goldman. 1966. Responses on Racial Attitudes as Affected by Interviewers of Different Ethnic Groups. *Journal of Social Psychology* 70:95–100.

Cahalan, D. 1968. Correlates of Respondent Accuracy in the Denver Validity Survey. *Public Opinion Quarterly* 32:607–621.

Cahalan, D., V. Tamulonis, and H. Verner. 1947. Interviewer Bias Involved in Certain Types of Opinion Survey Questions. *International Journal of Opinion and Attitude Research* 1:63–77.

Cannell, C. F. and F. J. Fowler. 1963. A Comparison of a Self-Enumerative Procedure and a Personal Interviewer: A Validity Study. *Public Opinion Quarterly* 27:250–264.

Cannell, C. F. and R. L. Kahn. 1968. Interviewing. In *The Handbook of Psychology*, G. Lindzey and E. Aronson, eds., rev. ed., Vol. 2. Reading, Mass.: Addison Wesley.

Carey, S. M. 1937. Signed vs. Unsigned Attitude Questionnaires. *Journal of Educational Psychology* 28:144–148.

Cisin, I. 1963. Community Studies of Drinking Behavior. *Annals of the New York Academy of Sciences* 107:610–616.

Clark, A. L. and P. Wallin. 1964. The Accuracy of Husbands' and Wives' Reports of Frequency of Marital Coitus, *Population Studies* 18:165–173.

Clark, J. P. and L. L. Tifft. 1966. Polygraph and Interview Validation of Self-Reported Deviant Behavior. *American Sociological Review* 31:516–523.

Colombotos, J., J. Elinson, and R. Lowenstein. 1968. Effect of Interviewers' Sex on Interview Responses. *Public Health Reports* 83:685–690.

David, M. 1962. The Validity of Income Reported by a Sample of Families Who Received Welfare Assistance in 1959. *Journal of the American Statistical Association* 57:690–695.

DeLamater, J. 1974. Methodological Issues in the Study of Premarital Sexuality. *Sociological Methods and Research* 3:30–61.

Dohrenwend, B. 1966. Social Status and Psychological Disorder: An Issue of Substance and an Issue of Method. *American Sociological Review* 31:14–34.

Dohrenwend, B. S., J. Colombotos, and B. P. Dohrenwend. 1968. Social Distance and Interviewer Effects. *Public Opinion Quarterly* 32:410–422.

Edwards, A. L. 1957. *The Social Desirability Variable in Personality Assessment and Research.* New York: Dryden.

Ehrmann, W. W. 1959. *Premarital Dating Behavior.* New York: Henry Holt.

Elinson, J. and V. T. Haines. 1950. Role of Anonymity in Attitude Surveys. *American Psychologist* 5:315–318.

Ellis, A. 1947. Questionnaire vs. Interview Methods in the Study of Human Love Relationships. *American Sociological Review* 12:541–553.

Erdos, P. and J. Regier. 1977. Visible and Disguised Keying on Questionnaires. *Journal of Advertising Research* 17:13–18.

Ferber, R. and H. Wales. 1952. Detection and Correction of Interviewer Bias. *Public Opinion Quarterly* 16:105–116.

Fisher, R. F. 1946. Signed vs. Unsigned Questionnaires. *Journal of Applied Psychology* 30:220–225.

Fowler, F. 1966. Education, Interaction and Interview Performance, Doctoral Dissertation, University of Michigan.

Fuller, C. 1974. Effect of Anonymity on Return Rate and Response Bias in a Mail Survey. *Journal of Applied Psychology* 59:292–296.

Goudy, W. J. and H. R. Potter. 1975. Interviewer Rapport: Demise of a Concept. *Public Opinion Quarterly* 39:529–543.

Hyman, H., et al. 1954. *Interviewing in Social Research.* Chicago: University of Chicago Press.

Johnson, W. T. and J. P. Delamater. 1976. Response Effects in Sex Surveys. *Public Opinion Quarterly* 40:165–181.

Katz, D. 1942. Do Interviewers Bias Poll Results? *Public Opinion Quarterly* 6:249–253.

King, F. W. 1970. Anonymous vs. Identifiable Questionnaires in Drug Usage Surveys. *American Psychologist* 25:982–985.

Kinsey, A. C., W. B. Pomeroy, and C. E. Martin. 1953. *Sexual Behavior in the Human Male.* Philadelphia: Saunders.

Knudsen, D. D., H. Pope, and D. P. Irish. 1967. Response Differences to Questions on Sexual Standards: An Interview-Questionnaire Comparison. *Public Opinion Quarterly* 31:290–297.

Koson, D. et al. 1970. Psychological Testing by Computer: Effect on Response Bias. *Educational and Psychological Measurement* 30:803–810.

Lenski, G. E. and J. C. Leggett. 1960. Caste, Class and Deference in the Research Interview. *American Journal of Sociology* 65:463–467.

Levinger, G. 1966. Systematic Distortion in Spouses' Reports of Preferred and Actual Sexual Behavior. *Sociometry* 29:291–299.

Levitt, E. E. and A. D. Klassen. 1974. Public Attitudes Toward Homosexuality. *Journal of Homosexuality* 1:29–43.

Locander, W. B., S. Sudman, and N. Bradburn. 1976. An Investigation of Interview Method, Threat and Response Distortion. *Journal of the American Statistical Association* 71:269–275.

LoScuito, L. et al. 1971. *Methodological Report on a Study of Public Attitudes Toward and Experience with Erotic Materials.* Technical Report of the Commission on Obscenity and Pornography, Vol. 6. Washington, D. C., Government Printing Office.

Lumby, M. E. 1976. Homophobia: The Quest for a Valid Scale. *Journal of Homosexuality* 2:39–47.

Ma, P. and Armstrong, D. 1984. *The Acquired Immune Deficiency Syndrome and Infections of Homosexual Men.* New York: Yorke Medical Books.

Metzner, H. and F. Mann. 1952. A Limited Comparison of Two Methods of Data Collection: The Fixed Alternative Questionnaire and the Open Ended Interview. *American Sociological Review* 17:491–496.

Nyberg, K. L. and J. P. Alston. 1976–1977. Analysis of Public Attitudes toward Homosexual Behavior. *Journal of Homosexuality* 2:99–107.

Oksenberg, L., A. Vinokur, and C. Cannell. 1975. *The Effects of Commitment to Being a Good Respondent on Interview Performance.* Survey Research Center, Institute for Social Research, University of Michigan.

Pearlin, L. I. 1961. Appeals of Anonymity in Questionnaire Response. *Public Opinion Quarterly* 25:640–647.

Pettigrew, T. F. 1964. *A Profile of the Negro American.* New York: Van Nostrand.

Phillips, D. 1971. *Knowledge from What?* Chicago: Rand McNally.

Pomeroy, W. 1963. The Reluctant Respondent. *Public Opinion Quarterly* 27:287–293.

Poti, S. J., B. Chakrabarti, and C. R. Malaker. 1962. Reliability of Data Relating to Contraceptive Practices. In *Research in Family Planning*, C. V. Kiser, ed., pp. 51–65. Princeton, N.J.: Princeton University Press.

Price, D. O. and R. Searles. 1961. Some Effects of Interviewer-Respondent Interaction on Responses in a Survey Situation. *Proceedings of the Social Statistics Section, American Statistical Association*, pp. 211–221. Washington, D. C.: American Statistical Association.

Reamer, F. G. 1979. Protecting Research Subjects and Unintended Consequences: The Effect of Guarantees of Confidentiality. *Public Opinion Quarterly* 43:497–506.

Rosen, N. A. 1960. Anonymity and Attitude Measurement. *Public Opinion Quarterly* 24:675–679.

Schofield, M. 1965a. *Sociological Aspects of Homosexuality: A Comparative Study of Three Types of Homosexuals.* Boston: Little Brown.

_____. 1965b. *The Sexual Behaviour of Young People.* Boston: Little Brown.

Selltiz, C. et al. 1959. *Research Methods in Social Relations.* New York: Holt, Rinehart and Winston.

Singer, E. 1978a. Informed Consent. *American Sociological Review* 43:144–161.

_____. 1978b. The Effect of Informed Consent Procedures on Respondents' Reactions to Surveys. *Journal of Consumer Research* 5:49–57.

Sorenson, R. C. 1972. *Adolescent Sexuality in Contemporary America.* New York: World Publishing.

Stouffer, S. A. 1950. *Studies in Social Psychology in World War II*, Vol. 4. Princeton, N.J.: Princeton University Press.

Sudman, S. and N. M. Bradburn. 1974. *Response Effects in Surveys: A Review and Synthesis.* Chicago: Aldine.

_____. 1982. *Asking Questions: A Practical Guide to Questionnaire Design.* San Francisco: Jossey-Bass.

Sudman, S. et al. 1977. Estimates of Threatening Behavior Based on Reports of Friends. *Public Opinion Quarterly* 41:261–264.

Summers, G. F. 1969. Toward a Paradigm for Respondent Bias in Survey Research. *Sociological Quarterly* 10:113–121.

Summers, G. F. and A. D. Hammond. 1966. Effect of Racial Characteristics of Investigator on Self-Enumerated Responses to a Negro Prejudice Scale. *Social Forces* 44:515–518.

Warner, S. L. 1965. Randomized Response: A Survey Technique for Eliminating Evasive Answer Bias. *Journal of the American Statistical Association* 60:63–69.

Weiss, C. 1968. Validity of Welfare Mothers' Interview Responses. *Public Opinion Quarterly* 32:622–633.

Welch, S. 1975. Sampling by Referral in a Dispersed Population. *Public Opinion Quarterly* 39:237–244.

Wildman, R. C. 1977. Effects of Anonymity and Social Setting on Survey Responses. *Public Opinion Quarterly* 41:74–79.

Williams, J. A., Jr. 1964. Interviewer-Respondent Interaction: A Study of Bias in the Information Interview. *Sociometry* 27:338–352.

———. 1968. Interviewer Role Performance: A Further Note on Bias in the Information Interview. *Public Opinion Quarterly* 32:287–297.

Wiseman, F. 1972. Methodological Bias in Public Opinion Surveys. *Public Opinion Quarterly* 36:105–108.

Chapter Two

Applied Methodology:
A Primer of Pitfalls and Opportunities in AIDS Research

Jane Zich and Lydia Temoshok

This paper is intended to be a guide to thinking about designing and implementing biopsychosocially oriented AIDS research. Both authors are integral members and among the founders of the University of California, San Francisco's Biopsychosocial AIDS-Research Project (UCSF-BAP), a group of scientist-practitioners committed to researching AIDS, AIDS-related complex (ARC), and the "worried well" from a multidisciplinary perspective. UCSF-BAP is composed of psychologists, medical and mental health practitioners, psychiatrists, and psychoneuroimmunologists, who also have collaborative ties with internists, nurses, medical anthropologists, health-department officials, and homosexual (gay) political activists in the United States and abroad. The majority of UCSF-BAP members are gay.

UCSF-BAP has generated several grants funded on national and regional levels and has developed both a paper-and-pencil self-report protocol for persons with AIDS, or ARC, and for the "worried well," as well as several forms of a structured interview aimed at needs assessment and interventions for these groups. In the course of initiating and conducting our research, a number of scientific, clinical, and political issues have arisen. Many of these issues seem to be inevitable and thus essential to consider in any AIDS-related research investigation. It is our intention to highlight these issues as well as possible goals and implementation strategies related to them.

We do not presume to have the answers to all the questions we pose, but we hope that by our raising the issues in advance the reader will be in a better position to avoid some of the major pitfalls and to move more effectively toward much needed biopsychosocial investigations of AIDS in a manner that is both scientifically rigorous and clinically sensitive to the populations studied and eventually served. Although the examples cited will be generated from our experience in conducting our own research on AIDS, which is primarily psychosocial research, we believe that the themes discussed will be relevant for other behavioral scientists. We should also note that the issues raised in this chapter are not unique to the study of AIDS but are perhaps highlighted by a subject of such magnitude, controversy, mystery, and tragedy.

THE POLITICAL, PROFESSIONAL, AND PERSONAL CONTEXT OF AIDS RESEARCH

In a recent article, Seymour Sarason (1984:477–485) posed the following question about the domain of scientific inquiry: If it can be studied or developed, should it be? Among the issues raised by Sarason was the possibility that researching some questions may lead to sociopolitical repercussions detrimental to the populations studied.

We find Sarason's article timely and relevant to AIDS research, for whenever a minority group that has been treated prejudicially is studied, there is a risk that the information may be used for political purposes. Much as the Bible can be quoted or misquoted to support any position, so too scientific findings may be cited out of context to bolster virtually any sociopolitical position on a topic. For example, considerable concern was generated in the San Francisco gay community over studies focusing on the drug and sexual practices of persons with AIDS and of gay men at risk for developing AIDS. Fears were voiced that sociobehavioral findings could be misused in support of initiatives to criticize gays as well as gay lifestyles or to curtail individual freedom in a politically repressive manner. Such anxiety was fueled, in part, by the issue of closing the San Francisco bathhouses and the question of who (the Public Health Department? the Mayor?) decides the risks an individual will be permitted to take.

We are not of the opinion that any research that has a substantial risk for misuse of findings should be left undone. Neither do we believe that research data are apolitical truths that must be judged solely on their "objective" scientific merits. Rather, we argue that the behavioral scientist venturing into a domain such as AIDS, which has such strong sociopolitical overtones, cannot claim exemption from responsibility for the ramifications of the research. We will go even further and assert that to ignore the sociopolitical context will severely limit a study's 1) development, 2) execution, 3) accuracy, and 4) impact. These points will be elaborated upon in subsequent sections. To better clarify the methodological issues, we will examine the topics in a question-and-answer format.

What are the professional problems, profits, and prognoses of studying AIDS? The behavioral or social scientist considering the study of AIDS is faced with the usual array of unstated professionally oriented questions: Is this an important topic? Am I asking significant or trivial questions? How will my colleagues and peers view my engagement in this research? Will the study I am contemplating boost or deflect my career trajectory? Will it help me get promoted? Certainly, few people would argue that AIDS is a trivial or untimely issue. Its very importance, however, also heightens the profile of any related research endeavor, opening the prospective AIDS researcher to accusations of being faddish, publicity seeking, or worse—an opportunist. The latter accusation is professionally poisonous, whether it comes from an external funding review committee, one's academic department, one's colleagues, the "public," which includes the gay community, or one's potential subjects. Therefore, we would strongly advise that the prospective AIDS researcher have a *context of concern* with some aspect of the problem or a related problem before attempting to launch a study. For example, the authors achieved credibility for our interest in the area through our psychosocial research, respectively, on depression and on cancer and for our similar longstanding involvement in clinical-health psychology and behavioral medicine.

A context of concern does not, however, immunize the prospective AIDS researcher from other problems related to academic politics. For example, within a conservative department, it is unlikely that the faculty member who mentions that he or she is thinking about researching AIDS will be embraced enthusiastically. First, any research on AIDS is "high-profile" research, likely to be reported in the popular press and not necessarily in a manner a researcher—or an academic department—would appreciate. Second, the topic of AIDS is laden with controversy. Fears of some sort of indirect contagion of AIDS or the related homophobic stigma can provoke even the more liberal of an organization's members to caution any colleague contemplating research in this area to reconsider. There may be more indirect behavioral reaction (for example, no financial support of pilot studies by a conservative department or university). Alternatively, those very hardships, risks, and warnings may stimulate the maverick in some potential AIDS researchers, which introduces the topic of personal motivation.

What are some of the motives of AIDS researchers? We recognize that questioning personal motives could be an issue for any behavioral or social scientist or, indeed, for any scientist. For AIDS, however, all issues are under the spotlight, and if one does not question one's own motivations, then one may be sure someone else will. It is our observation that many researchers have been brought to this area by intense personal concerns and a sense of mission: their friends and/or acquaintances are dying or have died of AIDS; their personal involvement has afforded them special insight into the disease process and its impact; as gays, many feel an obligation to join in a community effort to combat a health crisis that has hit the gay community heavily; they want to make an active contribution toward understanding and eventually controlling AIDS instead of grieving helplessly over its usually tragic consequences. We list these as examples of personal reasons that are no more or less valid than the reasons for which any other behavioral scientist chooses his or her field of inquiry. The highly emotional and, literally, life-or-death nature of this topic, however, makes personal motivation for working in this area particularly salient in the sometimes harsh light of scientific objectivity.

To use a poignant illustration from our own experience, the predecessor of our research effort, the first behavioral scientist at UCSF to begin investigating the psychosocial aspects of AIDS, was Paul Dague, Ph.D., who died in 1984 of AIDS. His death had an impact in terms of inspiring both determination and fear in other group members, some of whom knew him personally. Such events have an impact on our experience and subsequent interpretation of reality. We believe that the most personally and professionally adaptive strategy for the prospective AIDS researcher is to ask questions continuously of oneself about motivation, context, perspective, and interpretation. The goal in doing so is to achieve not an elusive, probably suspect, and possibly impossible "objectivity," but an *informed subjectivity*.

PLANNING A STUDY

Despite proclamations in the press, that "Research on AIDS Gets Big Dollars" (Weissman 1983), *social/behavioral*—in contrast to medical—research of AIDS has not been grandly financed. For a significant period of time, medical research was being federally funded, psychosocial intervention efforts were being locally funded, but behavioral science research was falling into an unfunded gap. Funding opportunities for behavioral science research were first made available through the National Institute of Mental Health (NIMH). This fact dictated a series of actions on the part of prospective AIDS researchers in the San Francisco Bay Area. First, it suggested that university-based researchers would probably have a better chance of getting these dollars than community-based practitioners. This interpretation led to the multidisciplinary strength of our research team, which is composed of both university-based, academically oriented researchers and community-based practitioners and students. Second, the fact that funding was provided by NIMH directed our approach toward the *mental health* aspects of this disease rather than, say, any possible somatopsychic etiology, hypothetical biological mediators of mind-body relations, or animal research. The focus of our first funded study in this area is on the mental health consequences and psychosocial needs associated with events in the disease process of persons with AIDS and with symptoms suspected of developing into AIDS. A secondary aim is to explore and evaluate contributions of psychosocial factors, and their possible interactions with immunological factors, to disease progression.

The process of writing a proposal to the National Institutes of Health (NIH) entails a rather relentless concentration upon a research question, general and specific aims, hypotheses, planned execution, and data analyses, as well as a detailed budget and justification. For a group as multidisciplinary in composition as ours, with a topic as big as AIDS, and with a perspective as comprehensive as one which is *biopsychosocial*, the discipline of writing an NIH proposal was both enormously helpful and arduous. It highlighted leaps of logic and flights of feasibility. Such a focusing and grounding process is recommended to any researcher or group attempting to study AIDS, even if the source of funding is local and does not require such extensive thought, planning, and justification.

Is funding necessary? Let us assume that the prospective AIDS researcher has asked some hard sociopolitical, professional, and personal questions of himself or herself and now is ready, with more or less open eyes, to pursue research in this area. From our experience, a strong personal motivation for studying AIDS often leads to a determination to do the work no matter what the obstacles. The need for funding is often the first—and it can be the last—obstacle encountered. Good will, personal commitment in and of itself, and volunteer time can, unfortunately, be stretched only so far before exhaustion, the need to earn a living, resentment, and other human limitations, take their toll. Beyond this, research involving many subjects, extensive telephone and postal communications, and computer analyses requires money. We believe it is important to recognize these realities early in the process and to seek funding without delay or guilt.

What about the politics of getting funded? A political platform on AIDS is as critical to the success of a research venture as is a starting philosophical position and a scientific stance. If you do not have a platform, someone else will construct one for you. Gay politics, which overlaps with medical, local, and even national politics, will determine to some extent: 1) whether or not your study is viewed as positive and therefore something in which gays, including persons with AIDS, will want to participate; 2) whether or not your study is supported for local funding or promoted at state or national levels; and 3) the ways in which your study—including its goals, specific aims, methods, and implications (even before you have results)—and your research team is depicted in the influential gay press, which will affect items 1 and 2 above.

Although we shall elaborate on the last issue in a subsequent section, the point to be made here is that gays, including persons with AIDS and ARC, read gay newspapers and derive much of their information about AIDS and AIDS research from these sources. This information is often more comprehensive and *accessible* than is that generated by public health, medical, or university sources. Because behavioral science theories and related research findings are more open to interpretation and possible distortion than are strictly medical statements, the behavioral science researcher in this area must respect the power of the press—gay or heterosexual (straight).

No less influential than the written word is "word of mouth." For example, we became aware of an undercurrent of disapproval regarding an AIDS researcher who was rumored to have violated the confidentiality of his research subjects. Whether or not this allegation was true, "word" went out to the gay community and to politically active persons with AIDS that this was a research study to avoid or possibly to undermine.

Approaching the Political Dimension

UCSF-BAP began to approach the political dimension by forming an explicitly collaborative group the stated objectives of which are 1) to help coordinate, systematize, and standardize psychosocial research efforts in San Francisco; 2) to ensure that these efforts will be congruent with and conducted in cooperation with medical research and treatment; and 3) to make participation in psychosocial research less duplicative for persons with AIDS or ARC.

Next, we recognized the importance of collaborative and cooperative arrangements beyond our task-defined groups. Early support of administrators, clinical directors, and researchers at the major sites of AIDS research and treatment was critical. Of course, letters from the appropriate persons in authority at these sites had to be included in our application to the university human research committee as well as in our proposal to NIMH. Our initial contacts and agreements had to be continually updated and revised as the project moved from the conceptual to the operational phase. We recognized that as the requirements of our study (e.g., to have doctors refer as potential subjects those patients who met our specified criteria or to have properly authorized access to certain pieces of medical information) made increasing demands upon site personnel, additional agreements had to be worked out. Often this took the form of paying those researchers or clinical directors who were rendering essential services as consultants or agreeing to have medical colleagues participating actively in our study as coauthors on future publications relevant to their specific contributions.

Information is shared with interested researchers and practitioners in the community through periodic open meetings, which are announced in gay newsletters, gay professional newsletters, and university periodicals. Interagency communication and local-to-national information sharing with kindred researchers is coordinated by one person, the administrative coordinator of UCSF-BAP (Jeffrey Mandel). We view this task as an essential, not a peripheral, component of our research enterprise.

In addition to letting other researchers and interested groups know what we are doing, we also actively seek feedback from these groups regarding our evolving research projects. For example, an ongoing advisory board, composed of gay leaders and medical personnel actively working with AIDS in the Bay Area, meets periodically to review our proposals and protocols. They have been especially helpful in addressing confidentiality issues as well as in facilitating pragmatic working relations at our research sites. In addition, voluntary ad hoc research review committees, composed of persons with AIDS or ARC, were formed to review preliminary drafts of our interview protocols and self-report packages. Members of these committees made extremely helpful suggestions (such as to delete or to change the wording of insensitive, incomprehensible, or duplicative items) and comments on order, length, and subject "debriefing."

In addition to these scientific contributions, we feel that the participation of persons with AIDS and ARC and of gay political leaders and health-care personnel in our research was an important factor in having the work accepted at our research sites and by potential subjects. Behavioral and social scientists remember that the primary function of medical hospitals and clinics, particularly those involved in the near-combat conditions of front-line AIDS treatment, is not behavioral or social research. Concomitantly, the primary tasks of patients in these settings are to get appropriately diagnosed and treated. No matter how important we feel that our research is, it must not interfere with medical goals. Ideally, the researcher and practitioner will view each other's goals as mutually compatible and will work toward these goals in a reciprocally enhancing manner.

Internal Politics

In any group, subtle, or not so subtle, competitions for power, status, or money will be waged. UCSF-BAP decided to devote time and energy to such process issues during our weekly meetings, even if to do so took time away from more strictly scientific concerns.

An important early issue was that of limited resources. Although our first proposal was funded, our already lean budget was trimmed to smaller than half its original size. Our way of dealing with this problem was, first, to acknowledge the situation and then to seek group suggestions. Members' needs, as well as past and future contributions, were voiced and weighed before reaching any conclusion on how funds would be spent.

What emerged as a workable solution was to reimburse members for hours worked on a proportional basis for as far as the budget would stretch. This meant that those who worked more than others would be paid more than others, but that time could not be fully compensated. This system was particularly pertinent to individuals who were using some aspect of the study as their dissertations, because resources from the larger study were, to some extent, being used for their individual benefit. UCSF-BAP members who, by virtue of faculty positions or senior status, had independent access to benefits such as travel funds, secretarial support, photocopying facilities, or even research or salary support, were asked to—and, in many cases, volunteered before being asked—utilize these resources before depleting the grant's scant reserves. As much as possible, opportunities to make presentations at workshops, conferences, and the like that have positive status or social value are distributed among interested group members. In general, our working position is to maintain an open, dynamic balance between the needs of individuals and the requirements of the study; between the individuals' resources and contributions and the study's monetary resources and other opportunities.

OPERATIONALIZING CONCEPTS AND DEVELOPING METHODS

We have adopted a biopsychosocial perspective in our investigations of AIDS. This theoretical framework made the most sense to us as a way of examining psychosocial variables affecting the development and progression of AIDS without denying, or being accused of denying, the stark biological realities of the disorder. A variety of clinical, scientific, and political considerations are likely to confront the biopsychosocially oriented AIDS researcher, regardless of whether the researcher's investigation focuses on assessment, intervention, epidemiology, program evaluation, or some combination of the above. For illustrative purposes, we will assume that the investigator reading this chapter is planning to employ some form of measurement involving a written or oral response from gay subjects who have AIDS, ARC, or sufficient personal concern about either to be classified as a member of the "worried well."

In the initial stages of developing tools and methodologies, the researcher has the luxury of pretending that all things are possible and that the only limiting factor is the scientific value of each alternative considered. During this first phase, the researcher builds an increasingly comprehensive and integrated domain of variables and related indices. During the second phase, this sophisticated packet of instruments and procedures is repeatedly whittled away and reshaped by the realities of conflicts between research and clinical demands, concern over the response burden on subjects, limited funding resources, and the politics involved in conducting research at multiple sites. Other necessary concerns at this point include: operationalizing subject eligibility into AIDS and ARC groups, recruiting subjects, working out solutions to confidentiality dilemmas, determining how to utilize the popular press, and finding an optimum level of communication with other AIDS researchers in the area who may be both colleagues and competitors for limited AIDS research funds.

You mentioned operationalizing eligibility into AIDS and ARC groups. Isn't that the domain of the medical profession? Shouldn't the researcher just verify the diagnosis in the subject's medical record? The criteria for a diagnosis of AIDS or ARC have shifted. It is possible that the Center for Disease Control (CDC) in Atlanta will continue to revise diagnostic criteria as research findings gather. Additionally, some physicians do not recognize ARC as a diagnosis, whereas others do. Some simply note "AIDS risk factors" in the medical record. There exists now no stable algorithm for what factors, in which combination and intensity, constitute a diagnosis of ARC, although efforts are underway to refine a diagnosis. Consequently, the researcher who relies on physician diagnoses for assignment of subjects to AIDS and ARC groups may end up with a significantly different sample of subjects in each group at the beginning of the study than at the end, as a function of the shift in diagnostic criteria in vogue at each time. Unless researchers record which symptoms and risk factors were present for each subject, it may be impossible, in retrospect, to determine if subjects in one AIDS study were indeed comparable to subjects in a different study that produced conflicting results. Identifying such subtle risk-factor differences among populations could have substantial heuristic value.

What do you suggest researchers do to operationalize these diagnoses? 1) For each subject, have a checklist of all risk factors and symptoms considered relevant to a diagnosis of either AIDS or ARC; 2) use, and note in the study, the CDC criteria for AIDS, as well as the most prevalent criteria for ARC at the time the study begins; and 3) retain the risk-factor information of all subjects so that subjects may be reassigned and data reanalyzed if results are compared to results from studies using somewhat different diagnostic criteria. This procedure may prove particularly useful in longitudinal studies, because it could lead to identification of ARC variables that, on an empirical basis, are most likely to predict subsequent diagnoses of AIDS.

How should the researcher determine whether or not risk factors are present in a given subject—through the medical record or through self-reporting? Self-reporting is inadequate, because several of the risk-factor indices involve findings from immunological assays and serological exams.

The medical record may also be incomplete. The physician may neglect to ask about, order tests for, or report all of the risk factors of interest. Consequently, we recommend securing the subject's consent for the physician and researcher to share data in the form of a symptom-and-risk-factor checklist that each subject's physician would routinely employ in their initial and subsequent examinations of the subject. Here is one means by which research may enhance clinical services by providing clinicians with an easy-to-use checklist that will improve the likelihood that each risk factor is at least considered briefly by the examining clinician. This checklist will not, however, guarantee that all assays and laboratory work of interest will be conducted for each subject.

What do you do about the subjects for whom no blood tests or immunological assays are ordered? We strongly suggest that the researcher work out some funding arrangements or scientific collaborations that will ensure that at least a subset of immunological assays are done on all subjects. If the researcher is truly interested in a biopsychosocial perspective, biological indices are imperative. Subjects' reports of physical distress are inadequate, because they do not correlate strongly with immunological findings. For instance, many subjects with grossly abnormal helper/suppressor T-cell ratios will report feeling surprisingly well, whereas some subjects with virtually all lab findings in the normal range will be convinced that there is something profoundly wrong with their health.[1] Indeed, to the biopsychosocially oriented researcher these subjects may prove to be most interesting: i.e., subjects who look fine from a biological perspective but feel sick and subjects who look sick from a biological perspective but feel fine. For this reason, we believe that reliance solely on self-reported data is a mistake. Other biological indices of interest to the AIDS researcher are number, types, and severity of opportunistic infections diagnosed, time from development of AIDS-related symptoms until time of diagnosis of AIDS, and length of survival.

What if the researcher's problem is an inability to limit the number of psychosocial variables that are interesting to examine as risk factors or moderating variables in the development or progression of AIDS, ARC, and other immunological disorders? Some of the guidelines UCSF-BAP utilizes in limiting the variable pool are: 1) use only measures that have been demonstrated to be reliable and valid in previous research; 2) "no fishing trips"—eliminate variables that have not been substantiated by previous research to be associated with immunologically related disorders or established risk factors for AIDS; 3) measures not meeting the requirements of 1 or 2 above will be included only if strong logical arguments can be

---

[1]The authors wish to thank George Solomon, M.D., for contributing this observation.

made for their relevance (e.g., to gay identity issues); 4) maximize chances for cross-study comparisons (i.e., when given a choice among measures for a specific variable of interest, choose the one in use, or likely to be used, by other AIDS researchers); 5) if the information sought is already present in the subjects' medical records or other archival sources, allow the subjects to sign release-of-information forms so that access can be gotten to this information and thereby avoid requiring subjects to answer the same or similar questions; and 6) keep in mind that the subjects are likely to be heavily taxed already by other research projects and that they may fatigue easily from this as well as from their physical status.

You mention using scales with good reliability and validity data, but I wonder how many scales have been standardized on gay samples. Is this an issue of concern to you? Given a choice between an attitude scale found to be reliable and useful with gays versus one shown to be reliable and useful only with general populations, we would choose the former. Such choices rarely emerge, however, because most of the scales for variables of interest to us do not report reliability and validity data specific to gays, so we select scales on the basis of findings with the general population. These scales may, however, require some modifications.

What kinds of modifications? For example, questionnaires with frequent references to spouses but with no mention of lovers, roommates, or friends may seem irrelevant to a respondent who is gay. Similarly, inclusion of social-support questionnaires focusing on ties to biological families and spouses but with no inquiries into the intensity or nature of ties to the gay community may be particularly inappropriate from the perspectives of both science and rapport. Subtle items failing to recognize the values and norms of gay versus straight society, (e.g., the acceptability of multiple sexual partners) may similarly jeopardize a questionnaire's credibility. Consequently, we invite persons with AIDS, as well as members of the gay community at large, to help develop and select instruments. They give us detailed feedback on items and procedures that they think are vague, irrelevant, naive, potentially offensive, or otherwise problematic. We then attempt to strike a balance between keeping instruments as close to the exact content and format used in the validity studies for the instruments and ensuring that the instruments are relevant and inoffensive to our study samples.

It seems that questions about subjects' drug and sexual practices could be offensive, and yet they seem to be important risk factors to consider. A research instrument that focuses exclusively on the subject's sexual and drug habits is likely to be viewed as intrusive and insensitive and could be interpreted by an oversensitive subject as an indication that the researcher is simply voyeuristic or plans to frame solutions for AIDS-related problems solely in terms of lifestyle changes in these two domains. These are domains in which an invasive, authoritarian stance have long been associated with political factions that are interested in curtailing the civil liberties, as well as lifestyle choices, of gays. Although both sexual practices and drug-use patterns have been identified as possible risk factors in the development of ARC and AIDS, exclusive attention to these variables may produce resentment, as well as suspicions, in potential research subjects. Such an orientation may be viewed by people with AIDS or ARC, or by individuals known to be at risk for these conditions, as failing to acknowledge and address the financial, social, medical, and emotional needs of these populations. Failure to acknowledge the existence of such stressors is hardly consistent with a message to subjects that the researcher is working in their behalf.

All these guidelines you mention sound fine in theory, but in reality, if a whole team of investigators is filled with investigators having favorite scales and questions, then isn't it difficult to have them volunteer to delete their favorite variables from the study? Rather early in the variable-elimination process, UCSF-BAP members began recognizing the rather obvious pattern of discarding the pet items and variables of whichever UCSF-BAP members were not present at the day's meeting. An alternative to this strategy is to flip a coin, use a random numbers table, or persuade a group of naive, would-be collaborators to "objectively" delete items that seem the most cumbersome, least clearly worded, or least relevant.

IMPLEMENTATION

Moving into the implementation stage, researchers may find themselves with only half the financial resources necessary to do the project proposed, with encouragement from funding sources to emphasize certain components of a project to the neglect of others more interesting to the researchers, while immediately ahead looms the ever-challenging task of changing grant proposal words into realities. In addition, the researchers may anticipate immersing themselves in the human side of AIDS research: the selection and training of research assistants and interviewers; interactions with medical providers and agency administrators; and the recruitment of face-to-face contact with prospective subjects, including some who are visibly ill and some who will die before the completion of the project.

The attractions to AIDS research here give way to the harsher realities of AIDS. The researcher may experience an increase in guilt, frustration, helplessness, self-doubt, or anxiety and may feel conflict between impulses to do therapy and to get on with the research. Determination to do *some*thing, however, is apt to intensity. Whichever the predominant reaction is, researchers are likely to find themselves more emotionally involved with AIDS at this stage than before. They are also more likely to become sensitive to the politics of AIDS and to their prospective subjects' marked concern about confidentiality and the protection of their rights.

How have UCSF-BAP subjects, especially those with AIDS, reacted to requests that they participate in lengthy questionnaires and interviews? Some subjects have found the procedures taxing, but cooperation has been generally high. We advise allowing breaks during the interview or dividing procedures into short periods, especially for subjects with AIDS, to minimize fatigue. Both AIDS and various treatment regimes for AIDS may interfere with cognitive abilities, including attention and concentration; we suggest that researchers recognize and assess this problem. It has been UCSF-BAP's experience that many subjects find the interview to be one of the few opportunities they have to discuss at length their concerns, needs, and feelings about AIDS and other emotion-charged issues with someone perceived as objective yet sympathetic. As such, the interviewer may feel torn between a desire to follow the interview protocol closely and an equally strong urge to take a therapeutic stance toward the subject. The two impulses are compatible only up to a point.

How have you dealt with this problem? First, we have attempted to assess the extent of the dual-relationship problem by having UCSF-BAP colleagues listen to tapes of interviews by the many different interviewers, asking them to identify those questions or situations during which interviewers are likely to stray from their research roles, and then having them suggest sensitive and tactful statements that could have been made by the interviewer at that point to acknowledge the subject's concerns without leaving the interviewer's role. Among the statements possible at such a point is, "I understand that you have been quite distressed by _____ . If you like, we can discuss that issue or other issues of concern to you in more detail after we finish the questions." In fact, at the end of all interviews, the interviewer asks the subject if there is anything that the interviewer has not addressed upon which the subject would like to comment. This serves the dual function of being able to postpone elicitation of material not directly relevant to the interview and of soliciting subjects' perceptions of variables that are important but largely unaddressed by the interview. Another intervention that may facilitate adherence to the structure of the interview and to the role-appropriate behavior of the interviewer is to describe the interview as a detailed and extensive study in which the interviewer will attempt to ask questions at a fairly brisk pace. Explain to the subject, however that time will be free at the end of the interview for the subject to discuss at more length, any topic he wishes, to ask questions, or to raise issues that he feels were not amply addressed in the interview. Such a preface allows the interviewer to feel comfortable about redirecting the subject to the intent of a question and about curbing irrelevant discourses. It may also help the subject know what is expected and to respond accordingly.

Neither of these interventions really changes the facts that AIDS can be devastating to the subject being interviewed, and questions about AIDS and related adjustment issues may stir up emotions of such intensity that failure to provide counseling opportunities to the subject would be irresponsible. We agree, and so would most human-subjects review committees. One method adopted by UCSF-BAP for handling this situation is to have the interviewer, at the end of each interview, say that he recognizes that the interview may leave the subject feeling as if there are things he would like to discuss in more detail. Alternately, the subject may find that he has questions that do not come to mind at the time but that may surface in a day or two. He is given the telephone number and name of his interviewer and encouraged to call if he does wish to discuss further any aspect of the interview or of his reactions to it. In the event that the subject does subsequently contact the interviewer and expresses an interest in some counseling, the interviewer facilitates a referral to one of numerous clinics and practitioners in the area that have been identified as able and willing to work with patients concerned about AIDS or who have AIDS. In cases in which the interview was particularly emotional, the interviewer makes a follow-up telephone call within the next day or two to ask the subject if any more questions or concerns have arisen since the interview and, again, makes a referral if the subject expresses an interest in counseling.

Is it important for the interviewers to be gay and to identify themselves as such? Initially some concern was raised by gay advisors that rapport might be best if all interviewers were gay and if they informed their subjects of this prior to the interviews. Pilot study interviews had already demonstrated, however, that it is not necessary for interviewers to identify themselves as gay in order to establish a good rapport with subjects. Consequently, we decided that interviewers would make no announcements to subjects about their sexual orientations but would answer simply and directly if asked whether they were gay or not. All UCSF-BAP interviewers are male but not all are gay.

Initially, UCSF-BAP was concerned that a straight interviewer might set a different tone or have poorer rapport with gay subjects, particularly when asking questions about sexual practices and feelings about being gay. In response to this concern, several UCSF-BAP members compared recordings of interviews to assess whether or not gay interviewers were eliciting different responses than was a straight interviewer. All reviewers concluded that no differences in rapport or interviewer effectiveness were attributable to whether or not the interviewer was gay. UCSF-BAP's impression is that it is essential to the development of rapport for interviewers to be "gay-sensitive," to be able to listen well, and to interact comfortably with gay subjects. This does not necessitate the interviewers' being gay. Furthermore, being gay does not automatically ensure that an interviewer will interact well with gay subjects. Poor interviewing skills, or prejudice and disdain toward gays or gay factions, can be evidenced in gay as well as in straight people.

Have any UCSF-BAP subjects died of AIDS? If so, how has the group dealt with this? On more than one occasion an interviewer has discovered that one of the people he had interviewed had subsequently died of AIDS. Because the interviews are extensive and personal, interviewers may feel as if they really had an opportunity to know the interviewee. Consequently, when news of an interviewee's death reaches the group, a loss is felt. The knowledge that any subject one interviews might die of AIDS within the year can be emotionally draining not only to the interviewer but to the whole research team.

Many of the researchers themselves, as well as their friends and colleagues, are at risk for AIDS. Although these concerns have been present throughout the investigation, when a subject or friend dies of AIDS, the group is mobilized to talk more directly than usual about personal anxieties and stressors associated with AIDS and to function more than usual as an emotional support group for each other. UCSF-BAP also recognizes the possibility that an interviewer may suffer symptoms of "burnout" in the course of the study. Group members have agreed to talk about such problems as they arise so that steps may be taken to alleviate the situation.

CONCLUSION

We have attempted in this paper to highlight some critical issues that could turn into major roadblocks for the unwary AIDS researcher. Some of these issues may seem to have more to do with politics than with science. As implied by some of our remarks, however, we believe that no AIDS researcher can steer clear of the political arena. Data on AIDS, by virtue of the deadlines of the disease, its epidemic proportions, and the minority status of the population most frequently associated with the disease, are inevitably politically significant. The AIDS researcher—like it or not—ends up with responsibilities for the sociopolitical ramifications of his or her data as well as for their scientific merits.

This situation calls for a fair bit of ethical soul-searching for the researcher from the moment of considering an investigation on through the various dissemination stages of the project. A high tolerance for sometimes compatible, sometimes antagonistic, ends and a flair for finding complex solutions to difficult problems are critical. Separation of research and clinical interventions is often difficult, and is at times desirable, at other times not. Gay community input and support may require multifaceted collaborations to ensure appropriate representation of various subgroups within the gay community and their respective viewpoints, which are not always compatible with others. The media are often a powerful influence throughout the investigation. They can be a tremendous resource to the AIDS researcher as well as a formidable foe, capable of destroying community support for a project or of mutilating data and quotes beyond recognition.

If at this point the reader has the feeling that the biopsychosocial investigator of AIDS should, optimally, be a public relations whiz, an ethicist, a clinician, a rigorous scientist, someone sensitive to and aware of gay issues, a possessor of substantial practical knowledge of psychoneuroimmunology, political science, diplomacy, medical anthropology, and administration, and a person imbued with an almost uncanny systems-level savvy, then we have made our point.

Now for the good news.

These talents and skills need not be concentrated in a single researcher, so long as the features are found in good measure within the investigative team and its collaborators and so long as a structure has been set up to ensure that the requisite skills will come into play at the appropriate times during the development, implementation, and dissemination phases of the study. It has been our experience that such a multidisciplinary team can be efficient and cooperative as well as stimulating.

Although the politics of AIDS can be frustrating, the influence of the media a perpetual source of anxiety, and the effects of AIDS—in terms of deaths and human suffering—profoundly distressing to researchers as well as to subjects, rewards can be gained as well. Findings may have a very real and immediate impact. The potential to use science in the service of the very subjects who have given their time and efforts to one's research project is gratifying, and the possibility that findings may have clinical relevance and primary and secondary prevention implications not only for AIDS but for a vast array of immunological disorders, holds a promise too great to dismiss outright or to sidestep because of inconveniences caused by muddying scientific waters with real-world dilemmas.

In conclusion, we hope that many prospective investigators of AIDS and related conditions will pursue research from a biopsychological perspective but only after considerable thought about the ethical responsibilities entailed in such pursuits. Furthermore, we hope such investigations will promote networking and collaborations among other AIDS and immunodeficiency researchers, so that what data are collected can be maximally utilized to alleviate human suffering.

ACKNOWLEDGMENTS

The authors wish to acknowledge our friends and colleagues in UCSF-BAP, without whom this paper could not have been written or, indeed, this work conducted. We are especially grateful to Jeffrey Mandel, M.P.H., Administrative Coordinator of UCSF-BAP, for his insights into and contributions to earlier drafts of the manuscript. Special appreciation is due to Faustina Shia for typing this manuscript. Time to prepare this paper was supported in part by National Research Service Award No. 1 F32 MH09046-01 to Jane Zich, Ph.D., from the Epidemiology and Clinical Services Division of NIMH and by NIMH Grant No. 1R01 MH39344-01 to Lydia Temoshok, Ph.D. The latter grant is also supporting the psychosocial AIDS research discussed in this paper.

REFERENCES

Sarason, Seymour B. 1984. If It Can Be Studied or Developed, Should It be? *American Psychologist* 39:477–485.

Weissman, Gerald. 1983. Research on AIDS Gets Big Dollars. *San Francisco Chronicle* October 1.

PART II
SOCIAL EPIDEMIOLOGY

Chapter Three

Behavior, Infection, and Immune Response: An Epidemiological Approach

Robin Flam and Zena Stein

Chronic disease epidemiologists have become accustomed to thinking in terms of complex models of causation, in which several factors acting together or separately form parts of the causal chain. By contrast, infectious disease epidemiologists have often been content with simpler models, in which the identification and characterization of an organism dominates both the study of cause and the approach to treatment and prevention. Yet, some infectious diseases, especially the more chronic ones, exemplified by malaria and schistosomiasis, have compelled investigators to develop models every bit as complex as those in use by chronic-disease epidemiologists.

Although recent work on AIDS provides evidence that the disease is associated with the transmission of a single, specific agent (specifically, LAV/HTLV-III), this disease will apparently require from the infectious-disease epidemiologist the kind of modeling that is the stock and trade of the chronic-disease epidemiologist. It is in this spirit that we approach the writing of this paper. Thus we start from the view that the epidemiological analysis of the pattern of AIDS occurrence suggests that no simple model of disease causation will describe the genesis and spread of AIDS and that certain behaviors and common infections (and the secondary effects of these) contribute to the causal chain. If this is true, the relevant behavioral, environmental, and biological factors must be identified and their roles in disease causation defined.

In this chapter we first define the framework and the uses of the general epidemiological approach. Next, we apply this approach to the case of AIDS, developing hypotheses of causation of AIDS that are concordant with this approach. Finally, we describe specific epidemiological study strategies that might be used to test the hypotheses posed.

I. THE GENERAL EPIDEMIOLOGIC FRAMEWORK

Epidemiology has been defined as "the study of the distribution and determinants of disease in human populations" (MacMahon and Pugh 1970). Implicit in this definition is the final goal of epidemiological investigation: disease prevention. Thus, epidemiological studies aim to describe the characteristics of a disease, discover its cause, and eventually interrupt the causal chain to make possible prevention of the disease.

A three-phase method has evolved to carry out the epidemiological investigation of a disease. The first phase is a description of the occurrence of the disease according to basic group characteristics (e.g., age, sex, ethnicity, race, occupation, geographic location). This is the *descriptive epidemiology* of the disease. The pattern of disease occurrence is then examined, and questions relating to the logic of this distribution emerge. For example, if people living in high altitudes get this disease more often than do people living in low altitudes, a question arises as to why this occurs.

Disease distribution can be studied by collecting any or all of three different "rates" of disease within a defined group. Each rate conveys a unique perspective. *Incidence* is the number of new cases of disease that arise in the group over a defined period of time; *prevalence* is the number of cases of disease that exist in the group at a given point in time; *mortality* is the number of deaths from the disease over a period of time. Regardless of which of these rates is used to describe the distribution of a disease, if rates are to be compared across groups, agreement must be had on the rate (incidence, prevalence, or mortality) to be used for each group. In addition, the definition of the disease, or the criteria for diagnosis of the disease, must be comparable across groups. Also, the procedures for reporting the disease must be standardized and rigorously specified for all groups.

Once specific patterns become apparent from the descriptive epidemiology of a disease, hypotheses that aim to explain these patterns are proposed. For example, if people living at high altitudes have a higher incidence of disease than do people living at low altitudes, one might hypothesize that the level of oxygen intake is a determinant of the disease. Various types of studies can be designed to test such a hypothesis. In a *case/control design*, people with and people without the disease are compared with regard to the amount of suspected exposure (in this example, oxygen intake). The hypothesis would be rejected if no significant difference in amount of exposure appears between the diseased and the nondiseased groups. In a *cohort or prospective design*, exposed and unexposed groups are compared with regard to the amount of disease that develops in each group over a period of time. The hypothesis would be rejected if there did not appear to be a significant difference in the amount of disease developing in the exposed group compared to the amount of disease developing in the unexposed groups. Each of these two basic study designs has its advantages and disadvantages as well as its variants (MacMahon and Pugh 1970).

As these analytic studies are conducted and hypotheses are either rejected or permitted to stand, more information regarding the disease is accumulated, new hypotheses are formed, and old hypotheses are refined. This iterative process of testing new hypotheses and refining old hypotheses, using appropriate study designs, is the second phase of epidemiological investigation and is called *analytical epidemiology.*

After accumulating results of several analytical studies, a point is reached at which statements regarding causality and consequent preventive action may be made. What kinds of statements are appropriate for causal inference, given epidemiological evidence? Because epidemiology is an observational and not an experimental science, can statements regarding causality be made at all? If so, what criteria must be met by epidemiological evidence in order to be reasonably sure that a causal relationship between a suspected exposure and a disease outcome exists?

The third phase of epidemiological investigation is devoted to causal inference and addresses these questions. A set of criteria has developed that allows a qualitative assessment of the probability that an observed relationship between a suspected exposure and a disease outcome is causal (Susser 1973). These criteria include the following: *time sequence* (the hypothesized cause must temporally precede the effect); *biological coherence* (laboratory experiments and animal studies must have yielded results that support the observations); *consistency* (studies done using different study designs and different populations must yield similar results); *strength of association* (exposure to the suspected cause must raise "considerably" the risk of contacting the diseases; *specificity* (either one agent, and no other, causes a particular disease or an agent or set of cofactors causes one disease and no other). The final step of public health action (recommendations for prevention) must be based on a careful weighing of the degree to which the criteria are met versus the invasiveness (in any sense: physical, social, moral, emotional, financial) of the proposed recommendation.

The three-phase epidemiological approach, as outlined above, can be used to investigate any disease with unknown etiology, including AIDS. With regard to AIDS, this paper seeks to answer the following questions: 1) What information regarding the descriptive epidemiology of AIDS is currently available? 2) What sorts of hypotheses emerge after analyzing the patterns provided by the descriptive epidemiology? 3) What sorts of analytical studies might be designed to test these hypotheses? 4) What are the implications of possible results of the studies vis-à-vis causal inference?

II. DESCRIPTIVE EPIDEMIOLOGY OF AIDS

As described above for the general case, uncovering the accurate descriptive epidemiology of AIDS involves determining the accuracy of the assessment of AIDS occurrence. Consistency of disease definition used, types of rates collected across groups, and rigor of reporting across groups are issues that must be considered in this determination.

A standard definition of AIDS that has been set forth by the Centers for Disease Control (CDC) is: "A condition of underlying immunodeficiency not explainable by genetic disease or drug therapy with the development of an opportunistic infection" (CDC 1982b:248–252). Use of this definition does decrease problems relating to the comparability of rates across groups, and it is widely adhered to as a standard; it does, nevertheless, create certain other problems that need to be made explicit.

First, the definition implies that the existence of actual immunodeficiency, although the central characteristic of the condition, does not in itself define the disease. Rather, the diseased condition is only ascertained in the presence of an opportunistic infection. Therefore, neither the clinical changes (generalized malaise, unexplained weight loss, rashes, night sweats) nor the serological changes (reversed ratio of helper to suppressor lymphocytes) that would ordinarily indicate and define immunodeficiency are in themselves considered diagnostic. Instead, these changes are almost incidental.

The absence of a primary role for the typical clinical and serological phenomena in the definition of AIDS raises issues that bear on whether or not an AIDS prodrome exists and what the consequences are of not counting these cases of prodrome if they do indeed exist. If, on the one hand, an individual with unexplained immunodeficiency inevitably goes on to develop an opportunistic infection, is the clinical or serological pattern a prodromal form of AIDS? Would not the study of this early stage (rather than just the final stage), because of its greater proximity to the inception of the disease, yield a clearer picture of the natural history and thus the etiology of the disease? By omitting these early cases the picture of individuals with AIDS that we draw from our studies reveals only the people with severe AIDS instead of the "true" picture of all people with AIDS. The possibility has been raised of a disease spectrum, which, at its broadest, would include subtle clinical and serological changes as well as more obvious serological changes coupled with opportunistic infection. If, on the other hand, these subtle clinical and serological changes do not necessarily lead to AIDS, perhaps they represent an unrelated disease, or perhaps they represent a mild nonprogressive variant of AIDS. In such a case, no information leading to the understanding of the etiology of AIDS might be lost by omitting these patients from study.

An analogous attempt to understand the relationship between subtle, possibly prodromal, changes and a severe disease was made when the Papanicolaou smear was introduced to screen for invasive cervical cancer. In addition to finding smears with no pathology and smears with invasive carcinoma (cellular neoplastic changes), two types of cell pathology, dysplasia (abnormal changes in the tissues covering the cervix) and carcinoma *in situ* (cellular anaplastic changes), were discovered in smears. The latter pathologies were assumed to be subtle, preinvasive cancer changes. However, verification of this assumption was necessary. Data were collected to see whether or not the more subtle pathologies appeared in the same risk groups as shown by invasive cancer. Similarities in the distributions of the pathologies by risk groups were found. The average age of women with each pathology was assessed, under the assumption that if one pathology leads to the other, then the average age at the first should be lower than the average age at the second. This correlation of increasing age with increasing severity was verified. Direct evidence for the progression of disease was sought from cohort studies that followed women with one of the earlier, more subtle pathologies over time to see the rate of progression to invasive cancer. Although progression from dysplasia to carcinoma *in situ* to invasive cervical cancer did occur, dysplasia that reversed to normal and dysplasia that neither reversed nor progressed were found, as well. The questions still remain whether or not each and every case of dysplasia indicates, is caused by, or leads to the same condition (Foltz and Kelsey 1978:426–462).

In AIDS research, the same approaches are being considered and used, but it is too soon to analyze survey data and data from cohort studies done on those individuals with the possible prodromal phase of AIDS. A study of the changes in incidence over time of these subtle clinical and serological changes, as compared to the changes in incidence over time of AIDS, might shed some light on any such relationship. The literature suggests a high level of these subtle changes occurring among the same risk groups as those showing AIDS (Seligmann et al. 1984). One cannot possibly determine, however, whether the current interest in certain risk groups that brings the groups under closer scrutiny thereby increases the detection of subtle symptoms or whether there is a true elevation in rates of the subtle changes in these risk groups.

The first criterion of the CDC definition of AIDS excludes those individuals with an immunodeficiency for which a known cause has been established. This exclusion category includes organ-transplant recipients; patients with systemic lupus erythematosus; and those who develop immune dysfunction in response to immunosuppressive drugs, in the presence of foreign tissue, or from a condition that has the secondary effect of immunosuppression. Unfortunately, individuals who are immunosuppressed with a known cause and individuals who are immunosuppressed with no known cause are clinically and serologically indistinguishable, even up to the point of developing the same types of opportunistic infections. If it is apparent, then, from looking at the "explained" immunosuppression, that clinically and serologically indistinguishable conditions can result from a large and diverse group of etiologies, then the question arises as to the validity of the assumption in the definition of AIDS that all remaining "unexplained" (or idiopathic) immunosuppressions have the same eitiology. With this consideration, we realize that if we consider all individuals who have "unexplained" immunodeficiency as AIDS patients and look at their characteristics as compared to a group of non-AIDS controls, our resulting picture of risk factors for AIDS might be a hodgepodge of risk factors for all yet-to-be-explained immune disorders (Sonnabend and Saadoun 1986).

Regardless of the resolution of these questions, we remain, at the moment, with a disease definition that is strict: that is, it defines a severe disease and one that lies possibly at the end of a disease spectrum. Restricting the count to the most severe cases does not affect the comparability of rates across groups, as long as the identically strict definition is adhered to for all groups studied. In general, however, epidemiologists prefer cases that represent the full spectrum of any disease, because the use of such cases gives inferences wider generalizability. For example, in many diseases, deaths represent the extreme end of a continuum of diseased people, so that the old, the very young, those disease types least responsive to treatment, and perhaps those people with least access to medical care are over-represented among deaths. This same type of selection bias will persist in those studies of AIDS that restrict case definition to the CDC criteria.

All new AIDS cases in the United States must be reported to local health departments and then to the CDC. Incidence rates based on such reports may be estimated for the total population, but in calculating incidence rates of AIDS for a specific group, one meets the difficulty of ascertaining accurate denominator information. This problem becomes virtually insurmountable when dealing with elusive groups such as IV-drug users, and the inaccuracy increases when attempting to separate the already uncertain group of IV-drug users into its subgroups (e.g., those who share needles versus those who do not). Although estimates of such denominator information are available and these estimates are the best and only way to calculate incidence rates, the possibility of inaccuracy must be considered.

Prevalence rates, as determined by surveys done at a single point in time, are not useful for investigating the cause of AIDS, because they do not reveal information regarding the time sequence of hypothesized cause and effect. Mortality data for AIDS would be a good estimate of AIDS incidence if AIDS was always immediately fatal, but because AIDS is not always immediately fatal, they cannot be regarded as more useful than morbidity-based incidence. In practice, mortality rates for AIDS can only be derived from incidence reports and not from death certificates (most commonly the source of mortality data for other diseases), because it is uncertain how consistently AIDS (and not the specific opportunistic infection) is coded as the cause of death on death certificates.

Because of the mandatory reporting of AIDS, once a case comes to the attention of health professionals, reporting is assumed to be consistent across groups. A question that must be considered is whether or not all groups who get AIDS are equally likely to come to the attention of health professionals. If one group has, for example, better access to medical care, rates of the disease might possibly appear higher in that group. This does not seem to be the case with AIDS, because the ultimate morbidity is so severe that medical attention, at least in the United States and in other developed countries, is undoubtedly sought in all cases, regardless of access to care. If, however, there are prodromal signs or symptoms, or milder conditions, then the available data are more likely to be biased by differential access to medical care.

Whether or not the AIDS syndrome, or a related form of it, is new in certain developing nations is unclear. Regions of Africa have long been known to have endemic Kaposi's sarcoma, but the relationship between AIDS and endemic Kaposi's sarcoma is not fully understood (Sonnabend and Saadoun 1986). Proof of an unprecedented high incidence of AIDS in the United States is important when examining etiological hypotheses. For example, if AIDS in male homosexuals is a recent and unprecedented phenomenon, a purely behavioral hypothesis is acceptable only if a recent and unprecedented change in behavior can be documented that would accompany the upsurge in the disease. Similarly, a single-agent hypothesis would only be acceptable if a new, previously nonexistent agent is found to exist. Even with such an agent (LAV/HTLV-III), unless the correlation between the agent and the disease is 100%, which it is not we can assume that cofactors or intervening variables that may be behavioral exist.

Several descriptive epidemiological studies have been undertaken both to identify risk factors more specific than group identity and to identify more consistent serological risk factors for, and possible indicators of, the syndrome. With regard to serological studies, small series of cases ($n = 3$ to 15) have been studied to establish serological attributes that make possible discrimination between cases and controls (Follansbee et al. 1982:705-713; Masur et al. 1981:1431-1438; Mildvan et al. 1982:700-704). For example, in one study, four previously healthy homosexual men with *Pneumocystis carinii* pneumonia were examined. In all four men, high levels of cytomegalovirus (CMV) and reversed T-cell ratios (helper to suppressor lymphocytes) were found (Gottlieb et al. 1981:1425). In another study, six previously healthy drug abusers with current opportunistic infections were examined. All were found to have reversed T-cell ratios (Moll et al.

1982:417–423). Similar serological changes have been found in individuals not experiencing full-blown AIDS but experiencing persistent generalized lymphadenopathy (Sonnabend 1983:1–22). This finding returns us to the question of whether or not an AIDS prodrome exists.

With regard to defining risk factors more specific than group affiliation, studies of drug use, sexual behavior, and evidence of other infection were conducted, most often within the risk group of male homosexuals. Conflicting data with regard to drug use were reported: one study that did yield a significant association between use of amyl nitrite and AIDS had these results called into question when sexual activity was controlled (Marmor 1985; Marmor et al. 1982).

The data on sexual activity are more consistent. Several studies have shown associations between large numbers of partners, the passive role in anal intercourse, and AIDS (Darrow et al. 1983:160; Jaffe et al. 1983: 145–151). The possible unique contribution of each of these practices has not been explored. Recent laboratory evidence (Richards et al. 1984:390) demonstrates an association between rectal exposure to semen and immune-system breakdown in mice, thereby suggesting a role for this secondary effect of a sexual practice as a cofactor in immune-system collapse. Several recent epidemiological studies (Hsia et al. 1984:1212; Mavlight et al. 1984:237) have shown significant associations between exposure to sperm alloantigens and immune dysfunction in male homosexuals (gays). Confirmation of this association in human being, creates a coherent hypothesis that includes a role for anal intercourse as a cofactor in AIDS causation.

The association between the presence of other infections and AIDS has been surveyed (Jaffe et al. 1983:145–151; Marmor et al. 1982:1083–1087). The data reveal that people with AIDS more often have evidence of a variety of sexually transmitted diseases than do non-AIDS controls. Specifically, CMV, Epstein-Barr virus (EBV), hepatitis B, and syphilis have been shown to have a significant association with AIDS. Recent studies have concentrated on various forms of human T-cell leukemia virus (HTLV), with results that point toward a causal role for a variant, HTLV-III (also called lymphadenopathy-associated virus, LAV) (Essex et al. 1983:859; Gallo et al. 1983:865; Mathez et al. 1984:799). An overwhelming majority of people with ARC are reportedly able to recover, but late-stage AIDS patients do not recover from the disease (Broder and Gallo 1984). HTLV, we would like to note, has been isolated as consistently from individuals with AIDS as from individuals with lymphadenopathy. This again points to a prodrome that requires the presence of HTLV-III in the first place but that also requires cofactors in order to progress to the severe stage. LAV/HTLV-III has also been isolated from many symptom-free members of high-risk groups (Laurence et al. 1984; Seligmann et al. 1984).

For current purposes, we feel that it is important to note that although women form only a small proportion of the total number of AIDS cases in the United States, they are by no means immune to the disease, and they do, in fact, manifest the disease in a way that is quite similar to the way men do (reversed T-cell ratios, elevated levels of IgG and IgA) (Masur et al. 1982:533–539). In an effort to pursue the hypothesis of transmissibility of AIDS, sexual contacts of female cases were traced to see whether or not the female cases could be connected to members of other high-risk groups. The connection could be made in a large number of cases (CDC 1983:697–698). In an effort to see whether or not those behaviors that are called risk factors in men (large numbers of partners, passive role in anal intercourse) could be associated with immune dysfunction in women, female prostitutes were studied. The data did suggest that these women had a degree of immune dysfunction (Wallace et al 1983:58–59). This evidence, although in no way conclusive, supports a role for behaviors and their secondary effects in the causal chain.

A study of clustering of AIDS among male homosexuals in Los Angeles (CDC 1982a:305–307) and the studies that link female cases sexually to male cases (CDC 1983:697–698) show clearly that the disease involves a transmissible agent. In addition, several case studies of AIDS in individuals who are not risk-group members suggest contact with risk-group members. For example, the investigation of AIDS in a white, 50-year-old Canadian woman revealed a stay in Haiti and a sexual contact while there (Rose and Keystone 1983:680–681). Several studies of AIDS in European men have revealed travel to, and sexual contact with individuals from, New York, Haiti, or central Africa (Brunet et al. 1983:700–701). In addition, the presence of AIDS in hemophiliacs and transfusion recipients suggests a blood product route of transmission. The presence of AIDS in children of high-risk individuals suggests transimissibility with close physical contact, probably in utero, prenatally, or in the early postnatal period.

If AIDS were transmissible in the same way as are other sexually transmitted diseases, the observed distribution of cases suggests that the circles of sexual contact among the risk groups have been sufficiently closed, preventing significant spread. On the face of it, this is unlikely, because bisexuality, for example, is not rare. If circles of sexual contact are not, then, as closed as a strictly transmissible pattern of AIDS occurrence might imply, necessary cofactors might possibly cluster within specific risk groups.

AIDS has been recognized in several other countries, most notably in Belgium, Zaire, and Haiti (Pape et al. 1983:945; Clumeck et al 1983:642). In those countries, cases do not cluster in the same high-risk groups found in North America. By contrast, most cases in other European countries can be linked by sexual contact to known high-risk groups (Brunet et al. 1983:700–701). These are puzzling inconsistencies that require further studies.

From the descriptive epidemiology of AIDS, three etiologic hypotheses emerge. As each of these are discussed in what follows, suggestions are made for appropriate analytic study designs.

III. ETIOLOGIC HYPOTHESES AND SUGGESTIONS FOR ANALYTIC EPIDEMIOLOGY

HYPOTHESIS 1. *A single agent, newly introduced or modified, probably LAV/HTLV-III, is "necessary" and "sufficient" to cause AIDS.*

Such a hypothesis would require for its unequivocal confirmation the demonstration of the presence of LAV/HTLV-III in all people with AIDS and the absence of LAV/HTLV-III from all who do not. LAV/HTLV-III has been isolated from a majority of people with AIDS but has also been isolated from a number of symptom-free individuals who are members of high-risk groups (Seligmann et al. 1984). Whether these symptom-free individuals will go on to develop AIDS or will remain symptom free as possible carriers is uncertain. Also uncertain is whether or not all individuals who are exposed to LAV/HTLV-III are equally as likely to develop AIDS. Because of the recency of the LAV/HTLV-III discovery, these uncertainties, and therefore this hypothesis, remain formally untested.

By attributing the distribution of cases entirely to the presence of an infective agent, it must be remembered that in crowded metropolitan areas smallpox, influenza, and rubella pass from person to person; polio, cholera, and typhoid are passed via water or excreta. In order for an infection to be confined to the risk groups observed for AIDS, this agent must be sexually transmitted. No other route (excluding blood transfusions) could be so exclusive. On the whole, infective agents of sexually transmitted diseases do not survive well in the open environment and are not found in contaminants of water or food. Usually, sexually transmitted diseases (e.g., chlamydia, syphilis, gonorrhea, herpes) are transmitted between the sexes, although manifestations and treatment responses vary in men and women. In the United States, AIDS is found mostly in men.

Three explanations are suggested. One is that the circle of transmission among exclusively homosexual men is a closed one and that not only women but also bisexual men are virtually excluded from this circle. This would be surprising on the face of it, because other sexually transmitted diseases are found among both men and women. On the other hand, hepatitis B appears frequently to be a sexually transmitted disease and is more common among homosexual men than among women. The second explanation is that the anal route favors the transmission of this particular agent. This explanation would be supported by the observation noted above of increased susceptibility to AIDS for the receptive partner of anal intercourse among male homosexuals. On the other hand, women exposed anally to many male partners should be equally susceptible as men. The third explanation is that women are in some way biologically protected from this organism. This is not entirely far-fetched, for there are conditions in which the possession of two, rather than one, X chromosomes by women has seemed to account for gender differences in incidence (Purtilo and Sullivan 1979:1251–1253). If this were true, the "new" epidemic of AIDS might be postulated to be a distant relation of the African Kaposi's sarcoma (which is, in general, more common among men than among women), but, again, based on the patterns of apparent transmission of AIDS in this country, AIDS and the African Kaposi's sarcoma are clearly quite different.

Choosing among these competing explanations has proven impossible. One might design a study that examined the boundaries of circles of sexual contact of high-risk groups in order to determine whether or not they are as closed as the distribution of AIDS suggests. One might also design an epidemiological study that would assess the effects of LAV/HTLV-III among men and among women. A group of men known to have LAV/HTLV-III could be compared to a group of women known to have LAV/HTLV-III, with regard to their immune functions. If these men and women show comparable immune function, the action of the agent is not sex dependent and the agent might be "sufficient" for AIDS causation. If the women display better immune function than do the men, perhaps although the agent might be "necessary," it is not "sufficient," because two X chromosomes are protective. It would be important in a study such as this to control for other factors that might be related independently both to immune function and gender; for example, use of certain drugs (hormones) or other unrelated health conditions (e.g., lupus).

HYPOTHESIS 2. *LAV/HTLV-III does not cause AIDS; its presence is virtually ubiquitous in already immunocompromised individuals. AIDS is the result of certain, specific sexual behaviors and their secondary effects (antibody formation, exposure and re-exposure to several common, sexually transmitted infections).*

This hypothesis emphasizes the role of sexual activity with multiple partners and the receptive role in anal intercourse, coupled with that of exposure and re-exposure to a variety of common sexually transmitted infections. The descriptive epidemiology of AIDS suggests that perhaps these factors alone are not "sufficient" for AIDS, because if they were, all groups that have these risk factors would also have AIDS. This is not the case, because female prostitutes, a group of people who are sexually active with multiple partners and who have high frequencies of re-exposure to common, sexually transmitted infections, have not emerged as a high-risk group for AIDS in the United States. Nor, it would seem, have female prostitutes who practice anal intercourse.

The question arises as to whether or not prostitutes experience any immune-system breakdown at all. If they do, but they do not acquire AIDS, it is possible to assert that immune system breakdown is not a direct prodrome to AIDS, and factors beyond large numbers of partners, anal intercourse, and re-exposure to common, sexually transmitted infections are "necessary" for AIDS to occur. The additional factor might be the absence of a second X chromosome (i.e., being male) or the presence of an exclusive infectious agent. In any case, a comparison of male homosexuals and female prostitutes who practice anal intercourse could separate the etiology of the possible AIDS prodrome from the etiology of AIDS itself.

In order to investigate further which factors are "necessary" for AIDS to occur, a comparison of prostitutes who have anal intercourse and prostitutes who do not (thus having only large numbers of partners and not anal intercourse) could be revealing. If immune dysfunction is greater in the former group, the practice of anal sex is highlighted. If the two groups demonstrate the same immune function, the anal mode adds nothing, given large numbers of partners. In addition, such a study would permit a contrast of the particular infections that flourish among women prostitutes in those who do and those who do not practice anal sex. If the organisms are the same, then the practice might simply modify the response of the host. If the organisms are different, then an important (if not "necessary") organism to immune-system breakdown might be discovered.

Sonnabend (1984: personal communication) has suggested that not merely behavior, but rather behavior in combination with the setting in which it is practiced, leads to immune system breakdown. That is, if re-exposure to a variety of common, sexually transmitted infections is a cofactor in AIDS causation and the prevalence of various common, sexually transmitted infections in male homosexuals is higher than it is in female prostitutes due to smaller, more closed circles of sexual contact, then even given similar behavior, the male homosexuals would be re-exposed to the same organisms more often and would thereby be at higher risk for AIDS than would female prostitutes. Ideally, the prevalences of the various sexually transmitted infections could be measured in the sera of the male homosexuals and in the sera of the contacts of the female prostitutes. This kind of comparison could shed light on the role of re-exposure to common, sexually transmitted infections in AIDS causation.

HYPOTHESIS 3. *A single, newly active agent, probably LAV/HTLV-III, is "necessary" but not "sufficient" to cause AIDS; AIDS is manifested only given specific behaviors and the presumed biochemical changes associated with them.*

This hypothesis seems to us to be the most likely, given the descriptive epidemiology of AIDS. It is testable epidemiologically by first specifying a model of cofactors for AIDS causation (agent plus sexual behaviors with their secondary effects plus exposure and re-exposure to common, sexually transmitted infections with *their* secondary effects), choosing AIDS cases and controls, and comparing groups with regard to adherence to the model. If the cases adhere to the model with more regularity than do the controls, then the hypothesis must be permitted to stand. If no significant difference in adherence to the model between cases and controls is found, then the hypothesis must be rejected (i.e., something "necessary" is missing from the model). This is a rigorous test of the hypothesis, because the model must be very precisely specified before data collection and the analysis begin. One small omission in the specified model will lead to the rejection of the hypothesis (even if all of the specified cofactors are "necessary"). In addition, observations that do not enable us to reject the hypothesis do not tell us whether or not the specified model is broader than it needs to be. This approach lends itself to iteration and is only truly practical after Hypotheses 1 and 2 have been rejected.

The ability to derive a valid explicit model for AIDS causation will be intimately tied to the ability to measure accurately the variables of interest. Measurement error can vitiate the results of even the most ingeniously designed study. Variables must first be precisely defined conceptually. Then the methods chosen to measure the variables should be tested for validity and reliability. Descriptions of methods of valid measurement and of the effects of measurement error are detailed elsewhere (Cook and Campbell 1979).

Why develop an explicit causal model for AIDS? Causal models have, historically (most notably in the cases of malaria and schistosomiasis), proven themselves indispensible for mapping options for disease control measures, planning resource allocation (based on the ability of the causal model to predict disease incidence), and presenting coherently and concisely, cutting across disciplinary lines, the mode of action and interaction of various cofactors. Thus, the model can be understood and used for different ends by professionals approaching the disease from a variety of perspectives (Susser 1973).

Thus, deriving an explicit causal model for AIDS is of great theoretical, and even greater practical, importance. Although biological research relating to a single agent is mandatory, attention must also be given to the other factors in the web of AIDS causation. Without these factors, in their proper proportions, AIDS possibly would not exist. In fact, this is precisely the point: with even a slight manipulation of the proportionate input of the factors, the incidence of AIDS could possibly be manipulated. We cannot realize this possibility until a carefully formulated model, which attributes to each cofactor its own share of input, is derived.

Sir Ronald Ross, in the 1890s, was in a situation with malaria that is analogous to the one we are now in with AIDS. While in the process of deriving the explicit mathematical model of causation for malaria, he realized:

> To say that a disease depends upon certain factors is not to say much, until we can also form an estimate as to how largely each factor influences the whole result. And the mathematical method of treatment is really nothing but the application of careful reasoning to the problem at issue (Ross 1910).

Let us not hesitate to apply this lesson from history to the investigation of AIDS.

REFERENCES

Broder, S. and R. Gallo. 1984. A Pathogenic Retrovirus (HTLV-3) Linked to AIDS. *New England Journal of Medicine* 311(20):1292–1297.

Brunet, J. B., E. Bovet, J. Leibovitch, J. Chaperon, and C. Mayud. 1983. Acquired Immune Deficiency in France. *Lancet* 1:700–701.

Centers for Disease Control. 1981a. Pneumocystic Pneumonia—Los Angeles. *Morbidity and Mortality Weekly Reports* 30:250–252.

_____. 1981b. Kaposi's Sarcoma and *Pneumocystis carinii* Pneumonia Among Homosexual Men—New York City and California. *Morbidity and Mortality Weekly Report* 30:305.

_____. 1982a. A Clutter of Kaposi's Sarcoma and *Pneumocystis carinii* Pneumonia Among Homosexual Male Residents of Los Angeles and Orange Counties, California. *Morbidity and Mortality Weekly Report* 31:305–307.

_____. 1982b. Epidemiologic Aspects of the Current Outbreak of Kaposi's Sarcoma. *New England Journal of Medicine* 306:248–252.

_____. 1983. Immunodeficiency Among Female Sexual Partners of Males with Acquired Immune Deficiency Syndrome. *Morbidity and Mortality Weekly Report* 31:697–698.

_____. 1984. Update: Acquired Immunodeficiency Syndrome—United States. *Morbidity and Mortality Weekly Reports* 32:688–690.

Clumeck, N., F. Mascart-Lemone, J. Demauberg, D. Brenez, L. Marcelis. 1983. Acquired Immune Deficiency in Black Africans, *Lancet* 1:642.

Cook, T. D. and D. T. Campbell. 1979. *Quasi Experimentation: Design and Analysis Issues for Field Settings.* Chicago: Rand McNally.

Darrow, W. W., H. W. Jaffe, J. W. Curran. 1983. Passive Anal Intercourse as a Risk Factor for AIDS in Homosexual Men. *Lancet* 2:160.

Essex, M., M. F. McLane, T. H. Lee, L. Flak, C. W. S. Howe, and J. I. Mullins. 1983 Antibodies to Cell Membrane Antigens Associated with Human T-Cell Leukemia Virus in Patients with AIDS. *Science* 220:859–962.

Follansbee, S. E., D. R. Busch, C. B. Wofsky et al. 1982. An Outbreak of *Pneumocystis carinii* Pneumonia in Homosexual Men. *Annals of Internal Medicine* 96:705–713.

Foltz, A. M. and J. L. Kelsey. 1978. The Annual Pap Test: A Dubious Policy Success *Health and Society* 56(4):426–462.

Gallo, R. C., P. S. Arin, E. P. Gelmann et al. 1983. Isolation of Human T-Cell Leukemia Virus in Acquired Immune Deficiency Syndrome. *Science* 220:865–867.

Gottlieb, M. S., R. Schroff, M. Schanker et al. 1981. *Pneumocystis carinii* Pneumonia and Mucosal Candidiasis in Previously Healthy Homosexual Men. *New England Journal of Medicine* 305(24):1425–1431.

Hsia, S., R. Shockley, C. Lutcher, D. Doran, P. Galle, and L. Hodge. 1984. Unregulated Production of Virus and/or Sperm Specific Antibodies as a Cause of AIDS. *Lancet* June 2:1212–1214.

Jaffe, H. W., K. Choi, P. A. Thomas et al. 1983. National Case-Control Study of Kaposi's Sarcoma and *Pneumocystis carinii* in Homosexual Men: Part 1—Epidemiological Results. *Annals of Internal Medicine* 99:145–151.

Laurence, J., F. Brun-Vezinet, S. Schutzer, C. Rouzioux, D. Klatzmann, F. Barre-Sinoussi, J. C. Cherman, and L. Montagnier. 1984. Lymphadenopathy-Associated Viral Antibody in AIDS. *New England Journal of Medicine* 311(20):1270–1273.

MacMahon, B. and T. F. Pugh. 1970. *Epidemiology—Principles and Methods.* Boston: Little Brown and Company.

Marmor, M. 1984. Risk Factors for AIDS. In *AIDS: A Basic Guide for Clinicians* Ebbesen, P., Biggar, R. J. and Melbye, M., eds. Philadelphia: W. B. Saunders.

Marmor, M., A. E. Friedman-Kien, L. J. Laubenstein et al. 1982. Risk Factors for Kaposi's Sarcoma in Homosexual Men. *Lancet* May 15:1083–1087.

Masur, H., M. A. Michelis, J. Greene et al. 1981 An Outbreak of *Pneumocystis carinii* Pneumonia. *New England Journal of Medicine* 305(24):1431–1438.

Masur, H., M. A. Michelis, G. P. Wormser et al. 1982. Opportunistic Infection in Previously Healthy Women. *Annals of Internal Medicine* 97(4):533–539.

Mathez, D., J. Leibowitch, P. Catalan, M. Essex, and D. Zaguri. 1984. HTLV and AIDS in France. *Lancet* I(8320):899.

Mavligit, G. M., M. Tapaz, F. T. Hsia et al. 1984. Chronic Immune Stimulation by Sperm Alloantigens. *Journal of the American Medical Association* 251(2):237–241.

Mildvan, D., U. Mathur, R. Enlow et al. 1982. Opportunistic Infections and Immune Deficiency in Homosexual Men. *Annals of Internal Medicine* 96 (Part 1):700–704.

Moll, B., E. E. Emeson, C. B. Small, G. Friedland, R. Klein, and I. Spigland. 1982. Inverted Ratio of Inducer to Suppressor T-Lymphocyte Subsets in Drug Abusers with Opportunistic Infections. *Clinical Immunology and Immunopathology* 25:417–423.

Pape, J. W., B. Liautaud, F. Thomas et al. 1983. Characteristics of the Acquired Immune Deficiency Syndrome (AIDS) in Haiti. *New England Journal of Medicine* 309:945–949.

Purtilo, D. T., J. L. Sullivan. 1979. Immunological Basis for Superior Survival of Females. *American Journal of Diseases of Children* 133:1251–1253.

Richards, J. M., J. M. Bedford, and S. S. Witkin. 1984. Rectal Insemination Modifies Immune Responses in Rabbits. *Science* 224:390–392.

Rose, J. B. and J. S. Keystone. 1983. AIDS in a Canadian Woman Who Had Helped Prostitutes in Port-Au-Prince. *Lancet* Sept. 17:680–681.

Ross, R. 1910. *The Prevention of Malaria*, 2nd Ed. New York: Dutton.

Seligmann, M. L. Chess, J. Fahey et al. 1984. AIDS — An Immunologic Reevaluation. *New England Journal of Medicine* 311(20):1286–1292.

Sonnabend, J. A. 1983. The Etiology of AIDS. *AIDS Research* 1:1–22.

_____ . 1984. Personal communication.

Sonnabend, J. A. and S. Saadoun. 1986. The Acquired Immune Deficiency Syndrome: A Description of Etiologic Hypotheses, In press.

Susser, M. W. 1973. *Causal Thinking in the Health Sciences*. New York: Oxford University Press.

Wallace, J., J. Downes, A. Ott et al. 1983. T-Cell Ratios in New York City Prostitutes. *Lancet* Jan. 1:58–59.

Chapter Four

The Case for a Haitian Origin of the AIDS Epidemic

Alexander Moore and Ronald D. Le Baron

There is an urgent need to understand AIDS better. The disease affects diverse populations: Haitians, black Africans, homosexual (gay) men, IV-drug users, hemophiliacs, users of blood products, and some infants. This paper focuses on the Haitian context of the disease.

Vieira et al. (1983:129), in a study of AIDS in Haitian immigrants, note that "the assumption that heterosexual Haitians and homosexual Americans have little in common may prove erroneous when epidemiologic and anthropologic surveys are completed."

A disease now recognized as AIDS was present in Zaire, Chad, and perhaps other central African nations in the mid 1970s. Indeed, a Danish surgeon died in Denmark in 1976 from a disease contracted in Africa and later diagnosed as AIDS (Siegal and Siegal 1983:99). At the same time it was almost certainly present in Haiti, where it was unrecognized initially for the same reasons that it went undetected in Africa: that is, in the general lack of public health care a subtle new disease resulting in a variety of opportunistic infections simply went unnoticed.

The virus probably causing AIDS has recently been identified as HTLV-III (human T-cell lymphotropic virus-III) (Gallo et al. 1984; Popovic et al. 1984; Sarngadharan et al. 1984). HTLV-III, a new agent or one seldom found heretofore in human hosts, could have originated by mutating through animals from closely related Type C oncoviruses to infect immunosuppressed humans. This agent could find its way into human hosts in Haiti, and in equatorial Africa, through the regular ingestion of uncooked animal blood sacrificed in spirit-possession ceremonies. However, the subsequent spread of the epidemic to Western populations was through international gay tourism to Haiti, not central Africa, which has comparatively little tourism. The probability of animal reservoirs of the ancestral AIDS agent and its regular entry into humans through blood sacrifice in Haiti or Africa or both is enough to warrant public health teams to work in both areas.

THE HAITIAN CONTEXT

An examination of social, cultural, and environmental conditions discloses that if any place in the world is ripe for the genesis of a major new pathogen, then that place is Haiti. The details of an exploding population's interaction with a deteriorating environment are extreme enough. Were Haiti to be classified with Africa in terms of development, its ranking would be quite low, and of all the New World nations, it is the least European in culture. Although nominally Roman Catholic in religion and nominally republican in government, it is in fact governed by a hereditary despotic monarchy closely allied with the priesthood of a spirit-possession cult of West African origin. This cult bolsters the regime through nationalistic symbols, which, in turn, the regime manipulate and imbue with terror through a special armed force, the *tonton macoutes*. In this context, the Haitian tourist industry is on an exotic frontier, yet is comparatively close to New York City, whose homosexual men it has welcomed as tourists with offers of abundant sexual recreation. The Haitian society, when understood as the systemic interrelation of underdevelopment, environmental—and consequently, physical and emotional—stress, a politically entrenched voodoo cult that thrives on the first two, and a small but distinctly offbeat tourist industry, is one in which the AIDS epidemic could well have originated.

Haiti ranks at the bottom of every standard index of development of all the nations in the Western hemisphere (Rotberg and Clague 1971). Its literacy rate of 11.5% is by far the lowest (Berry 1975). Only 2.6% of its dwellings had running water in 1969, and open drains, rather than sewers, are the rule in towns and outlying city districts (Rotberg and Clague 1971). Per capita income declined from $82 in 1955 to $70 in 1968 (Lundahl 1979). In 1969, the estimated population of 4.6 million was increasing at the rate of 2.3% annually; by 1984 the population stood at 6.6 million and should pass ten million before 1999. However, demographic data—and all other statistics—are hard to come by and must be treated cautiously, because Haiti has never had a reliable census. The last one, in 1971, has only been partially published. Population density—170 inhabitants per square kilometer in the late 1960s—has correspondingly increased; in the late 1960s Haiti was second in the hemisphere only to Puerto Rico in density (Bazile 1975). A major difference between the two nations however, is, that Puerto

Rico practices intensive agriculture and is highly urbanized and industrial-ized. Haiti, in contrast, is an overwhelmingly peasant society: 89% of the population lives on the land, mainly as subsistence farmers (Lundahl 1979:11–90), and industrial development is negligible.

The government of Haiti has consistently vacillated between brief con-trol by elite cliques and long-term rule by dictators (Nicholls 1979). Since 1957 Haiti has been ruled by two Duvalier Presidents-for-Life, first François ("Papa Doc") and now his son Jean-Claude ("Baby Doc"), who acceded to the presidency at age nineteen upon his father's death (Diederich and Burt 1969). Lundahl, borrowing the term from Myrdal, has called the Duvalier regime a "soft state," one based on spoils of the treasury. The Duvalier family is believed to have amassed enormous wealth abroad. In any case, all their development projects are believed to have failed (Lundahl 1979).

Haiti, a mountainous and once-fertile land, must confront critical problems of soil exhaustion and erosion. As its peasant population grows, the response has been not to intensify planting of erosion-resistant export crops such as sugar cane and coffee, but rather for peasant cultivators to ex-pand their subsistence plantings onto even steeper hillsides, removing rain-forest cover. The result has been deterioration of the soil and its eventual conversion to barren rock outcrops while the population that must subsist on that soil increases. The Duvalier regime has failed to enforce forestry legislation or to encourage soil conservation (Lundahl 1979).

Malnutrition is a problem in Haiti. One estimate of the average daily calorie and protein needs for the agricultural laborer is 2,200 calories and 55 grams of protein (Beghin et al. 1970). Surveys indicate daily caloric deficits of 35% and protein deficits of 12% (Lundahl 1979). Substantial deficits of vitamin A and riboflavin have been estimated, and nutrition has probably been declining over several decades. Preschool children suffer most; already high incidences of kwashiorkor (a severe protein-deficiency syndrome) and marasmus (acute starvation) are reportedly increasing (Lundahl 1979). Underfed adults are less able to work in the fields and have less resistance to disease than would their healthy counterparts (Beisel et al. 1982; King 1975; Miller 1980; Pekarek et al. 1979).

The incidence of disease in Haiti is high (Lundahl 1979). Yaws, former-ly endemic, was brought under control but not eradicated by a campaign launched under WHO and UNICEF auspices in 1950. A similar campaign to control malaria through insecticides, although having good initial results, has not succeeded in eradicating it. Significantly, malaria is an immunosup-pressive disease (Brasseur et al. 1983). Tuberculosis continues to be endemic, with 3% of the population suffering active cases and virtually all adults thought to have had the disease at one time in their lives. In the mid-1960s, evidence pointed to an intestinal parasite infestation rate of 100% in rural areas, and intestinal parasites may possibly have an immunosuppressive effect, too (Pearce 1983). Respiratory ailments other than tuberculosis are endemic, particularly during the rainy season.

Public-health services are virtually nonexistent in rural Haiti. In 1973, five physicians and fifty-seven hospital beds served every 100,000 inhabitants in the rural areas (Lundahl 1979). Nevertheless, the importation of inexpensive antibiotics and drugs has been sufficient to lower the death rate. This and the traditionally high birth rate have resulted in explosive population growth.

Although low rates of caloric consumption and high incidences of chronic disease may not be stressful for individual peasants who are in demographic and agricultural homeostasis with their environment, such is not the case in Haiti. Malnutrition and disease in the context of explosive population growth and deteriorating natural resources have meant disaster. Although data since 1975 are not available, we believe that conditions of individual stress in Haiti have been worsening steadily.

Crowding per se in human populations may not be stressful for individuals under conditions of urban industrial growth and expanding economic opportunity (thus, crowding in Hong Kong, for example, never became problematic). Crowding in Haiti, in contrast, is under conditions of rural degradation. Human stress is likely to have increased there over the last twenty years. (See the discussion of Calhoun's experiments in the crowding of rats in Hall 1969.) The recent, desperate taking to the seas in open boats of many Haitians without documents to brave a hostile reception abroad is dramatic evidence of that conclusion.

HAITIAN INGESTION OF ANIMAL BLOOD

In this situation of chronic stress caused by eroding farm soils, declining cash incomes, chronic malnutrition, and prevalent high rates of disease, observers should not be surprised to find that Haitians turn to their traditional religion for social and psychological support. The de facto religion of Haiti is a spirit-possession cult known as "voodoo." Although the Roman Catholic Church sporadically prevailed upon the state to persecute the cult in the past, the elder Duvalier, Papa Doc, early in his reign broke the power of the Catholic clergy and allied himself with the voodoo priests, *houngans*. Although some uncooperative *houngans*, together with other opponents of Duvalier, were killed during these early years, those who joined the Duvalier forces prospered. Today the cult is a major pillar of the regime, and in some areas voodoo priests are political bosses as well (Diederich and Burt 1969; Nicholls, 1979).

Although ostensibly Roman Catholic, all Haitians except the educated urban elite (scarcely 10% of the population) participate in the voodoo cult, at least by watching the spirit possessions and by dancing in the all night dances that follow the ceremony proper. Simpson (1934), an anthropologist, found that 10% of one rural district of 30,000 people and 200 priests actually entered into trance. Voodoo ceremonies are held weekly everywhere and are better established today than in the 1930s. Change over the last 50 years has brought intensification of traditional patterns in Haiti. Change has brought neither secularization nor Catholic evangelization to the countryside. The voodoo cult flourishes under conditions of intensifying stress.

Voodoo is not a superstition but a religion with a pantheon of gods derived in large part from Dahomey in West Africa. Closely related cults exist in Cuba, Trinidad, and the north coast of Brazil, all of which are also derived from Dahomey. All of these cults have adapted to New World conditions (Walker 1972). Only in Haiti in the New World, however, is the cult extensive enough to be termed *the* religion of an entire society. In Haiti, the pantheon has been expanded to include folkloric spirits with mythical attributes derived from Haitian history. The essential feature of spirit possession is the visitation of gods and spirits whose names and personalities are well known to priests. Spirits are believed literally to enter the communicants, who then enter hypnotic trances and exhibit personality traits imputed to the spirit. Spirits are believed to promote health and well being and, in some cases, to cure illness and trauma (Walker 1972). Some anthropologists have associated trance and spiritual possession with hysteria induced by malnutrition (Foulks and Katz 1973; Kehoe and Giletti 1981; Wallace 1972). Thus, beginners in the voodoo cult may be malnourished and particularly susceptible to infection.

In Haiti, spirits are summoned by blood sacrifice. Bulls, goats, pigs, pigeons, and chickens are sacrificed, but the most common and numerous offerings are chickens. In all cases the sacrificial animal is first offered food and drink. Acceptance by the animal of food and drink is interpreted as a sign that the spirit is about to descend. At that moment, the officiating priest and others go into trance-possession by a patron spirit. In frenzied trance, the priest lets blood: mammal's throats are cut; typically, chicken's heads are torn off their necks. The priest bites out the chicken's tongue with his teeth and may suck on the bloody stump of the neck. All sacrificed blood is collected immediately in a "gourd containing salt, ash, molasses or native rum" (Metraux 1958:156). This is stirred, allowed to coagulate, and then the priest and his or her assistants drink a spoonful. Some participants may also anoint their bodies with the blood. In curing ceremonies, the blood and the corpse of the sacrificed animal may be rubbed upon the afflicted part of the patient. Sacrificed animals are butchered on the spot and certain parts are buried as an offering to the spirits. The remaining parts are cooked and consumed by the participants (Metraux 1958:150–157). These rites do not constitute an orgy of bloodletting, but they do constitute an orderly and frequent opportunity for many Haitians to ingest uncooked mammalian and avian blood.

HOMOSEXUALITY IN HAITI

A high incidence of homosexuality is reported among male voodoo priests. Metraux (1958:55) implies that most of them are homosexual. During spirit possession the participant can quite possibly be possessed by a spirit of the opposite sex, in which case the participant exhibits transsexual characteristics during trance.

Furthermore, Herskovits reported in the 1930s that "the most prevalent Haitian attitude towards homosexuality . . . is one of derision rather than vindictiveness" (1971:118). He also reported that because of the high incidence of polygyny, whereby older men have several wives, many men remain unmarried, "some by preference, especially in the cities, where the incidence of homosexuality far exceeds that found in the country" (1971:119). He implies, however, that incidental homosexual behavior among young unmarried men was quite common even in the countryside. Ethnographers of Herskovits's generation were generally loath to report homosexuality among native populations whose reputations they consciously strove to enhance.

In the 1970s, international tourism brought homosexual men from New York City to Haiti in search of sexual recreation. In 1983, two gay guest houses were operating in Haiti and advertising in *The Advocate* ("The National Gay News Magazine"). One ad tells the prospective tourist that in Haiti "age does not count and *you are 21 again!*" and promises to "take care of all your needs!" including *"introductions."* Haiti is "a place where all your fantasies come true!" (*The Advocate* 1983:66, emphases in the original.) The gay tourist responding to this ad traveled to Haiti in the expectation of enjoying native delights.

The *Spartacus International Gay Guide, 8th Edition* (Stamford 1978:284–291) was no less explicit. It recommended Haiti to the gay tourist in lyrical terms: beautiful men "have a great ability to satisfy." However, "there is no free sex in Haiti." Male prostitutes charged $10–15 for an entire day. The guide listed one "rather seedy gay bar" and a house of male prostitutes. The 13th edition of *Spartacus* is less lyrical, warns of theft and violence, and no longer lists the house of prostitutes. Paid sex at "nominal" prices was still available in the early 1980s (Stamford 1983:770).

Investigative journalists have now discovered this link between Haiti and international gay tourists. The "NBC Nightly News" television broadcast of June 21, 1983, included a report direct from Haiti with a hidden camera in one of the bars listed in *Spartacus*, most of whose patrons were said to be male prostitutes eager to find clients among U.S. tourists.

Homosexual contact between Haitians and North American tourists thus has been going on at a small but constant rate for more than seven years. Given a high incidence of sexual activity with multiple partners among some homosexual men, the disease could spread very rapidly from only a few infected tourists. Data on the frequency of homosexual activities are limited, but one source cites Kinsey's 1970 survey of male homosexuals: two-thirds of his sample "had developed VD and two fifths had more than 500 sex partners" (Armytage 1980:167). Clearly, a new sexually transmitted disease could spread rapidly in this population.

PREDISPOSITION FOR IMMUNOSUPPRESSION

The etiology of AIDS is widely held to be multifactorial (Seligman et al. 1984). Among the possible predisposing factors are malnutrition; a history of multiple infections and of parasitic infestations—perhaps treated with antibiotics that may be immunosuppressive at therapeutic doses (Finch 1980); recreational drug use; and genetic predisposition. X chromosome-linked recessive genetic factors may predispose individuals to this disease. Several X chromosome–linked immunosuppressive disorders do affect males (Purtilo 1981; Purtilo et al. 1979).

Haitians are prey to malnutrition, multiple infections, and parasitic infestations. Some homosexual men in the United States are likely to use recreational drugs often, a practice known to be immunosuppressive (Brown et al. 1974; Goedert et al. 1982; McDonough et al. 1980). They are likely to have a history of multiple, sexually transmitted infections, of parasitic infestations (Gottlieb et al. 1981; Masur et al. 1981), and of repeated cytomegalovirus (CMV) infections, which are known to be immunosuppressive (Betts and Hanshaw 1977; Drew et al. 1981). Passive anal intercourse has been shown to be associated with abnormal cellular immunity. Homosexual men who engage primarily in passive anal intercourse are six times more at risk of developing AIDS than are those who do not (Detels et al. 1983). Malnutrition among homosexual men in the United States has not been reported.

Among the other groups currently at risk in the AIDS epidemic, intravenous drug users are predisposed to immunosuppression because of their drug taking (Brown et al. 1974; McDonough et al. 1980). Certain hemophiliacs suffer immune system abnormalities as a side effect of their treatment (Menitove et al. 1983), and infants experience developmental immune incompetence in utero and during early infancy.

DISCUSSION

An epidemic of a new disease, especially one infecting and killing adults, is usually caused by an agent new to the population suffering the epidemic (McNeill 1976). With increased global communications, viral epidemics of tremendous mortality (e.g., the flu epidemics of 1918–1919) have occurred with increased human travel (Koprowski and Koprowski 1975; Webster and Campbell 1974). The advent of jet travel in the late 1950s resulted in mass global tourism on an unprecedented scale.

Starting in the late 1940s with the independence of India and culminating in the 1970s with the liberation of the Portuguese colonies, the Third World nations gained their independence and joined the United Nations. A sizable migration of international bureaucratic elites throughout the Third World was one result. Both North Atlantic populations and Third World elites in the twentieth century have been raised in hygienic conditions that render them more susceptible to viral infections in adulthood than was the case for most persons in the last century. Moreover, in the 1970s tourism to the Third World took place in the context of the sexual liberation of the North Atlantic countries. Thus, AIDS may well be but the first of a number of strange and lethal new maladies borne by sexually active tourists. It is also one carried by that new traveler, the elite Third World native.

In evaluating the hypothesis that the current AIDS epidemic originated in Haiti, one might construct the following scenario: animals infected with one of the Type C oncogenic retroviruses, which are closely related to HTLV (Davis et al. 1982:1244), are repeatedly sacrificed in voodoo ceremonies, and their blood is directly ingested by priests and their assistants. These people could well suffer from conditions already predisposing them to immunosuppression, and could thus contract the new disease or become the passive hosts of a new virus, thereby enabling the animal virus to propagate itself in a human host. The virus could then spread in the Haitian population, already predisposed to immunosuppression, through sexual contact and unsterilized hypodermic needles.

Many voodoo priests are homosexual men who are of high prestige and who prosper economically. They are certainly in positions to satisfy their sexual desires, especially in urban areas. Moreover, because of the transsexual role of the homosexual voodoo priest (during spirit possession he *becomes* the goddess), the Haitian man who takes the active, insertor, sexual role with him during anal intercourse is *not* going to think of himself as homosexual. Such a man is quite likely to deny any homosexual identity to investigators with questionnaires.

The most recent studies of Haitian kinship stress that—in contrast to the stable marital unions of the hillside peasantry—few urban, working-class

Haitians can afford to maintain long-term marital unions. Urban, working-class men rely heavily on short, consensual unions and on prostitutes for sexual satisfaction. Urban rates of sexual activity with multiple partners are high (Legerman 1975). Thus, AIDS has likely spread in Haiti through both heterosexual and homosexual activities.

The "NBC Nightly News" television broadcast of June 21, 1983, featured a visit to the clinics of "folk doctors" operating in the poor districts of Port-au-Prince. These practitioners are trained in Western, not voodoo, traditions, and they commonly treat ailments by injections of antibiotics. They *do not sterilize* hypodermic needles. The broadcast showed a number of needles being cleaned with soap and water rather than being sterilized by heat or some other method. Such practices could contribute to the rapid spread of AIDS among poorer urban Haitians.

Thus, voodoo ceremonies and their blood sacrifices may have introduced AIDS into humans, but may be of less importance for the spread of the disease. Many Haitian people with AIDS may have never ingested animal blood in voodoo ceremonies; only the officiating priest and a few assistants do so. Ample other opportunities to contract AIDS in Haiti now exist, however.

One possible objection to the theory of a Haitian origin of AIDS is the argument that the disease spread to Haiti from New York City rather than the reverse. A "control" is nearby Puerto Rico. *Bob Damron's Address Book* is a gay tourist guide to North America. In contrast to *Spartacus's* mere two gay guest houses for Haiti, Damron (1983) lists for San Juan, Puerto Rico, eleven gay hotels and guest houses, eighteen gay bars, restaurants, and discos, and one gay bathhouse. By March 1984, the Pan American Health Organization had received official reports of 264 cases of AIDS in Haiti (OAS, PAHO 1985). Haitian immigrants in the United States represent 270 additional cases (CDC 1985a). Puerto Rico, which follows CDC domestic reporting procedures, reported only thirteen cases of AIDS as of October 5, 1983. By October 28, 1985 the number had grown to 164 (CDC, 1986). Thus, gay tourism, especially from New York City, is much more extensive in Puerto Rico than in Haiti yet the incidence of the disease in the two Caribbean countries is simply not proportionate. Gay tourists, therefore, likely did not bring the disease to Haiti.

Moreover, a recent report in the *Boston Globe* by two U.S. physicians doing volunteer work at a hospital deep in Haiti's interior discusses a case of AIDS in a young man who could not have had contact with homosexual men from the United States in the cities, reputedly did not have homosexual sex in the countryside, and who had had a history of repeated cures in voodoo ceremonies. He visited the Western physicians only with the permission of his voodoo priest. AIDS, they conclude, is present in isolated Haitian rural areas (Moses and Moses 1984).

There remain, however, cases of black Africans from Zaire and Chad diagnosed in Europe with AIDS (Clumeck et al. 1983; Clumeck et al. 1984; Offenstadt et al. 1983), the high rate of AIDS reported in Kinshasa, Zaire (Piot et al. 1984), and an even higher rate reported for Rwanda (Greenwood 1984). We want to discuss two epidemiological possibilities in this regard. First, elite Haitians, who have staffed the bureaucracy in Zaire for decades after its independence from Belgium (Piot et al. 1984) could have brought the disease to Africa. Second, it is possible that HTLV-III or its ancestral virus resides in animals in equatorial Africa and found its way into human hosts by routes parallel to those in Haiti: through blood sacrifice and ingestion of animal blood. In Africa, an additional potential to spread the infection exists in male initiation ceremonies that commonly involve circumcision and blood brotherhood by common sharing of the circumcision knife. Turnbull (1962:225–239) has reported such a ceremony in some detail for Zaire (then the Belgian Congo).

Blood sacrifice, especially of chickens, is also prevalent in Zaire and the rest of black Africa (Bohannan 1964:225–239). Chad has suffered both endemic civil war in the last decade, as well as severe famine, two conditions conducive to immunosuppression. However, in neither Zaire nor Chad is blood sacrifice combined with spirit-possession cults on the same scale as in Haiti. Spirit-possession cults are common, but they do not necessarily involve blood sacrifice. As one moves north and east in Africa, spirit-possession cults are increasingly associated with women and are quite marginal to the mainstream of society (Kehoe and Giletti 1981; Walker 1972). Indeed, no place in the world can rival Haiti for the intensity and extensiveness of spirit possession and blood sacrifice. Haitian voodoo represents a worldwide cultural climax of the two genres.

Coincidentally, Haiti offers a hospitable reception to international gay tourists. Such is not the case for Zaire and Chad. The latter is not mentioned in either edition of *Spartacus*. The 1983 *Spartacus* warns gay men *not* to have sex with natives in Zaire, because of the danger of blackmail and extortion (Stamford 1983). HTLV-III could well have originated from Type C retroviruses in animals of equatorial Africa. Because of the practive of blood sacrifice, it could find its way into human hosts there. But Africa is not the likely place for transmitting the infection to the U.S. populations currently suffering in the AIDS epidemic. That place, because of gay tourism, is almost certainly Haiti. The intermediate link, then, is the spread of an ancestral HTLV-III virus from African animals to Haitian ones. This is not unlikely, because African swine fever virus for instance, caused an epidemic among Haitian swine in 1979 so severe that a cooperative program sponsored by the governments of Mexico, Canada, and the United States is attempting to eradicate *all* Haitian swine (D'Eramo 1983a, 1983b).

There is then, yet that other possibility: The spread of AIDS from Haiti to equatorial Africa, given the patterns of migration concomitant with political upheavals, urbanization, and bureaucratization of these countries, especially Zaire, after independence.

In central Africa the period of European rule lasted less than a century. "Hardly more than a jubilee separated conquest from independence," in Goody's words (1973:342). Goody (1973) further points out that these were peoples without writing, the wheel, and plough agriculture when conquered by Europeans. They have gone very quickly from an iron age technology and a political system of decentralized kingdoms and chieftaincies to modernizing nations centered on bureaucratic-political elites (Foltz 1973). These elites have appeared very rapidly out of a rural, often tribal past. Their authority resides in their secondary school and university education in the "national" European language. Since independence these elites are the personnel holding the new nations together.

Zaire was given independence by the Belgians with almost no preparation. The country collapsed with the attempted secession of mineral-rich Katanga province and the consequent civil war. United Nations peacekeeping forces intervened and the country was unified around a strong central presidency (LeMarchand 1964). Because of the dearth of educated personnel, large numbers of educated Haitians entered Zaire to staff the civil service (Piot et al. 1984). They were of African descent and spoke French, the national language of Zaire.

The modern sector of Zaire's economy, like most of central Africa's, is extractive, depending on mining. Rapid urbanization has meant the migration of young, unmarried men in large numbers to the mining towns and the capital city. They leave behind them polygynous chiefs and elders with many wives. This pattern of large urban concentrations of unmarried young men and of scattered older men with many wives in the countryside is very common in Africa (See Epstein's (1973) ethnography of the politics of a preindependence Zambian mining town and his diagram for age and sex distribution.) The urban masses are mobile, the majority of them returning, especially in old age, to the tribal areas from which they came (Epstein 1973). Even married urban workers may leave their wives in their rural homes. The consequent importance of urban prostitutes can readily be imagined.

Finally, African elites, traditional rural ones and to a lesser extent modern urban ones, are both exogamous and polygynous: they marry widely, and important men marry many wives. This pattern of "marrying widely" provides many cross-cutting ties for the larger society (Goody 1973:352).

The central African context, like the Haitian one, is very different from that of North Atlantic culture, even though the African elites are all educated in European languages and professions. These elites are few in number compared to the urban masses. Kinshasa, Zaire's capital, has three million inhabitants, an almost overnight accumulation.

It is interesting that the African people with AIDS who have been diagnosed and treated in Belgium (Clumeck et al. 1984) are all elite persons with no history of homosexuality, drug use, or immunosuppressive diseases, except for common tropical intestinal parasites. Moreover, when Piot and his associates studied 38 people with AIDS in Kinshasa in 1983, they quickly determined that the disease was transmitted through heterosexual contact. Indeed, they identified two clusters of heterosexual partners with AIDS. The rate of 17 cases of AIDS per 100,000 people in Kinshasa puts the incidence of AIDS there at the same rate as in San Francisco or New York. Greenwood (1984), summarizing for Zaire and Rwanda, reports that half of the AIDS patients were female, that nearly all were upper or middle class, and that the disease is spread through *heterosexual* contact with multiple partners. Multiple sexual contacts that involve exchange of bodily fluids of both sexes would seem to spread the disease.

Many more data are needed, but we may be seeing in Africa the spread of the disease from elites downward to the urban masses, rather than from the countryside to the urban masses and then to the elites. The mode of transmission is through multiple heterosexual contacts, which have their own peculiar patterns in a society with widespread polygyny counterbalanced with intensive urban prostitution.

Broder and Gallo (1984) hypothesize that the human T-cell lymphotropic viruses originated in Africa and that HTLV-I spread to the Caribbean and the southern United States with the slave trade and to Japan with Portuguese missionaries in the sixteenth century. However, HTLV-III varies greatly in genetic make-up from HTLV-II (Nelson 1985). HTLV-III may have possibly come to Africa with Haitian elites, and in AIDS we may be seeing the spread of a New World disease.

We feel that the hypothetical origin outlined here of the current AIDS epidemic is plausible enough to provide potential key clues to laboratory investigators. We must stress, however, that we are not offering direct empirical evidence for our hypothesis. That is *not* the purpose of this paper, which is a survey of the literature only. Public health fieldwork must be done in Haiti to discover the rural incidence of AIDS and the role of voodoo ceremonies in the lives of AIDS victims. Such research must be conducted by a team including a veterinarian and an anthropologist. Research should include epidemiological surveys of farm animals commonly sacrificed in voodoo ceremonies. Initial research sites should focus on areas that have recently experienced unexpected high mortality rates among male voodoo priests.

An anthropologist could provide opportunities for constructive research with voodoo practitioners. Haitians are justifiably sensitive to sensationalism about voodoo; and an anthropologist could work to allay such fears. Researchers must make clear from the outset their conviction that no one is trying to blame either Haiti or spirit-possession cults for the disease. In a public health emergency blaming ongoing social realities is fruitless. Haitians are not to be blamed for sacrificing animals as they have always done, nor are gay tourists to be blamed for hiring sexual services in Haiti, nor further flamed for being sexually active with multiple partners before the outbreak of the epidemic. Such widely separated constellations of human behavior seem to have come together through AIDS. If so, the connection has happened through the random course of human social history, quite unintentionally and with disastrous results for public health. We must, therefore, return to the field in the search for the ancestral agent, and that field includes the Haitian farmyard.

ACKNOWLEDGMENTS

We are indebted to Richard B. Davidson, UCLA Biomedical Library, John Gluecker, USC Dental Library, and Norman Laurila, A Different Light Bookstore, Los Angeles, for bibliographic assistance. We thank Samuel Allerton, Ph.D., Isaac Beckor, Ph.D., Stephen Schoenfeld, D.D.S., Ph.D., Gary Trump, Ph.D., Otto von Mering, Ph.D., and Douglas A. Feldman, Ph.D., for comments on an earlier draft.

REFERENCES

The Advocate (San Mateo, Cal.). 1983. Jan 30:66.

Armytage, W. H. G. 1980. Changing Incidence and Patterns of Sexually Transmitted Diseases. In *Changing Patterns of Sexual Behavior* by W. H. G. Armytage, R. Chester, and J. Pell, P. 167. London: Academic Press.

Brazile, R. 1975. Demographic Statistics in Haiti. In *The Haitian Potential: Research and Resources of Haiti*, V. Rubin, and R. P. Schaedel, eds., pp. 3–10. New York: Teachers College Press.

Beghin, I., W. Fougere, and K. W. King. 1970. L'alimentation et la nutrition en Haiti. Paris: Les Presses Universitaires de France, p. 77.

Beisel, W. R., R. Edelman, K. Nauss, and R. M. Suskin. 1982. Single-Nutrient Effects on Immunologic Function. *JAMA* 245(1):53–58.

Berry, P. 1975. Literacy and the Question of Creole. In *The Haitian Potential: Research and Resources of Haiti*. V. Rubin and R. P. Schaedel eds., pp. 83–113 New York: Teachers College Press.

Betts, R. F. and J. B. Hanshaw. 1977. Cytomegalovirus (CMV) in the Compromised Host(s). *Ann Rev. Med* 28:103–110.

Bohannan, P. 1964. *Africa and Africans*. Garden City, N.Y.: Natural History Press.

Brasseur, P. H., M. Agrapart, J. J. Ballet, P. Briulhe, M. J. Warrel, and Savanat Tharavany. 1983. Impaired Cell-Mediated Immunity in *Plasmodium Falciparum* Infected Patients with High Parasitemia and Cerebral Malaria. *Clin Immunol Immunopathol* 27:38–50.

Broder, Samuel, and Robert C. Gallo. 1984. A Pathogenic Retrovirus (HTLV-III) Linked to AIDS. *N Engl J of Med* 311(20):1292–1297.

Brown, S. M., B. Stimmel, and R. N. Taub. 1974. Immunologic Dysfunction in Heroin Addicts. *Arch Intern Med* 134:1001–1006.

Centers for Disease Control (CDC). 1983a. Acquired Immune Deficiency Syndrome (AIDS) Activity: Cases Reported to CDC as of July 16. Mimeo report, 2 pages.

———— . 1983b. *Idem*, as of Oct. 5.

———— . 1984a. *Idem*, as of Jan. 10.

———— . 1984b. *Idem*, as of Nov. 30.

———— . 1985a. *Idem*, as of Feb. 15.

———— . 1985b. *Idem*, as of October 28.

Clumeck, N., F. Mascart-Lemone, J. De Maubeuge, D. Brenez, and L. Marcelis. 1983. Acquired Immune Deficiency in Black Africans. *Lancet* 1(8324):642.

Clumeck, N., J. Sonnet, H. Taelman, et al. 1984. Acquired Immunodeficiency Syndrome in African Patients. *N Engl J Med* 310(8):492–497.

B. Damron. 1983. *Bob Damron's Address Book*, 19th Ed. San Francisco: Bob Damron Enterprises.

Davis, B. D., R. Dubecco, H. N. Eisen et al. 1982. *Microbiology*, 3rd Ed. New York: Harper & Row.

D'Eramo, J. E. 1983a. Is African Swine Fever Virus the Cause? *New York Native*. May 23:28–29.

D'Eramo, J. E. 1983b. African Swine Fever Virus: Part II. *New York Native*. June 6:18–19.

Detels, R., K. Schwartz, B. R. Visscher, J. L. Fahey, R. S. Greene and M. S. Gottlieb. 1983. Relation between Sexual Practices and T-Cell Subsets in Homosexual Active Men. *Lancet* 1(8325):609–611.

Diederich, B. and A. Burt. 1969. *Papa Doc: The Truth about Haiti Today*. New York: McGraw-Hill.

Drew, W. L., L. Mintz, R. C. Miner, M. Sands, B. Ketterer. 1981. Prevalence of Cytomegalovirus Infection in Homosexual Men. *J of Inf Dis* 143(2):188–192.

Epstein, A. L. 1973. *Politics in an Urban African Community*. Manchester, England: The University Press (originally published in 1958).

Finch, R., 1980. Immunomodulating Effects of Antimicrobial Agents. *J Antimicrob Agents Chemother* 6:691–693.

Foltz, W. J. 1973. Political Boundaries and Political Competition in Tropical Africa. In *Building States and Nations*, Vol 2, S. N. Eisenstadt, and S. Rokkan, eds, pp. 357–383. Beverly Hills: Sage Publications.

Foulks, E. F. and S. H. Katz. 1973. Biobehavioral Adaptation in the Artic. In *Biosocial Interrelations in Population Adaptation*, E. S. Watts, F. E. Johnson, and G. W. Lasker, eds., pp. 1–11. New Orleans: Tulane.

Gallo, R. C., S. Z. Salahuddin, M. Popovic et al. 1984. Frequent Detection and Isolation of a Cytopathic Retroviruses (HTLV-III) from Patients with AIDS and at Risk for AIDS. *Science* 224:500–503.

Goedert, J. J., C. Y. Neuland, W. C. Wallen, M. H. Green, D. L. Mann, C. Murray, D. M. Strong, J. F. Fraumeni, and W. A. Blattner. 1982. Amyl Nitrate May Alter T-Lymphocytes in Homosexual Men. *Lancet* 1(8269):412–416.

Goody, J. 1973. Uniqueness in the Cultural Conditions for Political Development in Black Africa. In *Building States and Nations*, Vol 2, S. N. Eisenstadt and S. Rokkan, eds, pp. 341–356. Beverly Hills: Sage Publications.

Gottlieb, M. S., R. Schroff, H. M. Schanker, J. D. Weisman, P. T. Fan, R. A. Wolf, and A. Saxon. 1981. *Pneumocystis carinii* Pneumonia and Mucosal Candidiasis in Previously Healthy Homosexual Men: Evidence of a New Acquired Cellular Immunodeficiency. *N Engl J. Med* 305(24):1425–1431.

Greenwood, B. M. 1984. AIDS in Africa. *Immunology Today* 5:293.

Hall, E. T. 1969. *The Hidden Dimension*. Garden City, N.Y.: Doubleday/Anchor.

Haverkos, H. W. and J. W. Curran. 1982. The Current Outbreak of Kaposi's Sarcoma and Opportunistic Infection. *CA* 32(6):330–339.

Herskovits, M. J. 1971. *Life in a Haitian Valley*. New York: Doubleday/Anchor (originally published in 1937).

Kehoe, A. B. and D. H. Giletti. 1981. Women's Preponderance in Possession Cults: The Calcium-Deficiency Hypothesis Extended. *American Anthropologist* 83:549–561.

King, K. W. 1975. Nutrition Research in Haiti. In *The Haitian Potential: Research and Resources of Haiti*, V. Rubin, and R. P. Schaedel, eds., pp. 147–156. New York: Teachers College Press.

Koprowski, C. and H. Koprowski, eds. 1975. *Viruses and Immunity*. New York: Academic Press.

Legerman, C. J. 1975. Observations on Family and Kinship Organization in Haiti. In *The Haitian Potential: Research and Resources of Haiti*, V. Rubin, and R. P. Schaedel eds., pp. 17–22. New York: Teachers College Press.

LeMarchand, Rene. 1964. *Political Awakening in the Belgian Congo*. Berkeley: University of California Press.

Lundahl, M. 1979. *Peasants and Poverty: A Study of Haiti*. New York: St. Martin's.

Masur, H., M. A. Michelis, J. B. Greene, I. Onorato, R. A. Van De Stouwe, R. S. Holzman, G. Wornser, L. Brettman, M. Lange, H. W. Murray, and S. Cunningham-Rundles. 1981. An Outbreak of Community Acquired *Pneumocystis carinii* Penumonia: Initial Manifestation of Cellular Immune Dysfunction. *N Engl J Med* 305:1431–1438.

McDonough, R. J., J. J. Madden, A. Falek, D. A. Shafer, M. Pline, D. Gorden, P. Bokos, J. C. Kochale, and J. Mendelson. 1980. Alteration of T and Null Lymphocyte Frequencies in the Peripheral Blood of Human Opiate Addicts: *In Vivo* Evidence for Opiate Receptor Site on T Lymphocytes. *J Immunol* 125:2539–2543.

McNeill, W. H. 1976. *Plagues and Peoples*. Garden City, N.Y.:Doubleday/Anchor.

Menitove, J. R., R. H. Aster, J. R. Casper, S. J. Lauer, J. L. Gottschali, J. E. Williams, J. C. Gill, D. V. Wheeler, V. Piaskowski, P. Kirchner, and R. R. Montgomery. 1983. T-Lymphocyte Subpopulations in Patients with Classic Hemophilia Treated with Cryoprecipitate and Lyophilized Concentrates. *N Engl J Med* 303(2):83–86.

Metraux, Alfred. 1958. *Le Vaudou Haitien.* Paris: Gallimard.

Miller, C. L. 1980. Effects of Nutrition on Non-Specific Inflammatory and Specific Immune Host Defense System. *J Med* 11(4):267–273.

Moses, John, and Peter Moses. 1984. Medical Watch: The puzzle of AIDS in Haiti, Special to The Globe. *The Boston Globe.* Jan. 23:44.

Nelson, Harry. 1985. Third World Diseases: No Borders. *Los Angeles Times.* Feb. 22:1,16,18.

Nicholls, D. 1979. *From Dessalines to Duvalier: Race, Color and National Independence in Haiti.* Cambridge, England: Cambridge.

Offenstadt, G., P. Pinta, P. Hericord, M. Jagueux, F. Jean, and P. Amstutz. 1983. Multiple Opportunities Infection Due to AIDS in a Previously Healthy Black Woman from Zaire. *N Engl J Med* 308(13):775.

Pearce, R. B. 1983. Parasites and AIDS. *New York Native.* Aug. 29–Sep. 11:26–30.

Pekarek, R. S. H. H. Sandstead, R. A. Jacob, D. F. Barcome. 1979. Abnormal Cellular Immune Responses during Zinc Deficiency. *Am J Clin Nutr* 32(7):1466–1471.

Piot, P., T. C. Quinn, H. Taelman, et al. 1984. "Acquired Immunodeficiency Syndrome in a Heterosexual Population in Zaire. *Lancet.*, July 14, 2(8394):65–69.

Popovic, M., M. G. Sarngadharan, E. Read, and R. C. Gallo. 1984. Detection, Isolation and Continuous Production of Cytopathic Retroviruses (HTLV-III) from Patients with AIDS and Pre-AIDS. *Science* 224:497–500.

Purtilo, D.T. 1981. X-Linked Lymphoproliferative Syndrome. An Immunodeficiency Disorder with Acquired Agammaglobulinemia, Fatal Infectious Mononucleosis, or Malignant Lymphoma. *Arch Pathol Lab Med* 105(3):119–121.

Purtilo, D.T., L. Paquin, D. DeFlorio, F. Virzi, and R. Sakhuja. 1979. Immunodiagnosis and Immunopathogenesis of the X-Linked Recessive Lymphoproliferative Syndrome. *Sem in Hematology* 16(4):309–343.

Rotberg, R. I. and C. K. Clague. 1971. *Haiti: The Politics of Squalor.* Boston: Houghton-Mifflin.

Sarngadharan, M. G., M. Popovic, L. Bruch et al. 1984. Antibodies Reactive with a Human T-Lymphotrophic Retrovirus (HTLV-III) in the Serum of Patients with AIDS. *Science* 2224:506–508.

Seligman, M., L. Chess, J. L. Fahey et al. 1984. AIDS—An Immunologic Reevaluation. *N Engl J Med* 311(20):1286–1292.

Siegal, F. P., and S. Cummingham-Rundles. 1982. Opportunistic Infection in Previously Healthy Women. Initial Manifestations of a Community-Acquired Cellular Immunodeficiency. *Ann Intern Med* 97(4):533–539.

Siegal, F. P., and M. Siegal. 1983. *AIDS: The Medical Mystery.* New York: Grove Press.

Simpson, G. 1934. The Belief System of Haitian Vodun. *American Anthropologist* 47:35–59.

Stamford, J. D. 1978. *Spartacus International Gay Guide,* 8th Edition. Amsterdam: Spartacus.

———. 1983. *Spartacus International Gay Guide.* 13th Edition. Amsterdam: Spartacus.

Turnbull, C. M. 1962. *The Forest People: A Study of the Pygmies of the Congo.* Garden City, N.Y.: Doubleday/Anchor.

Vieira, J., E. Frank, T. J. Spira, S. H. Landesman. 1983. Acquired Immune Deficiency in Haitians. *N Engl J Med* 308:125–129.

Walker, S. S. 1972. *Ceremonial Spirit Possession in Africa and Afro-America.* Leiden: E. J. Brill.

Wallace, A. F. C. 1972. Mental Illness, Biology and Culture. In *Psychological Anthropology*, F. L. K. Hsu, ed., pp. 363–402. Cambridge, Mass: Schenkman.

Webster, R. G. and C. H. Campbell. 1974. Studies on the Origin of Pandemic Influenza IV. Selection and Transmission of "New" Influenza Virus In Vivo. *Virology* 62:404.

Chapter Five

The Social Origins of AIDS: Social Change, Sexual Behavior, and Disease Trends

William W. Darrow, E. Michael Gorman, and Brad P. Glick

INTRODUCTION

Epidemics do not happen by chance (Rosen 1973). They represent complex processes that occur as biological forces operate in social systems and cultural environments (Roueche 1980; Thomas and Morgan-Witts 1982; Zinsser 1935). One of the most curious aspects of the epidemic of acquired immune deficiency syndrome (AIDS) in the United States is its almost exclusive occurrence in seemingly disparate populations: homosexual and bisexual men, intravenous drug users, recent arrivals from Haiti, hemophiliacs, blood transfusion recipients, and the sexual partners of other risk-group members (Francis et al. 1983). Why AIDS has affected these groups at this time in U.S. history is a question that cannot be answered apart from the social and cultural attributes of the populations at risk or independently of the technological and behavioral changes that have occurred in our pluralistic society over the last twenty-five years.

Now that an etiological agent has been identified (Barre-Sinoussi et al. 1983; Centers for Disease Control [CDC] 1984a; Gallo et al. 1984), How has this agent evolved and become dispersed is a legitimate research question, but an extremely difficult one to answer. Some believe that the putative agent was imported into the United States from equatorial Africa; others have argued that an endogenous microorganism may have become pathogenic

Adapted from presentations to the annual meetings of the American Sociological Association, San Antonio, Texas, August 1984, and the American Anthropological Association, Denver, Colorado, November 1984.

through genetic mutation (Fromer 1983; Mayer and Pizer 1983; Siegal and Siegal 1983). To shed some light on these conjectures, we examined case reports and attempted to find indicators of annual trends in the social and cultural phenomena that had been epidemiologically associated with AIDS. We sought answers to two questions: 1) Why were certain populations, and not others, being affected? 2) What relatively recent social, behavioral, and technological changes might have facilitated the introduction and rapid dissemination of an infectious agent into various U.S. communities in the late 1970s?

METHODS

Available evidence suggests that the earliest cases of AIDS related to the outbreak were diagnosed in 1978 (Curran 1983; Jaffe et al. 1983a; Selik et al. 1984) and that the latency period before onset of symptoms ranges from several months to many years (CDC 1982; Curran et al. 1984; Feorino et al. 1984). Therefore, we sought indicators of social and cultural trends for at least 25 years before detection of the epidemic (i.e., from 1956 through 1981). Social indicators of epidemiological interest included homosexual men and their degrees of interaction, intravenous-drug use, migration and travel to and from places in which AIDS was known to occur, blood transfusions, and reports of venereal diseases. In order to answer our questions, we were compelled to use available indicators and accept all of the inherent limitations associated with the use of archival data.

To measure the number of homosexual (gay) men in the population and their frequencies of interaction, we looked at various studies of homosexual activities and found several indirect estimates of social encounters. No longitudinal studies of sexual activities with representative samples have ever been conducted in the United States, but most of the surveys conducted since Kinsey et al. (1948) published their preliminary report have come up with similar findings: approximately 4% of the male population is exclusively homosexual throughout their lives (Weinberg 1970). Therefore, we assumed that any increases in the number of gay men in the United States were directly due to natural increases in the population.

Although we postulated no increases in the proportion of gay men in the population, we posited that interpersonal and sexual contacts among gay men increased along with increases in social institutions such as bathhouses, gay bars, and private clubs (Weinberg and Williams 1974, 1975; William 1984). The number of social institutions patronized by gay men was measured by listings of establishments in *The Address Book* from its first publication (Damron 1964) through its most recent issue.[1]

Annual trends in intravenous drug use were estimated by the number of persons reported to the Drug Enforcement Administration as "physically addicted to narcotics use" (U.S. Bureau of the Census 1972:81). Immigrants from Haiti were persons who formerly resided in Haiti before admission as permanent residents of the United States (U.S. Bureau of the Census 1982:89), and immigrants from Africa were persons born in Africa (U.S. Bureau of the Census 1982:90). The number of U.S. citizens traveling overseas was estimated by the total number of passports issued (U.S. Bureau of the Census 1982:240); the number of foreign citizens visiting the United States was estimated by the number of visas issued (U.S. Bureau of the Census 1982:241). Reports of intercity and total passenger miles of air travel were obtained from the Air Transport Association of America (1983). Number of units of blood voluntarily donated to the American Red Cross was obtained from annual reports of the American Red Cross (U.S. Bureau of the Census 1982:346). Reports of hepatitis B infections (CDC 1981), cases of infectious syphilis among civilian men (CDC 1979), and cases of AIDS (CDC 1984b) were obtained from surveillance data collected by CDC from cooperating state and local health departments.

These and other variables were plotted and product-moment correlation coefficients were calculated with the assistance of various procedures available in the Statistical Analysis System (SAS Institute 1979). Correlation matrices were analyzed for available data and reanalyzed with estimates for missing values.

RESULTS

From 1956 to 1983, the population of the United States increased from 169 million to about 230 million. Assuming that the proportion of homosexual men remained constant, and assuming men who were exclusively homosexual were at greatest risk for developing AIDS, we estimated that the population of homosexual men at greatest risk of exposure to the retrovirus believed to cause AIDS increased from approximately 3.4 million in 1956 to 4.6 million in 1983. As shown in Figure 5.1, the number of social institutions for gay men listed in Bob Damron's *Address Book* increased much more rapidly

---

[1]Bob Damron and Patrick McAdams kindly provided us with background information and a complete set of back issues of *The Address Book*. *The Address Book* now lists a wide variety of establishments, ranging from bars for lesbians to shoe stores open to the general public. The coding scheme used to identify places has changed over the years; therefore, we could not reliably identify gathering places frequented primarily by gay men. However, the guide published by Damron continues to be directed primarily at gay men; therefore, we included all listings in our analyses.

Figure 5.1.   Homosexual Men and Listings in the Address Book: 1956–1983.

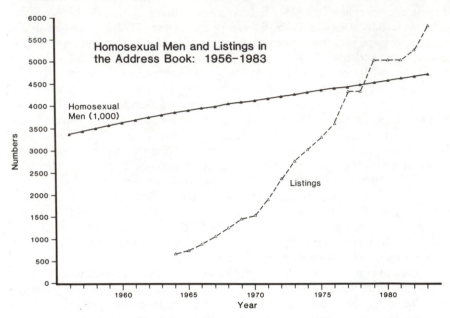

than did the population at risk: from 690 places in 1964 to 5,800 in 1983. Furthermore, the number of establishments listed increased most dramatically during the decade of "Gay Liberation" that followed the "Stonewall Riot" of June 28, 1969.[2] However, many of the other social indicators we examined also increased during the decade before AIDS was recognized in this country. For example, units of blood donated to the American Red Cross increased from 2.4 million in 1960 to 3.2 million in 1970 and to over 6 million in 1983.

In an effort to identify the social trends most highly associated with the outbreak of AIDS, we calculated zero-order product-moment correlation coefficients for all available indicators. High correlations between indicators of male homosexuality and sexually transmissable diseases (STD) were expected and found (see Figure 5.2). As the number of establishments for gay men increased, reported cases of syphilis, hepatitis B, and, later on, AIDS, also increased in the United States. However, units of blood donated to the American Red Cross and the number of foreign travelers in the

---

[2]The "Stonewall Riot" was a confrontation between gay men and police during a raid of the Stonewall Inn, then a gay bar in New York City. This event marked the beginning of the "Gay Liberation Movement."

Figure 5.2. Trends in Male Homosexuality and Diseases in the United States: 1956–1983.

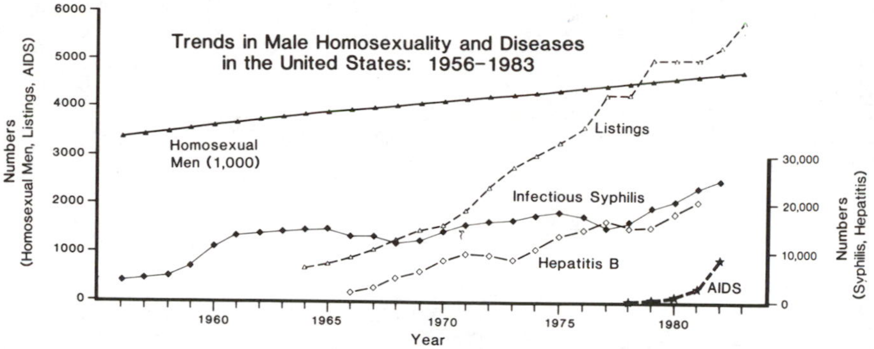

United States were also highly correlated with the number of cases of STDs reported among U.S. men, and listings in *the Address Book* were significantly correlated with both blood donations and foreign travelers (Table 5.1). In contrast, the number of immigrants from Haiti was not associated with any other trends.

Indicators of international travel were of particular interest because some investigators had suggested that the retrovirus etiologically associated with AIDS had been imported into the United States from equatorial Africa (Saxinger et al. 1985), perhaps by way of Europe or Haiti (Bygbjerg 1983). Since the initiation of international travel by jet aircraft in 1959, both the number of U.S. citizens traveling overseas and the number of citizens of foreign nations traveling to this country have increased rapidly. Intercity air-passenger traffic within the United States has also increased, and the number of immigrants from distant continents, such as Africa, has increased as well. As shown in Figure 5.3, indicators of foreign travel were highly associated with the outbreak of AIDS.

Further support for the hypothesis that the virus was imported from elsewhere and spread very quickly can be found in reports of early cases. Attached to one of the 7,609 case reports received by the CDC as of December 31, 1984, was the travel itinerary of a foreign visitor (see Figure 5.4). This man had had recurrent bouts of diarrhea for nine months when he reentered the United States in March 1983. He was scheduled to visit twelve American cities in forty-seven days. However, he was hospitalized with *Pneumocystis carinii* pneumonia (PCP) in Florida during the last week of April 1983 and died ten days later. Although atypical, this case clearly illustrates how an infectious agent might have been seeded in various urban populations in a relatively short period of time.

In one cluster of forty patients linked by sexual contacts (Auerbach et al. 1984) were six men who developed symptoms of AIDS before 1980: four from New York City, one from Los Angeles, and a foreign citizen, "Patient

TABLE 5.1. Product-Moment Correlation Coefficients for Social Indicators Associated with the Outbreak of AIDS: 1956–1983.

Social Indicator	Homosexual men	Listings in *Address Book*	Donations to ARC*	Narcotic Drug Users	Intercity Air Miles	Foreign travel to US	U.S. Citizens Overseas	Immigrants from Haiti	Immigrants from Africa	Cases of Syphilis	Cases of Hep B	Cases of AIDS
Homosexual Men in U.S.	1.000	0.989	0.968	0.636	0.886	0.913	0.968	0.082 (ns)	0.916	0.912	0.975	0.434
Listings in *Address Book*		1.000	0.991	0.536 (ns)	0.888	0.966	0.934	0.033 (ns)	0.903	0.842	0.955	0.514
Blood Donations to ARC*			1.000	0.607	0.934	0.976	0.921	0.059 (ns)	0.922	0.845	0.956	0.530
Narcotic Drug Users				1.000	0.723	0.574	0.727	0.471 (ns)	0.675	0.492 (ns)	0.671	—
Intercity Air Miles					1.000	0.978	0.891	0.111 (ns)	0.957	0.836	0.866	0.729
Travel to US by Foreigners						1.000	0.914	0.094 (ns)	0.954	0.802	0.912	0.562
Travel Abroad by U.S. Citizens							1.000	0.109 (ns)	0.927	0.814	0.927	0.352 (ns)
Immigrants from Haiti								1.000	0.381 (ns)	-0.118 (ns)	0.188 (ns)	0.248 (ns)
Immigrants from Africa									1.000	0.653	0.851	0.653
Syphilis										1.000	0.849	0.503
Hepatitis B											1.000	0.537

*American Red Cross.

Figure 5.3. Travel and AIDS: 1956–1982.

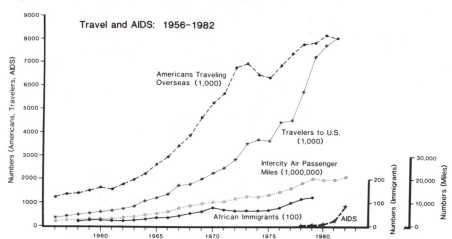

0," who was associated with cases in New York City and California (see Figure 5.5). Although patients NY1 and LA1 could not be linked directly with Patient 0, all were employed by airlines involved in international travel. LA1 traveled to Kenya and Tanzania in 1976, Italy and Greece in 1977, and France and England in 1978, and first noticed a lesion in February 1979 that subsequently was diagnosed as Kaposi's sarcoma. NY1 traveled to Haiti and other Caribbean countries while employed as a flight attendant from 1974 until he developed the lesions of Kaposi's sarcoma in December 1978. Before he died, he reported having sexual contact with another man who had been diagnosed with Kaposi's sarcoma, and this other man reported sexual contacts with other flight attendants, including Patient 0. Patient 0 developed lymphadenopathy in December 1979 and Kaposi's sarcoma in June 1980. Thus, these men could have passed an infectious agent from one to another while engaging in sexual activities during the late 1970s.

CONCLUSIONS

Our exploratory study of relationships among social conditions and social diseases is obviously limited by the kinds of information that we could obtain. Nonetheless, it appears from our crude indicators that many of the social phenomena epidemiologically linked to AIDS are significantly correlated. Upward trends in many variables occurred before the outbreak of AIDS, particularly in the mid-1970s. Trends in international travel, male infectious syphilis cases, and listings in Bob Damron's *Address Book* were

Figure 5.4.   Travel Itinerary (Forty-Seven Days and Twelve Cities) for a Man with AIDS (PCP) from March 1983 to May 1983.

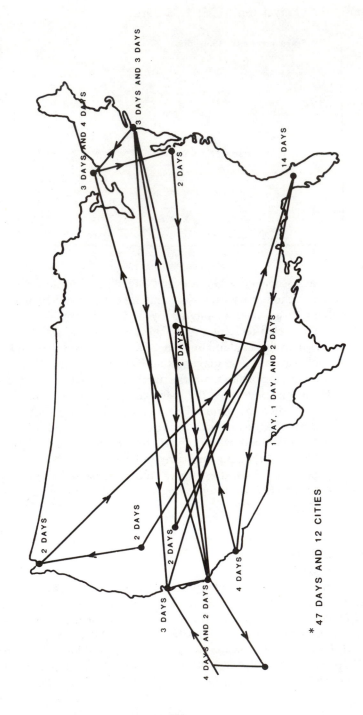

3 DAYS AND 4 DAYS

3 DAYS AND 3 DAYS

2 DAYS

14 DAYS

2 DAYS

1 DAY, 1 DAY, AND 2 DAYS

2 DAYS

2 DAYS

2 DAYS

4 DAYS

3 DAYS

4 DAYS AND 2 DAYS

* 47 DAYS AND 12 CITIES

Figure 5.5. Cluster of People with AIDS Linked by Sexual Contacts.

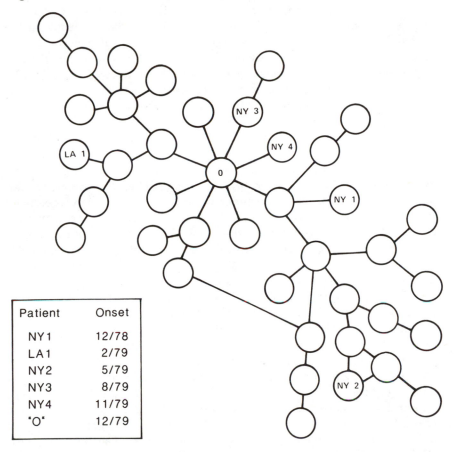

Patient	Onset
NY1	12/78
LA1	2/79
NY2	5/79
NY3	8/79
NY4	11/79
"O"	12/79

highly associated. These findings do not mean that there is a causal connection among these variables, but they clearly suggest that social conditions in the late 1970s in many urban areas of the United States may have been conducive for the introduction and rapid dissemination of a completely new and different sexually transmissible infectious agent into a susceptible population of gay men.

Good evidence exists to show that the infectious agent that causes AIDS is a previously unrecognized retrovirus, called lymphadenopathy-associated virus (LAV) by investigators at the Institut Pasteur (Barre-Sinoussi et al. 1983) and human T-cell lymphotropic virus-type III (HTLV-III) by investigators at the National Institutes of Health (Gallo et al. 1984). This virus has been recovered from saliva (Groopman et al. 1984), semen, and blood (Ho et al. 1984), and appears to be spread by sexual contact (Goedert et al.

1984; Jaffe et al. 1983b) or by exposure to contaminated blood or blood products (Curran et al. 1984; Feorino et al. 1984). Serologic surveys of antibodies to the virus indicate that infection was rare among people in the United States before 1978, but now high proportions of gay men (Jaffe et al. 1985) and intravenous-drug users (Spira et al. 1984) in large, densely populated cities of the United States have been infected with HTLV-III/LAV. Thus, epidemiological evidence strongly suggests that the virus was present in the United States in the mid-1970s and is now widely dispersed in selected populations.

In our analyses, we found that the earliest cases included gay men involved in international travel. Some of these men may have had sexual contacts with one another, but, more importantly, each reported many sexual exposures with other gay men in cities in which AIDS is now a major health problem. It is impossible to conclude that any one of these men is responsible for introducing the virus to the United States. In fact, the virus may have evolved or arrived in some other way. Our purpose is not to pinpoint the source or cast blame, but to show that social conditions in the mid-1970s provided a unique opportunity for the introduction and transmission of an insidious and highly fatal viral disease.

Although the agent could have been introduced before the advent of the Gay Liberation Movement and the jet age, the rapid dissemination of the virus would have been difficult before the development of geographically distinct gay communities and their interconnection by transcontinental air travel (Levine 1979). The number of gay men in the United States has increased, but, more importantly, the numbers of social and sexual contacts among gay men have increased, as well. Before AIDS was detected, health authorities recognized an increasing incidence in infectious syphilis, rectal gonorrhea, hepatitis B, amebiasis, and a host of other STDs among gay men living in major metropolitan areas (Conant et al. 1984; Darrow et al. 1981; William 1984). These diseases were relatively benign, easily treated, or infrequently fatal; thus, infection or fear of infection with one or more of these diseases rarely modified sexual behaviors. Now AIDS, AIDS-related conditions, and HTLV-III/LAV infections are being found in gay men who have characteristics very similar to those infected with other STDs and many high-risk gay men are attempting to dramatically alter their behaviors (McKusick et al. 1985).

Research on all aspects of AIDS continues. Traditionally, social scientists have related changes in patterns of social interaction to cross-cultural contacts and technological innovations well after these social processes have begun. In contrast, we are continuing to collect information on alterations in human conduct in response to a public-health crisis as these changes occur. As applied social scientists working on a specific sociomedical problem, our course is being charted by evolving discoveries in related disciplines as well as by traditional sociological and anthropological concepts, theoretical perspectives, and methodological approaches. For example, the recent report of a simian T-lymphotropic virus very similar to HTLV-III/LAV (Kanki et al. 1985) suggests another hypothesis regarding the social origin of AIDS: transmission from a reservoir of infected Old World monkeys to one or more susceptible human beings. Although our primary task is to stop the spread of AIDS, our efforts and those of other scientists may lead to a more basic understanding of the social and cultural processes that underlie the spread of all infectious diseases in human populations.

REFERENCES

Air Transport Association of America. 1983. *Air Transport 1983*. Washington, D.C.: Air Transport Association of America.

Auerbach, D.M., W.W. Darrow, H.W. Jaffe, and J.W. Curran. 1984. Cluster of Cases of the Acquired Immune Deficiency Syndrome. *Am J Med* 76:487–92.

Barre-Sinoussi, F., J.C. Chermann, F. Rey et al. 1983. Isolation of a T-lymphotropic Retrovirus from a Patient at Risk of Acquired Immunodeficiency Syndrome (AIDS). *Science* 220:868–871.

Bygbjerg, I.C. 1983. AIDS in a Danish Surgeon (Zaire, 1976). *Lancet* I:925.

Centers for Disease Control (CDC). 1979. *STD Fact Sheet*. HEW Publication No. 79-8195. Atlanta, Ga.: Centers for Disease Control.

_____ . 1981. *Hepatitis Surveillance Report No 47*. Atlanta, Ga.: Centers for Disease Control.

_____ . 1982. Possible Transfusion-Associated Acquired Immune Deficiency Syndrom (AIDS)—California. *Morbid Mortal Weekly Rep* 31:652–654.

_____ . 1984a. Antibodies to a Retrovirus Etiologically Associated with Acquired Immunodeficiency Syndrome (AIDS) in Populations with Increased Incidences of the Syndrome. *Morbid Mortal Weekly Rep* 33:377–379.

_____ . 1984b. Acquired Immunodeficiency Syndrome (AIDS) Weekly Surveillance Report—United States. December 31.

Conant, M.A., A. Moss, S. Dritz, and D. Schild. 1984. Changing Pattern of Sexually Transmitted Diseases over the Past 15 Years. In *AIDS: The Epidemic of Kaposi's Sarcoma and Opportunistic Infections*, A.E. Friedman-Kien and L.J. Laubenstein, eds., pp. 261–278 New York: Masson.

Curran, J.W. 1983. AIDS—Two Years Later. *N Engl J Med* 309:609–611.

Curran, J.W., D.N. Lawrence, H.W. Jaffe et al. 1984. Acquired Immunodeficiency Syndrome (AIDS) Associated with Transfusions. *N Engl J Med* 310:69–75.

Damron, B. 1965. *The Address Book*. San Francisco: Pan-Graphic.

Darrow, W.W., D. Barrett, K. Jay, and A. Young 1981. The Gay Report on Sexually Transmitted Diseases. *Am J Pub Health* 71:1004–1011.

Feorino, P.M., V.S. Kalyanaraman, H.W. Haverkos et al. 1984. Lymphadenopathy Associated Virus Infection of a Blood Donor-Recipient Pair with Acquired Immunodeficiency Syndrome. *Science* 225:69–72.

Francis, D.P., J.W. Curran, and M. Essex. 1983. Epidemic Acquired Immunodeficiency Syndrome: Epidemiologic Evidence for a Transmissible Agent. *JNCI* 71:1–4.

Fromer, M.J. 1983. *AIDS: Acquired Immunodeficiency Syndrome*. New York: Pinnacle.

Gallo, R.C., S.Z. Salahuddin, M. Popovic et al. 1984. Frequent Detection and Isolation of Cytopathic Retroviruses (HTLV-III) from Patients with AIDS and at Risk for AIDS. *Science* 224:500–503.

Goedert, J.J., R.J. Biggar, D.M. Winn et al. 1984. Determinants of Retrovirus (HTLV-III) Antibody and Immunodeficiency Conditions in Homosexual Men. *Lancet* II:711–716.

Groopman, J.E., S.Z. Salahuddin, M.G. Sarngadharan et al. 1984. HTLV-III in Saliva of People with AIDS-Related Complex and Healthy Homosexual Men at Risk for AIDS. *Science* 226:447–449.

Ho, D.D., R.T. Schooley, T.R. Rota et al. 1984. HTLV-III in the Semen and Blood of a Healthy Homosexual Man. *Science* 226:451–453.

Jaffe, H.W., D.J. Bregman, and R.M. Selik. 1983a. Acquired Immunodeficiency Syndrome in the United States: The First 1,000 Cases. *J Infect Dis* 148:339–345.

Jaffe, H.W., K-W. Choi, P.A. Thomas et al. 1983b. National Case-Control Study of Kaposi's Sarcoma and *Pneumocystis carinii* Pneumonia in Homosexual Men: Part 1, Epidemiologic Results. *Ann Intern Med* 99:145–151,

Jaffe, H.W., W.W. Darrow, D.F. Echenberg et al. 1985. The Acquired Immunodeficiency Syndrome in a Cohort of Homosexual Men: A Six-Year Follow-Up Study. *Ann Intern Med* 103(2):210-4.

Kanki, P.J., M.F. McLane, N.W. King, Jr. et al. 1985. Serologic Identification and Characterization of a Macaque T-Lymphotropic Retrovirus Closely Related to HTLV-III. *Science* 228:1199–1201.

Kinsey, A.C., W.B. Pomeroy, and C.E. Martin. 1948. *Sexual Behavior in the Human Male*. Philadelphia: W.B. Saunders.

Levine, M.P., ed. 1979. *Gay Men*. New York: Harper & Row.

Mayer, K.H., and H.F. Pizer. 1983. *The AIDS Fact Book*. Toronto: Bantam.

McKusick, L., W. Horstman, and T.J. Coates. 1985. AIDS and Sexual Behavior Reported by Gay Men in San Francisco. *Am J Pub Health* 75:493–496.

Rosen, G. 1973. Health, History and the Social Sciences. *Social Science and Medicine* 7:233–248.

Roueche, B. 1980. *The Medical Detectives*. New York: Times Books.

SAS Institute. 1979. *SAS Users Guide*. Raleigh, N.C.: SAS Institute.

Saxinger, W.C., P.H. Levine, A.G. Dean et al. 1985. Evidence for Exposure to HTLV-III in Uganda before 1973. *Science* 227:1036–1038.

Selik, R.M., H.W. Haverkos, and J.W. Curran. 1984. Acquired Immunodeficiency Syndrome (AIDS) Trends in the United States, 1978–1982. *Am J Med* 76:493–500.

Siegal, F.P. and M. Siegal. 1983. *AIDS: The Medical Mystery*. New York: Grove.

Spira, T.J., D.C. DesJarlais, M. Marmor et al. 1984. Prevalence of Antibody to Lymphadenopathy-Associated Virus among Drug-Detoxification Patients in New York. *N Engl J Med* 311:467–468.

Thomas, G. and M. Morgan-Witts. 1982. *Anatomy of an Epidemic.* Garden City, N.Y.: Doubleday.

U.S. Bureau of the Census. 1972. *Statistical Abstract of the United States, 1972.* Washington, D.C.: Government Printing Office.

_____ . 1982. *Statistical Abstract of the United States, 1982–83.* Washington, D.C.: Government Printing Office.

Weinberg, M.S. 1970. Homosexual Samples: Differences and Similarities. *J Sex Research* 6:312–325.

Weinberg, M.S. and C.J. Williams. 1974. *Male Homosexuals: Their Problems and Adaptations.* New York: Oxford.

_____ . 1975. Gay Baths and the Social Organization of Impersonal Sex. *Social Problems* 23:124–136.

William, D.C. 1984. The Changing Life-Styles of Homosexual Men in the Last Fifteen Years. In *AIDS: The Epidemic of Kaposi's Sarcoma and Opportunistic Infections,* A.E. Friedman-Kien and L.J. Laubenstein, eds. pp. 259–262. New York: Masson.

Zinsser, H. 1935. *Rats, Lice and History.* Boston: Little, Brown.

PART III
LIFESTYLES AND BEHAVIORAL CHANGE

Chapter Six

AIDS and Needle Sharing within the IV-Drug Use Subculture

Don C. Des Jarlais, Samuel R. Friedman, and David Strug

Intravenous (IV)-drug users constitute the second largest group of persons who have developed the acquired immune deficiency syndrome (AIDS) in the United States. Of the 9,405 U.S. cases reported to the Centers for Disease Control (CDC) through April 5, 1985, persons with IV-drug use as their primary risk factor accounted for 1,573 (17%) of the cases (CDC 1985). An additional 850 cases (9%) occurred in homosexual/bisexual men who also injected drugs.

IV-drug users also appear to be the link to two other groups with increased risk for AIDS. Of the 108 cases of AIDS in children reported to the CDC through April 5, 1985, slightly over half (55) have occurred in children for whom at least one parent was an IV-drug user. The heterosexual partner's risk group consists of people whose only known risk for AIDS is heterosexual relationships with a member of a previously identified risk group. Almost three-quarters (53/73) of the heterosexual-partners AIDS cases have involved sexual relationships with an IV-drug user (CDC, 1985).

Transmission of the LAV/HTLV-III virus by sharing needles for injecting drugs appears to be the primary means by which IV-drug users contract AIDS (Cohen, et al. 1985, Weiss, et al. 1985). Risk reduction behavior in this group may influence the likelihood of spread to other groups, also.

The drugs injected by IV-drug users who have developed AIDS, or have been exposed to LAV/HTLV-III, are primarily heroin and cocaine (Cohen, et al. 1985, Friedland, et al., 1986). Injection of amphetamines has been infrequently reported and does not appear to be a major factor

111

in AIDS among females and heterosexual males.[1] In our studies of IV-drug users who have been exposed to HTLV-III, almost all have used both heroin and cocaine, often together in a "speedball." In this they do not differ from "control" IV-drug users who have not been exposed to HTLV-III. Thus, the particular drug injected does not appear to be of much importance in the spreading of the LAV/HTLV-III virus. Because the IV-drug users who have been exposed to HTLV-III appear basically similar to the traditional heroin injectors, most of the previous research on heroin addiction can be applied to IV-drug users at risk for AIDS.

In this chapter, we shall examine the prospects for lasting behavioral change within the IV-drug-use subculture in response to the AIDS epidemic. These prospects for change are conditioned by the "pre-AIDS" social context of needle sharing and knowledge of AIDS among IV-drug users.[2]

SOCIAL ORGANIZATION OF IV-DRUG USE

Prior to an examination of the social contexts of needle sharing among IV-drug users, background consideration of the social organization of IV-drug use in the United States will be helpful. IV-drug use has traditionally been described as a "subculture" within sociological and anthropological research (e.g., Agar, 1973, Coombs et al. 1976, DuToit 1977, Johnson 1980, Weppner 1977). Although the concept of "subculture" does not have an overly precise definition, it is used to denote a distinct group with a singular set of values, roles, and status-allocation rules and that exists within a larger society (Johnson 1973:1980). From the perspective of its members, participating in the subculture is a meaningful activity and not an "escape from reality" or an "illness" (Preble and Casey 1969).

IV-drug use clearly constitutes a deviant subculture within the United States. Possession and sale of the drugs are violations of the law, as are many of the activities undertaken to obtain money for purchasing the drugs. In addition to legal differences between IV-drug users and members of conventional society, there is an empathy barrier. Most members of conventional society, even though they may use illicit drugs, have great difficulty imagining themselves injecting drugs or imagining themselves doing what IV-drug users are believed to do to obtain money for drugs. Most members of conventional society find it easier to empathize with victims of drug-related crimes than with IV-drug users. Thus, IV-drug users are not merely

---

[1] A small possibility exists that amphetamine injection may play an important role in homosexual/bisexual men who inject drugs, but this has not been documented.

[2] Original data presented were a part of our ongoing study of AIDS among IV-drug users. Direct quotations are from current and/or former IV-drug users. The methods used in this study are discussed in a section at the end of the chapter.

considered different, but are often objects of fear, mistrust, hostility, scorn, and to a limited extent, pity. This psychological and social distance between the IV-drug use subculture and conventional society contributes to a climate of generalized mistrust between the two groups that will greatly hinder public health efforts at controlling the epidemic among IV-drug users.

A certain minimum of interpersonal trust is needed to conduct the business of providing drugs and the equipment and locations for injecting, and for the social validation of the worth of "getting high." The interpersonal trust is in precarious balance with a generalized mistrust among members of the IV-drug use subculture. Among the many reasons for this mistrust are competition for scarce goods (drugs and the money to buy them), use of informants by law enforcement agencies, carryover of the "hustling" of "straights" to the hustling of other drug users, and the use of violence to settle disputes. A feeling for this generalized mistrust can be obtained from the activities of Bill, who operated one of the "shooting galleries" we studied.

In the past, Bill has been involved in "taking off" customers with the help of Chuck, his crime partner. Chuck would bring unsuspecting clients to the gallery to shoot heroin. At a moment agreed upon by Bill and Chuck, Bill would "yoke" (grab by the neck) the unsuspecting client while Chuck would go through the client's pockets and steal his money. They would then throw the client out.

Not long ago, a client whom Bill and Chuck had robbed returned with friends, a Doberman pinscher, and guns. They were ready to kill Bill and burn down the gallery. Inside the gallery, the client pressed a cocked pistol against the head of a man awakening from a drunken stupor. Fortunately, the would-be murderer realized that it was another man and not Bill or Chuck. Bill, who was not at the gallery that evening, learned of the event, and stayed in hiding a number of days.

Bill reports that he no longer rips off potential clients, because "it's bad for (his gallery's) business." His previous activities, and the reaction of one former gallery client, do provide a feeling for how interpersonal disputes arise and are settled within the IV-drug use subculture.

Some emotionally positive relationships are needed within the IV-drug use subculture in order to balance the general mistrust. As noted below, the emotionally positive relationships often involve needle sharing. These social contexts of "pre-AIDS" needle sharing will shape the possible ways in which significant reductions in needle sharing might occur.

NEEDLE SHARING

Because the sharing of needles is believed to be the major mode of transmission of the LAV/HTLV-III virus among IV-drug users, we want to examine the social and social psychological conditions of needle sharing among IV-drug users in detail. We will examine the three primary social contexts for needle sharing initiation into IV-drug use, sharing with "running partners," and sharing in "shooting galleries."

Before describing these three contexts, however, we should more fully describe exactly what is and can be shared. The needle ("spike") itself is the most likely item for transmission of a virus. The narrow width of the needle makes this the most difficult place from which to clean blood.[3] To the extent that not all blood is removed from the needle, the likelihood that a blood-borne virus like LAV/HTLV-III would be transmitted to the next user increases. To indicate how well needles are sometimes cleaned, we note the practice of using lamp wires to remove clotted blood from a needle so that it may be reused. LAV/HTLV-III has recently been found in saliva (Groopman et al. 1984), so that the practice of cleaning a needle by blowing through it may be another means of viral transmission.

The needle is not, however, the only part of the "works" (the apparatus used by the IV drug user) that may transit virus. Clearly, the syringe would be capable of transmitting virus, as would an eye dropper with a rubber "binkie" (pacifier) that is sometimes used. Sharing of the "cooker" in which the drug is heated and dissolved prior to injection, as well as the cotton used for straining the drug solution when it is taken into the syringe, may also be methods through which the virus might be transmitted. Thus, the possibilities of viral transmission go well beyond just the sharing of needles; sharing of almost any part of the entire works used for injecting might be a possible means of transmitting a blood/saliva-borne virus. We will refer to these different ways of possibly transmitting the virus generically as "needle sharing," while noting that more than the needle itself might be important.

Initiation

An IV-drug user's first injection is typically not self-administered. It is done by a friend who already has experience in injecting, and it is done with the friend's set of works. Within the IV-drug use subculture, initiating people into drug injecting is termed "giving them their wings." The initial motivation for taking the injection varies across individuals, though peer acceptance, risk taking, and curiosity may be the most important reasons. One of our informants, who had previously sniffed heroin, described his induction into needle use by his friend Tom and Tom's older brother Jim:

> When Jim came home from school, he was the first junkie that I knew, who had a habit. I knew Jim well, so it was easy for me to cop heroin whenever I wanted some. I used to watch Jim shoot up, and I became

---

[3]If cleaning is not attempted, this is also the place where blood is most likely to clot. Thus, if the needle is to be reused, some minimal cleaning probably will be done.

very curious about the rush and the high. So one night, I was alone with Jim and Tom and before I knew it, Jim was preparing the dope, and Tom was holding my arm. I was excited. My best friend's older brother was "giving me my wings." We put on the stereo in Jim's bedroom. While Lou Reed sang, "I'm waiting for my man," Jim inserted the number 25 needle into my arm. He got a fast hit, and I went flying off into heaven. Ooh, It was nice and euphoric. I fell in love with heroin that night in my good friend's house. I felt very secure. Like I wasn't alone anymore. I realized that things wouldn't be the same for me, now that I've used the needle.

Other informants describe their initial injection in similar terms. It was "exciting, dangerous, romantic." There was a feeling of "getting away with it, putting something over on parents and other people, so you walk down the street and think, 'They don't know.'" The identification with friends who were already injecting was stressed: "It's like a secret society. They seduce you. My friend had been shooting up for several weeks, and I wanted to be part of that society."

Our informants did not necessarily plan their initial drug injections in terms of setting a specific time and place, but it is clear that they had developed an expectation of its occurring, and a desire that it be a positive experience. One informant compared initial injection to initial sexual intercourse: "It's like the first time you have sex. You don't know what it will be like, but it's a big experience. You want it to be perfect."

The first drug injection appears to be an expected, but not a planned, event. It develops from association with others who are already injecting and, although expected, seems to be a spur-of-the-moment decision. Thus, the planning needed to insure a separate set of works for the initiate would likely not be undertaken. Such planning would require a deliberateness inconsistent with the "romantic, exciting" emotional tone of being given one's wings. It would call into question whether one is really going to "get away with it." The analogy with sexual initiation holds: the need for a positive emotional tone for the experience reduces the chances that initiates will take birth control/venereal disease precautions.

Running Partners

As noted earlier, a generalized mistrust runs throughout the IV-drug-use subculture. The most important exception to this mistrust is between "running partners" or "shooting buddies." Being an IV-drug user involves much more than injecting drugs; one must also "hustle" the money to purchase the drugs and then locate a source of supply. Because much hustling and all dealing are illegal activities, these are not simple tasks. Very often they can be more effectively accomplished by small teams rather than by individuals.

Running partners "scheme, hustle, and boost" together as well as "get off" together. They might often spend jail time together as well. If they are of the opposite sex, they will probably have a sexual relationship (the sharing of works or the partners' injecting each other may have strong sexual connotations in this context). If the partners are both males they may have serial sexual relationships with the same women. Not only do the common activities serve as a bonding force, but so does the synchronicity of intense emotional experiences. They will be "getting sick" (entering withdrawal) together, and then, often through joint efforts, be experiencing euphoria together. Within the subculture, the running partner becomes the substitute for family.

Because needles and works are often in short supply, and withdrawal creates a sense of urgency, the teamwork of running partners often extends to sharing works. The order in which the partners use the works reflects a mixture of concerns. Going first indicates higher status and/or a more important role in obtaining the drugs to be injected. Going first—even before AIDS—was generally considered safer in that it reduced the possibility of receiving a variety of infectious agents. This was believed even though whoever went first took the greatest risk with respect to a "hot shot" that might cause an overdose or other fatal reaction.

Even if each individual has his or her own works for injecting, "cookers" are typically shared. IV-drug users generally believe that dissolving all of the drug to be injected in a single cooker, with each person then filling his or her syringe from the common cooker, leads to a stronger drug effect than the use of separate cookers.

The running partner relationship is the strongest positive relationship within the IV-drug use subculture. The concept of blood brothers—persons who mix their blood together as a symbol of bonding—is found in a variety of cultures and probably can be applied to running partners. Actions that create the suspicion that the partner's blood is "bad" would symbolically threaten the relationship. It would be considered a major insult to refuse to use one's partner's works if one did not have works of his or her own readily available. Refusal to share one's own works so that the partner remained in a state of withdrawal would place a severe strain on the relationship. It would undermine the teamwork and synchronicity of intense experience that are the bases of the running-buddy relationship.

Shooting galleries

IV-drug users must have places in which they can inject drugs without fear of interruption. Homes, cars, and abandoned buildings are all popular. The most notorious location for drug injecting is the "shooting gallery." In a shooting gallery one pays a fee for the use of a (relatively) safe place to inject and may also rent works with which to inject the drugs. The charge for renting works is typically only a few dollars. New (unused) works, when available, will rent or sell for about twice the cost of used works.

Because shooting galleries have the potential for spreading a virus to large numbers of IV-drug users, we have been conducting observational study of galleries in New York City. As part of our research, we have observed several galleries:

What appears to be an abandoned building is, in fact, home to several individuals who permanently reside there and is the location of shooting galleries and a flop house used by prostitutes. The building is an eyesore. Its dull, gray exterior is in need of repainting. There are cracks in the front stoop.

The building is furnished with electricity brought into individual rooms with a wire that residents have attached to the lamp post on the street in front of the house. A "men at work" sign has been placed above the wire on the pavement in front of the house to give the impression that the wire was put in place by city employees working inside. A number of the rooms in this semi-abandoned building have ovens that work because the city has never turned off the gas in the building. The gas burners are kept on all the time to provide warmth inside the shooting galleries and to heat water to inject drugs.

On the first floor is a shooting gallery run by two women who themselves inject cocaine. Myra has lived in this building for years; she remembers when, only four years ago, it was "a good place to live, you couldn't get into the building without being buzzed in." Her apartment–shooting gallery now looks extremely deteriorated.

The ceiling of the apartment has a large hole in it and the paint is peeling. A window frame is covered over with a cloth nailed down to prevent wind and rain from entering. The front door is buttressed with thick pieces of wood to prevent intruders from forcing entry. A fluorescent light fixture diffuses sickly blue light throughout the room. The room's furniture consists of a couch, a number of plastic milk crates for chairs, a small, metal table for holding drug paraphernalia, and a folding bed. A list on the closet door gives the costs to clients for injecting drugs ($2), "piggybacking" (unscrewing the syringe from a needle in a vein and then screwing a second syringe onto the needle so that two syringes of drugs may be injected through only a single puncturing of a vein) ($1), and "being hit" ($1). Myra will also assist the client in finding a vein still useful for injecting drugs for $1. The bathroom has a hole in the floor which serves as a toilet.

Myra has a friend, Sarah, who assists her in running the gallery. Sarah is a 37-year-old woman who lives with her five children. She supports herself by working at Myra's. Sarah is also a prostitute and supplements her income by working as a seamstress. She injects cocaine daily and is a heavy drinker. She left a methadone program five years ago.

A large part of Sarah's day is spent helping Myra run the gallery. Sarah's assistance is critical because the continual flow of clients day and night exhausts Myra. Sarah's presence also makes it easier for Myra to run her gallery. Last year a client banged on the door with a pistol and threatened to rob Myra. With Sarah's help, they scared him off.

This building also contains another shooting gallery upstairs. To get there, one climbs the stairs using a flashlight. The hallway has no electricity and the floorboards are missing in many places. The hallways are filled with trash as well as human feces.

The next gallery is located a short distance from the top of the stairs. It is a single room about 20 feet long by ten feet wide and is divided into two sections by a blanket hung from a clothes line. In the front section drugs are injected, and in the section behind the blanket is a bed that L.T., an alcoholic, sometimes uses. The bed is covered with old clothes and the personal belongings of L.T. Bill, who runs this gallery, describes the place as so filthy and rat infested "that not even the cops will go in. They're afraid of getting AIDS."

Bill is very heavily involved with cocaine and claims to inject cocaine "all day long." When not attending to his customers, Bill often sits on the steps of the building and talks with the prostitutes in the area, chats with his friend L.T., or socializes with other neighborhood people.

Bill always empties out the contents of the glassine bag that holds the cocaine he will inject, and ritualistically rubs the empty bag on his nose to inhale any of the white cocaine powder that may still be in the bag. Sometimes he forgets to wipe the cocaine dust off his nose, and he looks clownish sitting on the steps of the building in which his gallery is located.

Clients enter Bill's "crib," as he refers to his shooting gallery, at all hours of the day and night. Bill charges $2 for the use of the gallery, and charges another $2 to "rent works." It costs another dollar if clients need Bill's assistance in finding and hitting a vein. A small metal bowl containing two hypodermic syringes and a small amount of water sits on top of a wooden table. Next to the bowl are several wads of cottony upholstery padding from the couch across the room. This material is used to wipe the needles "clean" before they are used for further injections. A cooker, jerry-built from a soda bottle cap and a woman's hair clip, is near the upholstery material.

The room has no running water; water for dissolving the drugs prior to injection is obtained from a fire hydrant near the building. The water is heated over the jets of an old gas stove, which also provides the only heat for the room.

It has not been possible for us to study a random sample of shooting galleries in New York. Some are more amenable to infection control and others are less. The descriptions of these galleries raise the question, Why do IV-drug users risk robbery, assault, and a multitude of diseases besides AIDS in order to inject drugs at shooting galleries? There are several reasons. First, the galleries do provide privacy and the water needed for injecting. The galleries are relatively safer than injecting in public places, where one might be interrupted by the police or by others who would "take one off." A second reason is the reduced time from purchase of the drugs to injection. Galleries are typically close to "copping areas," so that the purchaser of drugs can use a gallery to inject very soon after the purchase. This is of great importance if the user is in a state of withdrawal. This proximity also permits the purchaser to return quickly to the dealer when the purchaser wants to seek redress or take revenge if he or she was "burned" (sold inactive ingredients rather than real drugs).

The galleries also provide places for social interaction with other IV-drug users. This may include practical information about sources of drugs or police activities, and it provides social reinforcement for membership within the subculture.

Finally, renting works means that one does not have to risk arrest by carrying works.[4] Our informants have noted that the AIDS epidemic has increased the dangers of carrying around one's own works in the eyes of street IV-drug users. The IV-user fears being beaten by the police if a police officer should prick himself or herself on a needle while searching the IV-drug user.

Shooting galleries, both as locations for injecting and as suppliers of works for injecting, clearly meet practical needs of IV-drug users. What distinguishes shooting galleries from the sharing of works and of places to inject among running partners is both the payment for these services and the relatively large number of people who may use a single set of works. This change from providing needed services on a friendship basis to providing them on a monetary basis is partly an economies-of-scale factor. In areas with a large number of IV-drug users, running a shooting gallery can be a lucrative business.

The sharing of works for injecting drugs is thoroughly integrated into the IV-drug subculture. It starts with initiation into injecting, is an important practical and symbolic part of the running-partner relationship, and becomes a business in the shooting galleries, in which sharing of works extends to persons who may not know each other. The sharing of works symbolizes a wide range of positive relationships among IV-drug users, from the romantic initiation, to the social bonding of running buddies, to the practical mutual advantages for a user and a gallery owner. Significant

---

[4]Because many IV-drug users are engaged in crimes immediately prior to purchasing drugs, the chances of being stopped by police are comparatively high.

reductions in the sharing of needles may thus require fundamental changes throughout the subculture.

POTENTIAL CHANGES IN THE IV-DRUG-USE SUBCULTURE

Even though IV-drug injecting is frequently seen as an intractable habit at the individual level, there have, nevertheless, been numerous evolutionary changes in the IV-drug-use subculture over time (Courtwright 1983; Courtwright, Joseph and Des Jarlais 1981; Musto 1973). Within the last fifteen years, major adaptions in the IV-drug use subculture have occurred in response to the development of methadone maintenance as a large-scale treatment modality (Goldsmith et al. 1984; Hunt et al. 1985). Thus, it is reasonable to expect changes in the subculture as a response to the AIDS epidemic.

A prerequisite for AIDS-related reduction in needle sharing would be knowledge among IV-drug users that the AIDS virus is spread through the sharing of needles. Our field studies indicate that this knowledge has already been incorporated into the folklore of IV-drug use in New York City (Friedman et al. 1985).

Many currently unknown factors will influence the impact and course of the AIDS epidemic among IV-drug users. Among these are the effects of limited reductions in needle sharing, the characteristics of a carrier state for the virus, the percentage of exposed IV-drug users that develops AIDS, and possible development of effective treatments or vaccines.

Despite these uncertainties, we believe that the present structure of the IV-drug use subculture makes some types of changes much more likely than others. As noted earlier, a balance between a generalized mistrust and positive interpersonal relationships exists within the IV-drug use subculture. The social functions of needle sharing before AIDS were primarily associated with positive social relationships. Sharing needles at initiation is one of the changes in self that occur as one identifies with other IV-drug users. It is part of seeing oneself as "getting away with something" and belonging to a special group. Needle sharing among running partners symbolizes a close, caring, "family" relationship. Needle sharing within shooting galleries reflects economic-utilitarian cooperation among members of the subculture. From this analysis of the social functions of needle sharing, we see the possibility of two qualitatively different types of cultural changes in response to the AIDS epidemic: adaptation or radical disruption.

By adaptation we refer to a level of change in which the basic values and central activities of the subculture would be maintained. In the fall of 1983, we conducted extensive interviews with eighteen IV-drug users about AIDS and possible reductions in needle sharing (Des Jarlais et al. 1986).

These drug users were aware of AIDS and believed that it was spread through sharing needles. They also reported increased attempts by themselves and by others to reduce needle sharing.

Probes on the specifics of the reported reduction in needle sharing indicated that it occurs within specifiable conditions. One condition was that "new" or unused needles had to be available at the time that the person had drugs to inject. Motivation to inject once one has successfully obtained drugs becomes very strong, and we consider unreasonable the expectation that an experienced IV-drug user will not inject—and thus forgo the expected euphoria and/or relief of withdrawal symptoms—simply because the only needles available had been used by others.

A second condition limiting reduction in needle sharing concerned running partners—close personal relationships among IV-drug users. Refusing to share a needle with someone whom one wanted to maintain a close personal relationship with was considered very difficult or impossible. Refusal to share implies that one believes that the other person has and/or can transmit AIDS. Such an implication would severely strain a personal relationship among IV-drug users, just as it would among members of conventional society.

These limits on behavioral change are best understood within the context that AIDS is only one more cause of death among IV-drug users. IV-drug users can die in many ways—from violence, from overdoses, from a variety of diseases other than AIDS (Goldstein and Hunt 1986). Through February 1985, slightly over a thousand AIDS cases had been reported among persons with a history of IV-drug injection in New York City (Friedman et al. 1985). This number includes homosexual men who also inject drugs. Approximately half of these patients have died, and the prognosis for the rest is certainly very poor.[5] As serious as this epidemic is, over 2,500 people have died from "chronic/acute intravenous narcotism" during the same time period (NYS Division of Substance Abuse Services 1984). AIDS is less understood, less familiar, and probably more feared than other causes of death for IV-drug users, but it is still only one among many.

In the spring of 1985, we conducted interviews with persons selling needles in the major "copping areas" of New York City (Des Jarlais et al. 1986). These needle sellers reported an increased demand for new needles among IV-drug users and said that the demand was specifically linked to fear of contracting AIDS. Risk-reduction behavior is occurring among IV-drug users, but the present form seems to be primarily increased use of new needles rather than a reduction in drug injecting itself. Thus, adaptation to the epidemic is occurring within the existing value system—emphasizing

---

[5]The number of IV drug users with AIDS in New York City rose to 1,628 by October 30, 1985. (New York City Department of Health 1985).

injection to get high—and within the existing market system for the distribution of drugs and drug use paraphernalia.

Although the percentage reduction in needle sharing due to increased use of new needles cannot yet be quantified, it could be substantial. Our respondents report that a single needle may be used up to fifty times in a shooting gallery before the needle becomes too clogged for further use and that shooting galleries are most used by persons at the high-frequency levels of drug injection. We estimate that at least an order-of-magnitude reduction in needle sharing could occur through an adaptive response by the IV-drug use subculture to the AIDS epidemic. Whether such a reduction in needle sharing would significantly affect the course of the epidemic cannot be determined now.

The AIDS epidemic also has the potential for radical disruption of the IV-drug use subculture. This would be catastrophic change, both in the sense of discontinuous change as described in catastrophe theory, and in the human suffering that would cause such a change. The current rate of increase in AIDS cases among IV-drug users in New York City is a doubling approximately every nine months (Friedman et al. 1985). An "adaptive" response may greatly reduce needle sharing with only a minor effect on the spread of AIDS among IV-drug users.

If the current rate of increase in new cases in New York City should continue for even a few more years, AIDS would undoubtedly become the predominant cause of death among IV-drug users. Prior to AIDS, needle sharing at initiation seemed to be a "romantic getting away with something." Needle sharing among running partners symbolized a caring "family" relationship, and needle sharing at shooting galleries reflected utilitarian cooperation. If the epidemic continues at its present rate of increase, these views would be replaced by a view of needle sharing as inviting a protracted, painful, socially isolated death. Recruitment into the subculture would become exceedingly difficult, and the most important positive social relationship within the subculture would be effectively undermined.

In addition to possibly changing the symbolic meanings of sharing needles, the AIDS epidemic may undermine the IV-drug-use subculture in a second way. The ratio of males to females among IV-drug users is approximately three to one. The majority of male IV-drug users have their primary sexual relationships with females who are not IV-drug users (Des Jarlais et al. 1984). Male IV-drug users also frequently depend upon non-IV-drug using females for food, shelter, and small amounts of money. Increasing evidence points to a heterosexual transmission of the LAV/HTLV-III virus. Harris and colleagues studied female sexual partners of male IV-drug users and found that about one-third of the females had antibody to LAV/HTLV-III (Harris et al. 1984). Heterosexual transmission has not yet received widespread media attention. If knowledge of heterosexual transmission were to lead non-IV-drug-using females to refuse sexual relationships with male IV-drug users, then the result could be greatly reduced material support and undermined macho sexual identities.

If the adaptive changes in reducing needle sharing are not effective in reducing AIDS cases among IV-drug users so that AIDS becomes the primary association to needle use, or if the fear of AIDS leads non-IV-drug using females to refuse sexual relationships with IV-drug using males, then a real possibility of a radical disruption of the IV-drug use subculture exists. Recruitment into IV-drug use might fall to levels at which the subculture could not be sustained.

Were this to happen, the experiential base for a deviant-addicted drug subculture would probably switch to "freebasing/smoking" of drugs. Various forms of cocaine (particularly cocaine paste) can be inexpensively smoked, and there is extensive illicit research on narcotic analogs (Shafer 1985) which may produce inexpensive versions that could be smoked. Smoking as a method of administration does produce intense drug effects. It can easily be adapted to sharing rituals that facilitate the social bonding needed for the formation of a distinct subculture. Finally, smoking drugs would also permit social and sexual relationships between members of the subculture and others in more conventional society without the fear of transmitting a fatal disease.[6]

REFERENCES

Agar, M. H. 1973. *Ripping and Running: A Formal Ethnography of Urban Heroin Addicts.* New York: Seminar Press.

Centers for Disease Control (CDC), AIDS Surveillance. 1985. Personal communication to D. C. Des Jarlais, April.

Cohen, H. et al. 1985. Behavioral Risk Factors for HTLV-III/LAV Seropositivity among Intravenous Drug Users. Unpublished paper presented at the International Conference on the Acquired Immunodeficiency Syndrome, Atlanta, Georgia, April.

---

[6]The original data presented in this chapter were collected under a National Institute of Drug Abuse funded study of "Risk Factors for AIDS among Intravenous Drug Users" (grant 5 RO1 DA03574-01). The study involves laboratory analyses of blood samples, structured questionnaires, nonstructured interviews and nonparticipant observation. The research is being conducted in New York City, which has reported over 60% of all IV-drug use AIDS cases thus far in the epidemic. To date, approximately 450 IV-drug users have been interviewed as part of this study. All material within quotations marks are direct quotations from either current or former IV-drug users. The observations of the shooting galleries were conducted by David Strug. We would particularly like to acknowledge the assistance of the Street Research Unit of the New York State Division of Substance Abuse Services, and the New York City Department of Health.

Coombs, R. H., L. J. Fry, and P. G. Lewis (eds.) 1976. *Socialization in Drug Abuse.* Cambridge, England: Schenkman.

Courtwright, D. T. 1983. *Dark Paradise: Opiate Addiction in America before 1940.* Cambridge, Mass.: Harvard University Press.

Courtwright, D. T., H. Joseph, and D. C. Des Jarlais. 1981. Memories from the Street: Oral Histories of Elderly Methadone Maintenance Patients. *Oral History Review* 9:47–64.

Des Jarlais, D. C., S. F. Friedman, and W. Hopkins. 1986. Epidemiology and Risk Reduction for AIDS among Intravenous Drug Users, In press.

Des Jarlais, D. C. et al. 1984a. Heterosexual Partners: A Large Risk Group for AIDS. *Lancet* 2:1346–1347.

———. 1984b. Immunologic Abnormalities Related to Lymphadenopathy Associated Virus (LAV) among Intravenous Drug Users at Risk for AIDS. Submitted for publication.

DuToit, B. M. (ed.) 1977. *Drugs, Rituals and Altered States of Consciousness.* Rotterdam: A. A. Balkema.

Friedland, G. et al. 1986. Intravenous Drug Abusers and the Acquired Immune Deficiency Syndrome (AIDS): Demographic and Drug Use Patterns. unpublished manuscript.

Friedland, G. et al. 1984. Intravenous Drug Users and AIDS: Knowledge, Views, and Behavioral Changes. Unpublished paper presented at annual meetings of the Society for the Study of Social Problems, San Antonio, Texas.

———. 1985. AIDS among Intravenous Drug Users: Threat and Response. Unpublished paper presented at annual meetings of the Eastern Sociological Society, Philadelphia.

Goldsmith, D., D. E. Hunt, D. Strug, and D. S. Lipton. 1984. Methadone Folklore: Beliefs about Side Effects and Their Impact on Treatment. *Human Organization.* 43:330–340.

Goldstein, P. and D. E. Hunt. 1986. Health Consequences of Drug Use, in press.

Groopman, J. E. et al. 1984. HTLV-III in Saliva of People with AIDS-Related Complex and Healthy Homosexual Men at Risk for AIDS. *Science* 226:447–449.

Harris, C. et al. 1984. Antibodies to a Core Protein of Lymphadenopathy Associated Virus and Immunodeficiency in Heterosexual Partners of AIDS Patients. Unpublished paper presented at the Interscience Conference on Antimicrobial Agents and Chemotherapy, Washington, D.C.

Hunt, D. E., D. Goldsmith, D. Strug, and D. S. Lipton. 1985. It Takes Your Heart: The Image of Methadone among Street Addicts and Its Effects on Recruitment into Methadone Treatment. *International Journal of the Addictions* 21:75–89.

Johnson, B. D. 1973. *Marijuana Users and Drug Subcultures.* New York: John Wiley.

———. 1980. Toward a Theory of Drug Subcultures. In *Theories on Drug Abuse,* NIDA Research Monograph 30, D. J. Lettieri, ed., pp. 110–119. Rockville, Md.: National Institute on Drug Abuse.

Musto, D. F. 1973. *The American Disease: Origins of Narcotic Control.* New York City Department of Health. 1985. AIDS Surveillance Update, October 30, 1985. New Haven: Yale University Press.

New York State Division of Substance Abuse Services. 1984. Heroin Update for New York State. Unpublished manuscript.

Preble, E. and J. H. Casey. 1969. Taking Care of Business: The Heroin User's Life on the Street. *International Journal of the Addictions* 4:1–24.

Shafer, J. 1985. Designer Drugs. *Science 85* 6:60–67.

Weppner, R. S. (ed.) 1977. *Street Ethnography.* Los Angeles: Sage Publications.

Weiss, S. et al. 1985. Risks for HTLV-III Seroprevalence and AIDS among IV Drug Abusers in New Jersey. Unpublished paper presented at the International Conference on the Acquired Immunodeficiency Syndrome, Atlanta, Georgia, April.

Chapter Seven

Gay Lifestyle Change and AIDS: Preventive Health Care

Joseph A. Kotarba and Norris G. Lang

The purpose of this paper is to examine the popular notion that the AIDS phenomenon has led to a widespread movement among homosexual (gay) men toward conservative lifestyles. Data will be presented that indicate that, on the contrary, cognitive and behavioral responses to AIDS have been much more varied and complex than previously alleged. The paper will also examine the common assumption that any conservative lifestyle change observed among gay men can be attributed to the AIDS phenomenon. By applying established social scientific models of preventive health care behavior to this issue, a number of critical factors—such as the relevance of aging, commitment to the more culturally pervasive value of healthism, and geographic mobility—can be shown to be associated with the change, or lack of change, in gay lifestyle patterns.

Mass media coverage of AIDS, which has tended to frame this phenomenon with an aura of sensationalism (Streitmatter 1984:22), has indicated a widespread movement towards conservative lifestyle patterns. The explanation commonly given for this behavioral shift is that gay men as a result of tremendous fear of contracting this highly fatal disease, have overwhelmingly adopted the prevailing epidemiological theory of AIDS. This theory argues that the risk of contracting AIDS is highest among those gay men who live in the "fast lane" of extensive and sometimes indiscriminate sexual activity and recreational drug abuse (Schier 1983:11). During the summer of 1983, which was the height of media coverage of AIDS, for example, *Time* magazine featured a cover article with the following lead: "The Real

---

The order of authorship on this paper is strictly alphabetical.

Epidemic: Fear and Despair . . . AIDS isolates many of it victims and is changing the gay life-style" (Leo 1983:56). The article stated:

> AIDS has clearly changed the rules of the sexual game for homosexuals. Anonymous and casual sex can be fatal . . . . Some gays are attempting to remain celibate or turning their attention to older partners . . . . Others have set up sexual collectives . . . . Some footloose gays are turning to monogamy (Leo 1983:57–58).

This type of generalization has been common in the general media (e.g., Coppola 1983:80).[1]

Two major assumptions help to explain the mass media's premature assertion that the AIDS phenomenon has led to dramatic changes in the gay man's lifestyle. First, AIDS is treated as an overwhelmingly "homosexual" phenomenon—although other at-risk subpopulations for AIDS clearly exist—instead of being framed medically as a "disease" phenomenon. Because homosexuality is still largely a stigmatized status in our society, the media has become unusually dependent upon public gay leaders, spokesmen, and "experts" for information about the impact of AIDS on the gay community. What appears to have occurred is a confusion between the ideological/political position of the organized gay community—generally espoused by these leaders—and actual, everyday gay sexual behavior. The ideological/political position of the organized gay community is to promote "safe sex" and preventive health care (KS/AIDS Foundation of Houston 1984; Goodstein 1984). Even when gays adopt these attitudes in the abstract, one would expect some variation in the impact of these attitudes on actual sexual behavior, as McKusick et al. (1984:2) have discovered.

Second, a commonsense, causal link between the AIDS phenomenon and lifestyle is made in the media. Any reasonable person would conclude that the horrible and tragic consequences of contracting AIDS, which by all accounts are almost universally understood by gays (D'Eramo 1984), would automatically lead a gay male to do everything possible to eliminate known high-risk behaviors. Put differently, the assumption is made that the "fear of AIDS" would cause a national response. The media reports, therefore, tend to ignore the immense complexity of human behavior in a case like this, especially the irrational component of this behavior. The cigarette-smoking-and-cancer phenomenon is the prototypical model in this regard

---

[1]Streitmatter (1984) provides an insightful analysis of the mass media coverage of the AIDS phenomenon during the summer of 1983. He concludes that, with the exception of a very few major news organizations, the media tended to overdramatize the risk of AIDS, ignore the impact of AIDS on local communities, and missed coverage of key events in the development of the phenomenon.

(Graham 1968). The turnaround associated with the surgeon general's report and the decrease in cigarette smoking has been gradual and has varied according to gender, age, and other factors.

A few systematic studies of gay men's attitudes toward and behavioral adaptations to AIDS have been conducted by social and behavioral scientists; these studies point a bit more realistically to the variability and complexity of responses to AIDS. Feldman (1983) conducted a questionnaire survey of 403 homosexual and bisexual men in New York City and found the responses to AIDS very mixed in his sample. Half of those surveyed reported that they altered their sexual behavior in response to AIDS; only 16.5% had undergone a laboratory test for AIDS (i.e., an immunodeficiency test), and 61% said that they were familiar with the commonly acknowledged symptoms of AIDS. Although the mean number of different sex partners (per month) dropped from 6.8 to 3.6 after the advent of AIDS, the 3.6 figure does not support the popular claim of wholesale movement towards celibacy and monogamy in the gay community. As Feldman (1983:10) indicates:

> It could be argued . . . that if one is told that every time he has sex with someone new, he is playing "Russian roulette" by putting his life on the line, you might ask why any male homosexual would want to have any sex with any other male homosexual. From that viewpoint, 3.6 new people each month is still high.

McKusick et al. (1984) conducted a questionnaire survey of 655 gay men in San Francisco in November 1983. They found that, although a movement toward "true" monogamy among those respondents engaged in relationships commonly referred to as monogamous appeared, the proportion of "single" men increased after the advent of AIDS. Those respondents who frequent gay baths and/or bars tend to continue, and in some cases actually increase, high-risk sexual behaviors.

In addition, it should be noted that psychological and psychiatric therapists working with gay men have witnessed this behavioral variability among their clients. Clinically observed reactions range from adaptive acceptance of AIDS to depression, risk bargaining, and even the denial of personal risk (Morin et al. 1984:1292–1293).

Although early social and behavioral studies have been very useful in discovering variability to responses to AIDS, they raise certain methodological and theoretical issues that must be addressed if we are to extend this important line of inquiry. The primary methodological issue is sampling. With the exception of Feldman's (1983) study, which includes a small subsample from Pittsburgh, research on the AIDS phenomenon focuses on San Francisco and New York City.

Although these two cities are home for large gay communities, generalizing research findings of gay men in New York and San Francisco to gay men across our society is presumptuous. The incidence of AIDS appears to have developed more rapidly in these two cities than in other locations, and much of the early media reporting on responses to AIDS was based on events occurring in these two cities. Thus, research should be conducted in contrasting communities and geographic regions. In this regard, the city of Houston is more than just a convenient setting for our study. Like San Francisco and New York City, Houston has a large and influential gay community, but unlike these two cities it maintains a distinctively Southern/Southwestern cultural style and has felt the impact of the AIDS epidemic much more recently.

A related sampling problem is locating subjects within the target community. A typical sampling procedure used in surveys of the gay community, including McKusick et al.'s (1984) study, consists of questionnaires handed out or made available to gay males at the most obvious public locations at which gays are thought to assemble (e.g., baths, bars, health clinics, gay churches, clubs, and organizations). Gay males who do not frequent these public settings are left unaccounted for in the analysis. The development of networks of subjects through personal contacts can reduce this sampling bias by providing the researcher with access to gay men for whom privacy of lifestyle is a concern.

Finally, the common use of questionnaires should be complemented with open-ended interviews. Such interviewing allows the researcher to discover those values, attitudes, constraints, and goals that respondents see as relevant to *their* methods for coping with the AIDS phenomenon. For example, the McKusick et al. (1984) questionnaire included a forced-choice item asking respondents to choose between two popular theories of AIDS transmission: the immune-overload theory and the one-contact infection theory. Although it may be true that these two theories are the most popular in the gay community, the forced-choice item precluded the possibility that some respondents may in fact adhere to other, perhaps more esoteric, folk theories of AIDS, which influence their adaptive behavior. As an illustration of this phenomenon, one subject in our study recalled, "I remember the thoughts also came through my head—somebody has planted something in the gay community to kill the queers off!"

Theoretically, researchers, like mass media reporters, should exceed their thinking beyond framing the relationship between AIDS and lifestyle in simple, monocausal terms. We are suggesting the need for theory to guide research and to account for the complexity of the AIDS phenomenon. Within the social psychology of health and illness behavior, two specific approaches—the Health Belief Model (Rosenstock 1966) and the locus-of-control theory (Rotter 1966)—are relevant to this topic. The Health Belief

Model is noteworthy because it theoretically assembles a comprehensive set of varibles that interact to determine preventive health-care behaviors, whereas the locus-of-control theory provides insight into the issue of whether or not an individual perceives the ability to intervene in areas such as health risk.

The remainder of this paper undertakes three tasks. First, the Health Belief Model and the locus-of-control theory will be discussed to demonstrate their potential application to the AIDS phenomenon. Second, a team-oriented ethnography and interview study designed to deal with the issues raised in this paper will be described. Third, some preliminary findings from this study will be provided; they indicate the future directions of our research.

THE HEALTH BELIEF MODEL

The Health Belief Model (HBM) has become the most influential psychosocial approach for understanding the ways in which healthy people seek to avoid illness. Originally developed by Rosenstock (1966) and refined by his colleagues (Becker 1974), the HBM is largely derived from decision-making theory in psychology. Within this theoretical framework, human behavior is viewed as being dependent upon two primary variables: the value a person places on a particular outcome and the person's belief that a given action will result in that outcome. Accordingly, the HBM argues that preventive care taken by an individual to prevent a particular disease is due to that individual's perception that he or she is personally susceptible and that the occurrence of the disease would have at least some severe implications for him or her.[2]

The perceived threat of the disease, however high, is insufficient impetus for taking preventive health action. Certain modifying factors come into play, including demographic (e.g., age and ethnicity), psychosocial (e.g., personality and reference-group pressure), and structural (e.g., knowledge about the disease) variables. If the threat of the disease remains high, the individual may still not be sufficiently motivated to take action. He or she must weigh the perceived benefits of preventive action (e.g., whether or not the action will eliminate or reduce risk) against the perceived costs of taking action (e.g., expense, unpleasantness, pain, inconvenience, and trauma). Finally, even a positive cost-benefit ratio will require a "cue to action" stimulus that triggers the appropriate preventive health care action. These triggers may include mass media campaigns, advice from significant others, illness of a family member or friend, or newspaper articles.

---

[2]See Becker (1979) for a comprehensive review of the empirical applications of the HBM.

There are at least three reasons that the HBM is relevant to the analysis of lifestyle change among gay males. First, it is designed to explain *preventive* health care behavior, which we can assume is one, if not the primary, reason for lifestyle change among gays. Second, the HBM is designed to incorporate a wide range of social and psychological variables that can influence the decision to modify lifestyle behaviors. This allows for the introduction of insights and hypotheses from a well-developed social-scientific literature on health and illness behavior into the analysis of AIDS. Third, and perhaps most important, the HBM demonstrates the ways in which the absense or dysfunction of one factor can preclude preventive action, even in the presence of other, strong factors in an individual's experience. This dimension of the model is especially relevant to the AIDS phenomenon, because researchers need to explain the reasons for which the tremendous fear and threat of AIDS, in and of themselves, are insufficient causes for modifying lifestyles for certain gay males.

Thus, the HBM points to the following research issues. We would not expect the perceived seriousness of AIDS to be problematic for most respondents. Because AIDS is known to be a disease that kills frequently, the fear of AIDS is probably a near-universal one in the gay community (see also Graham 1973). We would, however, expect to find variation in perceived susceptibility to AIDS. Susceptibility would be a function of the fit between the individual's "member" theory of AIDS and the ways in which he interprets his lifestyle in face of that theory.

Although all of the modifying factors listed in the HBM could be relevant to gay men, we would expect the impact of reference group pressure to be especially relevant. As we indicated earlier, the gay identity is largely a stigmatized identity in our society. Therefore, the gay person's immediate reference groups (e.g., the gay community) are critical sources to counteract the stigma. Self-esteem, definitions of gayness and political orientations play an important role (Warren 1980:130–135). We would anticipate that reference group expectations of lifestyle modification, or lack of it, have an impact upon the individual's decision making.

The cues to action would be relevant, given the widespread mass media coverage of AIDS qua epidemic. We find the illness of a family member or friend to be an interesting cue, because of reports that the memory of the sight of a person with AIDS in the advanced stages of disease deterioration is related to reduction in high-risk behavior (McKusick et al. 1984:2).

Finally, the cost-benefit ratio of taking preventive action may be the key to understanding variation in responses to AIDS. The benefits of eliminating high-risk behaviors may not be overwhelming if, for example, an individual endorses a theory of AIDS that states that susceptibility to the disease is genetically inherited or endemic to homosexuality. Moreover, we can hypothesize a number of cognitive barriers to preventive action, such as the belief that one is "addicted" to the fast-lane, gay lifestyle or the belief that one is going to die someday anyway, so why not make the most out of life now?

LOCUS-OF-CONTROL

Locus-of-control theory was first developed by Rotter (1966) as part of his work on personality and learning. He argued that long periods of exposure to uncontrollable reinforcement may lead an individual to believe that he or she is helpless in general. Some people believe that what happens to them is largely the result of *external* occurrences—that is, events beyond their control—and some people believe that what happens to them is largely the result of *internal* circumstances—that is, their own decisions. Rotter designed a 23 item scale to measure generalized orientation toward internal or external control called the "I-E scale." Phares (1976) reviewed the massive research conducted with the I-E scale and found that, compared with people who are more internal in their beliefs, external individuals feel more anger, are less popular socially as children, are less active in solving mental problems, and are more likely to make lower estimates of their success, even if their success is equal to that of internals. With respect to physical health, internals experience less illness, are less likely to be cigarette smokers, experience less depression, engage in more physical exercise, and are more likely to engage in preventive health care.

Although research conducted on locus-of-control is clearly correlational at best, we contend that this theory can provide insight into lifestyle responses to AIDS. Many homosexuals believe that their sexual orientation is beyond their control, that is, it is genetically or hormonally determined or fixed within the psyche early in life (Altman 1982; Gagnon and Simon 1973). This sense of fatalism/determinism may extend to health-related issues like AIDS. Furthermore, we would expect locus-of-control orientation to be highly related to an individual's personal theory of AIDS—which may differ from the prevailing medical theory—at least to the degree that, in general, people attempt to be consistent in their thoughts about the world (see Festinger 1957).

A DESCRIPTION OF THE STUDY

During the Summer of 1984, we assembled a field research team to begin a preliminary investigation into various psychosocial dimensions of the AIDS phenomenon. The team comprised the authors of this paper, who served as principal investigators, and four student members. We designed the study to focus on a number of subtopics. Included among the topics were the issue of lifestyle change discussed in this paper, the political responses of the gay community to the AIDS phenomenon, the impact of AIDS on intimate, gay relationships, and gays' perceptions of the heterosexual (straight) community's reaction to AIDS and the impact of these perceptions on the everyday life of gays.

Our team was unusually blessed by its diverse composition. It included gays and straights, men and women, teachers and students. This blend afforded us two unique benefits of investigative team research, as outlined by Douglas (1976). First, team research allows for a practical division of labor. Social researchers tend to vary in their skills. Some are more adept at interviewing, or developing contacts with subjects, or writing reports, or reviewing the literature, or interacting with members of the opposite gender than are others. On our team, several members had well-developed social and occupational contacts with the gay community, an advantage that helped us locate subjects and gain access to the political facet of the gay community. The gay members of our team were most useful in providing us with an understanding of the semantics and subcultural nuances of gay life. Finally, the interweaving of sociological and anthropological perspectives enriched the study both methodologically and conceptually.

Second, team research allows for a multifaceted approach to social phenomena. This approach is especially useful for studying groups notably marked by conflict or social phenomena for which participants maintain differing meanings, values, opinions, and goals. In general, the team approach provided us with a good sense of the immense complexity of the AIDS phenomenon and the differing effects it has wrought on the behavior and self-identities of gay men.

Our personal concerns for the rights and safety of our subjects—in addition to the conditions of our agreement with the University of Houston, Committee for the Protection of Human Subjects—greatly affected data-collection strategies. Although we generated a snowball sample based upon our personal contacts, no member of the team interviewed any subject known personally to him or her. In order to protect our subjects' rights of privacy, we had interested, prospective subjects initiate contact and arrange interviews by telephone. No subject identifying information was included on notes or transcripts, and the audiotapes will be destroyed upon completion of the entire study.

Each interview lasted approximately one-and-one-half hours. The interview schedule consisted of three parts.[3] First, we began with a series of objective questions seeking information on 1) socioeconomic/demographic characteristics; 2) health status and behavior before and after the onset of

---

[3]Copies of the interview schedule are available upon request.

the AIDS phenomenon; and 3) sexual attitudes and behavior before and after the onset of the AIDS phenomenon. Second, we asked a series of specific, open-ended questions regarding, for example, 1) experiences of homophobia (fear of gay men and women) since the onset of the AIDS phenomenon; 2) sources of information on AIDS; 3) the nature of the subject's political involvement with the gay community's collective response to AIDS; and 4) the subject's initial thoughts and feelings when first learning of the existence of AIDS.

Third, we engaged our subjects in a grounded-theory exercise that forms the basis for the present report. According to its originators (Glaser and Strauss 1967), the grounded theory method stresses discovery and theory development rather than logical-deductive reasoning (see also Charmaz 1983). Data collection and analysis proceed simultaneously, so that one's theoretical understanding of a phenomenon is constantly revised as more data are collected. Grounded theory was specifically designed for the analysis of qualitative data, because it views the discovery of social life as an *interpretive* endeavor.

The basic strategy in grounded theory construction necessitates that the researchers approach the phenomenon with as few preconceptions as possible. Three major components of grounded theory are 1) *coding*, which is the process of categorizing and sorting data according to emerging patterns; 2) *memo writing*, which is the continuing, written elaboration of ideas and insights; and 3) *theoretical sampling*, which is an inductive system by which new data and subjects are sought, either to test out ideas derived from existing data or to exhaust analytical categories.

As Charmaz (1983:125) clearly indicates, each researcher develops his or her own variations on grounded theory to suit personal style and the demands of the phenomenon in question. During our initial interviews, we became aware that the effects of the AIDS phenomenon on the gay male lifestyle were many and varied. We, therefore, decided to code our dependent variable, lifestyle change, into simple categories. We refer to a *private lifestyle* as one operationalized by a tendency toward monogamous or closed group relationships, moderate or no recreational drug use, and concern for personal health. We refer to a *public lifestyle* as one operationalized by high levels of sexual activity with multiple and/or anonymous partners, multiple drug use or abuse, and an effective disregard for personal health. The public lifestyle is commonly referred to as the "fast lane" in the gay community.

When we introduce a dimension of change, that is, lifestyle before and after the onset of the AIDS phenomenon, we can place any subject in one of four possible dimensions: Public-Public, Public-Private, Private-Private, and Private-Public. Our sampling procedure was primarily based upon the search for subjects fitting each category and, secondarily, to test out possible psychosocial variables that could account for, or at least correlate with, change or the absence of change. We concluded this preliminary study with a total *n* of 48, predominantly composed of white, middle-class, gay males in the 22 to 67 age range.

The list of psychosocial variables that provided direction for subsequent interviews came from two sources: the social science of health and illness literature, specifically the HBM and locus-of-control theory discussed above, and, in accord with the spirit of grounded-theory analysis, insights gathered from our initial interviews. Among the more important lines of inquiry derived from these latter insights were: 1) relevance of aging, 2) whether or not the subject is or has been in psychological or psychiatric therapy, 3) awareness of and/or adherence to the dictates of healthism, and 4) perception of the moral essence of homosexuality. The following are some of the more interesting preliminary findings.

PUBLIC-PUBLIC

The Public-Public dimension (*n* = 13) consists of gay men who were in the "fast lane" before the onset of the AIDS phenomenon, yet remain there in spite of awareness of AIDS. There tends to be some lifestyle accommodation to the AIDS phenomenon, albeit quite minor, such as efforts to reduce the exchange of body fluids during sex. Nevertheless, high levels of sexual activity with multiple and/or anonymous partners ordinarily continues.

All of the Public-Public subjects acquired sophisticated knowledge of the AIDS phenomenon and perceived great pressure from the media and some significant others to turn to a private lifestyle. Nevertheless, we observed two cognitive schemes used by these subjects to account, both to themselves and to us, for their continued high-risk behaviors. Each scheme can be denoted by locus-of-control orientations.

First, those subjects who are "internal controls" tend to adhere to a *systemic* theory of AIDS. Regardless of the cause of AIDS or the vehicle for the transmission of AIDS, the focus of attention for the prevention of AIDS is the holistic well-being of the human system. Put differently, one can continue to engage in high-risk behaviors so long as the body is strong and its resistance to disease is strong. Some of the strategies discussed for maintaining strength are 1) regular visits to the doctor, 2) exercise, 3) sufficient sleep, and 4) stress management. One subject voiced the belief that the key to avoiding AIDS is the maintenance of psychological well-being:

> I think that a lot of it [susceptibility to AIDS] is psychological I
> think that a certain percentage of the [gay] population is prone to conditions like AIDS . . . . A need to be sick, a need to get it [AIDS], who

knows. I often think that there are people, for whatever psychological reason or reasons, who need to have some kind of physical breakdown, or they need attention, or they tell themselves it's not OK to be well.

This subject has been engaging in psychological therapy at the time of the study.

Second, those subjects who are "external controls" are fatalistic about the risk of AIDS. Preventing AIDS is beyond their control because, they feel either 1) some people have a genetic predisposition to AIDS, or 2) the risk of contracting diseases like AIDS is endemic to being homosexual. One respondent even went so far as to describe a completely fatalistic relationship between AIDS and the gay lifestyle:

> I think we [gays] have always lived with risk. This is just another risk on a list of risks that we all live with. And I'll tell you when it [AIDS] first appeared, we were all in a state of shock, then we put it on a list of things that we have to think about and that we know that we are running a risk of every time we go out. And I think that's very much a part of the gay lifestyle is that element of knowing that you are doing things at risk.

The sense of fatalism displayed by these gay males helps explain the early media reports of widespread movement towards sexual conservatism. In general, many members of the Public-Public category attempted to adhere to the rules of "safe sex" at the onset of the AIDS phenomenon—when the gay community was under constant scrutiny by the media—but have since returned to previous sexual practices. Eventual resignation to fate has been enhanced to some degree by the growth of medical/epidemiological understanding of AIDS. Knowledge of the lengthy and asymptomatic incubation period of the AIDS virus, for example, has led to a new concept in the gay vernacular, the "fatal fuck," that was observed during several of our interviews. The "fatal fuck" concept refers to the belief that the AIDS virus may have been contracted through one, discrete sexual encounter sometime in the indeterminable past. Thus, the "fatal fuck" concept has become a readily available account for justifying a return to a Public lifestyle, because, "I ain't got nothing to lose," as one respondent expressed it.

In summary, the HBM process can break down at any of several points for the Public-Public subjects. There may be reference group pressure to continue in the fast lane. Effective cues to action are missing; in fact, remembrance of the visual image of a deteriorating AIDS victim, which McKusick et al. (1984) found to be related to reductions in high-risk behavior, was missing in most of these interviews. Those people who are "internal controls" see themselves engaging in preventive care, although not by the most highly recommended means offered by the medical profession. The key to understanding the Public-Public category, however, is the perceived cost-benefit ratio of comprehensive preventive action. In general, these gay men feel that they either cannot or will not sacrifice their high levels of sexual activity. As one respondent noted, "I need my hot sex. Sometimes I think I'm addicted to it."

PUBLIC-PRIVATE

The Public-Private dimension ($n = 20$) consists of those gay men who have moved toward quite conservative lifestyles. In general, they no longer frequent gay baths, bars, or bookstores for the purpose of sexual encounters. They tend toward the highly selective engagement of sexual partners, and they no longer abuse recreational drugs. In general, they adhere to the medical model for minimizing risk of AIDS, such as minimizing the exchange of bodily fluids during sex. They are very high on internal control, as would be expected.

Two subtypes appear within this category. On the one hand, there are those now-"classic" gay men for whom the dramatic cues to action available since the onset of AIDS have been sufficient final cause for drastically modifying lifestyles. On the other hand, there are those men for whom the movement toward a private lifestyle did not originate with the AIDS phenomenon; for example, those subjects over the age of thirty who have become concerned with their state of health largely as a result of perceptions of aging. As one subject indicated:

> I've begun over the past few years taking better care of my health. It's not solely because of the AIDS scare. A lot of it has to do with the fact that my body has started to tell me that I'm getting older, and I can't quite do it like I used to . . . . I think a lot of it is simply the process of physical aging and needing to keep a better eye on that.

In the above case, as well as in others, concern over aging occurred around the age of thirty, an age at which respondents felt that they were losing the "boyish good looks" needed to be a desired sexual partner in the fast lane.

In summary, it is clear that any observed movement from Public to Private lifestyles cannot be simply attributed to AIDS as a cue to action, whether or not this movement coincided temporally with the AIDS phenomenon.

PRIVATE-PRIVATE

The Private-Private dimension ($n = 10$) consists of those gay men who felt that they have not had to modify their lifestyles in any significant way in response to the risk of AIDS. These subjects tend to be older (35 and above), in monogamous relationships or highly selective sexual encounters, relatively conservative in their sexual tastes, and concerned with health and aging. They reflect strong internal control, which is demonstrated in their adherence to the medical theory of AIDS. It is within this category, however, that we witnessed a distinctly moral dimension, couched sometimes in homophobic tones, to perceptions of homosexuality in general and the AIDS phenomenon in particular. Private-Private subjects tended to talk about two types of gays: those, like themselves, who are responsible to themselves and the gay community, and those who are irresponsible. As one respondent described the situation: "Those who can't see beyond the backs of their partners are going to get what they deserve."

Those who remain in the Public lifestyle and are causing all the headlines about AIDS, they argue, are destroying all the gains made by gays in our society over the past few years. As one respondent indicated:

> I'm hoping it [the AIDS phenomenon] is making them [the gay community] look at themselves. To me, the gay community has so much potential as a minority that is just wasting away . . . . The AIDS thing can help take the blinders off the gay community. They know of nothing except their work and their partying. Very little community work, anything like that. The primary motivation is to go out, have a good time, get drunk or do drugs, and pick up a trick. Sure, that's OK, but that cannot be what you live for.

PRIVATE-PUBLIC

The Private-Public category ($n = 5$) consists of gay men who, since the advent of the AIDS phenomenon, have actually moved into the fast lane. Although it would be extremely difficult to estimate the extent of this apparently maladaptive behavior in the gay community, there are a few references to it in the literature. Leo (1983:58), for example, cites a study conducted in San Francisco that found that 10% of the gay male respondents have increased high-risk sexual behavior since learning of AIDS. Morin et al. (1984:1292) indicate that some gay men will even seek "unsafe sex" immediately after attending group therapy sessions. Ironically, these sessions are organized as support groups to help gay men without AIDS learn to cope with stress associated with the AIDS phenomenon.

The explanations offered for this behavior locate the cause at the psychological level. Leo (1983:58) suggests that this behavior may be a sign of unconscious defiance of the medical establishment that, before AIDS, maintained a long and infamous history of defining homosexuality itself as a pathological disease. Morin et al. (1984:1292) suggest that this behavior is very similar to that of individuals facing death. Specifically, movement into the fast lane is an act of denial. Life-threatening activities are used as a recourse for those gay men who cannot or will not face the realities of the AIDS threat.

Our preliminary investigation has discovered two explanations, perhaps primarily sociological and situational, for at least some of the observed movement into the fast lane that occurs largely independent of the AIDS phenomenon. First, the dissolution of long-term, intimate relationships is often the occasion for a rapid return to a Public lifestyle. Several respondents have stated that anonymous or indiscriminate sex is a way of coping with the stress, anger, hurt, and other feelings associated with breaking up. One respondent did indicate, however, that the AIDS phenomenon was a minor, precipitating factor during a recent breakup. Specifically, the respondent insisted that his lover abandon his various "side affairs" and practice true monogamy in response to the AIDS threat. The lover refused and the relationship ended. The respondent admitted, though, that there were a number of other problems in their relationship before the breakup, such as his lover's abuse of alcohol. Nevertheless, this example raises an important issue for further research, namely, the degree to which the AIDS phenomenon has placed undue stress on intimate gay relationships.

Second, geographic relocation is often the occasion for entering the Public lifestyle. This phenomenon is particularly visible in a growing city like Houston, which has a large gay community. Many respondents in all categories indicated that moving to Houston provided them with previously unavailable opportunities for living in the fast lane. Gay newcomers, especially those from conservative or small town backgrounds, are amazed at the number of bars, bookstores, and baths in the gay community. Regularly visiting these establishments to engage in a great deal of sex with many partners becomes the vehicle for nurturing and freeing a previously constrained self-identity. As one respondent noted:

> There is a tremendous sense of isolation among gays who don't live in a real gay community. When a young stud comes to Houston from the farm, he feels the sense of celebration just being able to be in a gay bar publicly with other gays. The fast lane just feeds this sense of freedom he has for the first time in his life.

We have observed a number of reasons for gay men's migration to Houston, including job opportunities, efforts to be with a lover, and previous knowledge of sexual and social opportunities there. In any case, the cognitive irrelevance of the AIDS phenomenon to these men is plausible, because entering a large gay community like that in Houston is: ". . . a lot like a little kid being locked up in a candy store overnight," as one respondent described his experience.

In summary, the Private-Public dimension may well turn out to be the most analytically useful in our continuing investigation. It illustrates both the strongest and weakest influence of the AIDS phenomenon on gay males. A dramatic shift in locus-of-control, from internal to external, may have occurred for those gay men to whom the psychological explanations apply. On the other hand, the perception of personal susceptibility to AIDS—the first step in seeking preventive health care according to the HBM model—is effectively blocked for many gay men whose lives are preoccupied with exploring the newly discovered gay community.

CONCLUSIONS

In the course of collecting data for this study, we have often heard the comment that gays are so different that the only characteristic they share is sexual preference. The essence of diversity, which this paper has attempted to portray, should be a guiding assumption of all future research on gay reactions to AIDS. Early reports of this phenomenon, especially in the mass media, have tended to assume that social scientists refer to as the *ecological fallacy* (Babbie 1983:80): the danger of making assertions about one unit of analysis based upon an examination of the other, most commonly, by attributing a characteristic of the group to individual members of the group. Although the gay community—through its political organizations, leaders, and spokespersons—has clearly mobilized to reduce the threat of AIDS through efforts like the "safe-sex" campaign, we cannot assume that this shift in values reflects the everyday-life concerns of all gay men.

The Health Belief Model and the locus-of-control theory appear to be useful tools in the analysis of gay lifestyle change as preventive health care. The HBM in particular, though, offers a weak explanation for the Private-Public dimension, because it calls for a more general sociopsychological theory to account for the complex ways in which AIDS can be defined by some gay men as virtually irrelevant to everyday-life concerns.

Several issues raised in this preliminary study will inform the next stage of research. As we expand our data to account for gay men in all socioeconomic groups, we need to expand our simple typology to reflect *rates* of change in lifestyle behavior. Furthermore, this expanded data base will allow us to extrapolate the proportions of gay males that fall into each dimension, particularly the Private-Public dimension.

We also need to explore some intriguing findings not reported above. We have encountered a number of highly unusual, if not esoteric, folk theories of AIDS. For example, we have heard various kinds of conspiracy theories, such as, "Someone planted a virus to kill all the gays"; and "It's all a CIA plot to kill gays . . . they developed a virus in Africa and transplanted it to Haiti . . . ." Although it appears that these theories were much more common at the onset of the AIDS phenomenon, an examination of the rationale behind them can increase our understanding of the process by which an at-risk population accounts for an otherwise mysterious and tragic health threat.

In summary, the search for health care, whether preventive or curative, is most essentially a search for practical meanings that work (Kotarba 1983). As Antonovsky (1979) argues, coping activities—that is, the search for health care meanings—must occur within a personally meaningful context of community, tradition, or cosmos that sets a limit to personal control and makes "affectively comprehensible" the many uncontrollable and tragic aspects of human life. Therefore, in order to flesh out our preliminary findings, we must examine the ways in which gay men seek meaning for AIDS from all available sources, such as the gay community, gay tradition, and the dominant U.S. culture.

ACKNOWLEDGMENTS

The Center for Public Policy at the University of Houston provided support for the preparation of this paper. We would also like to acknowledge the invaluable assistance and dedication of the student members of our research team in the construction of this chapter; they are Cindy Underwood, Allen Snyder, Kevin Olive, and Jeanmarie Theine.

REFERENCES

Altman, Dennis. 1982. *The Homosexualization of America, The Americanization of the Homosexual.* New York: St. Martin's Press.

Antonovsky, Anthony. 1979. *Health, Stress and Coping.* San Francisco: Jossey-Bass.

Babbie, Earl. 1983. *The Practice of Social Research.* Belmont, Cal.: Wadsworth.

Becker, Marshall H. 1974. *The Health Belief Model and Personal Health Behavior.* San Francisco; Society for Public Health Information, Inc.

———. 1979. Psychosocial Aspects of Health Related Behavior. In *Handbook of Medical Sociology*, Howard E. Freeman, Sol Levine, and Leo G. Reeder, eds., pp. 253-274. Englewood Cliffs, N.J.: Prentice-Hall.

Charmaz, Kathy. 1983. The Grounded Theory Method: An Explication and Interpretation. In *Contemporary Field Research*, Robert M. Emerson, ed., pp. 109–126. Boston: Little, Brown.

Coppola, Vincent. 1983. The AIDS Epidemic: The Change in Gay Life-Style. *Newsweek* 101(16):80.

D'Eramo, James E. 1984. African Swine Fever Virus and AIDS: Promising Questions But No Real Answers. *Christopher Street*, Vol. 7, No. 7.

Douglas, Jack D. 1976. *Investigative Social Research*. Beverly Hills, Cal.: Sage.

Feldman, Douglas A. 1983. AIDS: Differential Response to a Health Epidemic. Unpublished paper presented at the annual meeting of the American Anthropological Association, Chicago.

Festinger, Leon. 1957. *A Theory of Cognitive Dissonance*. Stanford, Cal.: Stanford University Press.

Gagnon, John and William Simon. 1973. *Sexual Conduct*. Chicago: Aldine.

Glaser, Barney G. and Anselm L. Strauss. 1967. *The Discovery of Grounded Theory*. Chicago: Aldine.

Goodstein, D. B. 1984. Opening Space. *The Advocate*, 398. July 10.

Graham, Saxon. 1968. Cancer of Lung Related to Smoking Behavior. *Cancer* 21 (March): 523–530.

———. 1973. Studies of Behavior Change to Enhance Public Health. *American Journal of Public Health* 63:327–334.

Kotarba, Joseph A. 1983. *Chronic Pain: Its Social Dimensions*. Beverly Hills, Cal.: Sage.

KS/AIDS Foundation of Houston. 1984. Safe Sex Catches On. *KSA Lifeline*. Volume 1, Number 1 (February): 1.

Leo, John. 1983. The Real Epidemic: Fear and Despair. *Time* 122 (1): 56–58.

McKusick, Leon, William Horstman, and Arthur Cafagni. 1983. Reaction to the AIDS Epidemic in Four Groups of San Francisco Gay Men. Unpublished report prepared for the Department of Public Health, City and County of San Francisco. November, 1983.

Morin, Stephen F., Kenneth A. Charles, and Alan K. Malyon. 1984. The Psychological Impact of AIDS on Gay Men. *American Psychologist* 39: 1288–1293.

Phares, E. J. 1976. *Locus of Control in Personality*. Morristown, N.J.: Central Learning Press.

Rosenstock, Irwin. 1966. Why People Use Health Services. *Milbank Memorial Fund Quarterly* 44: 94–127.

Rotter, J. B. 1966. Generalized Expectancies for Internal Versus External Control of Reinforcement. *Psychological Monographs* 80 (1, Whole No. 609).

Schier, Mary Jane. 1983. Syndrome Called Worst of Century. *The Houston Post* (February 21): 11.

Streitmatter, Roger. 1984. AIDS: It's Just a Matter of Time. *The Quill* 72 (5): 22–27.

Warren, Carol. 1980. Homosexuality and Stigma. In *Homosexual Behavior*, Judd Marmor, ed., pp. 123–141. New York: Basic Books.

Chapter Eight

AIDS Health Promotion and Clinically Applied Anthropology

Douglas A. Feldman

INTRODUCTION

One of the major roles for clinically applied anthropologists is the area of health promotion and education (Christman and Maretzki 1982; Phillips 1985). The sudden emergence of AIDS, from its first mention in the medical literature in 1981 (*Morbidity and Mortality Weekly Report* 1981a, 1981b), to Health and Human Services Secretary Heckler's categorization of the disease as the United States' number one health problem in 1983, to the well-founded fear and despair that is found in much of the homosexual (gay) community in the United States today (March 1985) (Feldman 1985a), has created a profound gap in the need for AIDS health promotion and education from governmental agencies.

If Horn and Waingrow's (1966) model for personal-choice health behavior is utilized to explain behavioral change as a response to AIDS, we can perhaps better understand the complexity of the issue. The model was originally applied to cigarette smoking behavioral change, but has been extended to cover the gamut of health-impairing behaviors. It is a refinement of the Health Belief Model (cf. Kotarba and Lang's chapter—Chapter Seven—this volume) and consists of: 1) factors that would motivate individuals to change their behaviors, 2) the perception of the threat from the behavior, 3) factors associated with the psychological usefulness of the behavior, and 4) factors facilitating or inhibiting continued reinforcement. This paper will use this model to generate a framework for a health promotion program for AIDS prevention and will discuss the results of the author's study of behavioral change within the New York City gay community.

Before applying this model to AIDS, the behavior or behaviors that need to be changed must be specified. In the case of cigarette smoking, the desired changes for health promotion would be to have the individuals stop smoking, or at least cut down the number of cigarettes consumed, or switch to a low-tar, low-nicotine brand. In the case of AIDS, identifying behaviors to be changed is not simple. Even though hemophiliacs are currently the most susceptible high-risk population for AIDS, with an incidence rate now above one in 280 for hemophilia A patients (Shore et al. 1985), the risk to their health would be greater if Factor VIII concentrate were to be made unavailable. Thus, no such behavioral change is recommended for hemophiliacs.

The same applies to recipients of blood transfusions who are at considerably higher risk of death by refusing a transfusion in order to avoid AIDS than of death from AIDS by having the transfusion (*Lancet* 1984). Intravenous (IV)-drug users would, however, decrease their risk for contracting AIDS by avoiding shared hypodermic needles (Ginsburg 1984; also see Des Jarlais, Friedman, and Strug's chapter—Chapter Six—in this volume).

Heterosexual partners of IV-drug users and any other at-risk individuals should avoid the exchange of bodily fluids (Altman 1985). Female prostitutes may transmit or be at risk for AIDS (*Oncology Times* 1985; Ortleb 1985). If this proves to be correct, the exchange of bodily fluids with this population should also be avoided.

The mode of AIDS transmission among Haitian-Americans, Haitians, and Central Africans requires substantially greater study before any recommendation for behavioral change can be offered. One theory holds that AIDS is predominantly spread among heterosexuals through anal sex (Krim 1984; Altman 1985). If this proves accurate in Haiti, Central Africa, and among Haitian-Americans in the United States, alternative birth-control information and devices would reduce AIDS mortality and morbidity in these populations.

Homosexual (gay) and bisexual men account for the vast majority of people with AIDS in North America and Europe (Centers for Disease Control 1985; *Morbidity and Mortality Weekly Report* 1985). Generally, AIDS health promotion and education has emanated from self-help and other groups—such as the Gay Men's Health Crisis, People with AIDS, the National Gay Task Force, the Shanti Project, and New York Physicians for Human Rights—and through information published in the gay press. Some state and municipal governments, most notably the states of California and New York and the city of San Francisco, have also developed health-promotion and education programs.

Advice to gay men for reducing the risk of contracting AIDS has included improved nutrition, adequate sleep, lowered stress, increased exercise, and avoidance of recreational drugs, including amyl nitrate, butyl nitrate, and isobutyl nitrite (Marmor et al. 1982; Mayer and D'Eramo 1983). The sexual transmissibility of AIDS, however, has prompted most health-promotion and education advice to be directed at modifying sexual behavior among gay men. These efforts have ranged from promoting total celibacy[1] to advocating sex with different partners but without exchanging bodily fluids.[2]

New York Physicians for Human Rights, a gay physicians organization, has issued guidelines to the gay community for "safe" sex, which include reducing the number of different sexual partners, use of condoms during sex, avoidance of swallowing semen, and cessation of analingus, "gantizing,"[3] and ingestion of urine.[4] Very little research has been undertaken to determine actual patterns of LAV/HTLV-III transmissibility among gay men. How safe is oral sex without swallowing semen? Will LAV/HTLV-III from the saliva of someone performing oral sex infect his sexual partner? What is the likelihood of becoming infected through receptive anal sex without a condom and without an ejaculation? Is it safe if a condom is used? LAV/HTLV-III has been found in the saliva of people with AIDS: should kissing, or even sharing of the same glass in a gay bar or a cup of popcorn in a movie theater, be avoided? Is frequent hugging, cuddling, or mutual masturbation with a person with AIDS or ARC totally safe? These limitations of available epidemiological data will handicap the clinically applied anthropologist or health educator in any effort to develop a comprehensive program for AIDS prevention, but should not thwart the further implementation of such programs.

Another area of concern has been the number of different sexual partners required to reduce one's risk to AIDS. A cure for AIDS may not be found for years (D'Eramo 1984). Most gay men should not be encouraged to completely abstain from sex until a cure is found, because doing so would severely curtail the quality of their lives. Moreover, giving up customary patterns of sexual behavior is no easy task. Carnes (1983) indicates that a segment of both homosexual and heterosexual populations are addicted to compulsive sexual behavior. Quadland (1984) and other psycho therapists

---

[1]Beldekas (1985) quotes Dr. Mervyn Silverman, former San Francisco Public Health Director who banned sex in that city's gay bathhouses and other public places, as saying that gay men should cease all sexual contacts, "wet or dry," with other gay men.

[2]A popular Gay Men's Health Crisis poster in New York City reads, "Healthy Sex is Great Sex."

[3]Gregersen (1983) prefers the term "gantizing" to "fisting." "Gantizing" is derived from the French *gant*, glove, and refers to the practice of using a body cavity (i.e., the rectum) as a glove into which a hand is placed.

[4]However, in an AIDS safe sex guidelines card distributed by the San Francisco AIDS Foundation, the Bay Area Physicians for Human Rights describe "watersports—external only" (urinating upon a sexual partner, but not ingesting the urine) as a possibly safe sex practice.

are working with gay men who find alteration of their sexual behaviors especially difficult. Though many heterosexuals are astonished by the numbers of same sex contacts possible in one night at a gay bath,[5] sexual frequency with multiple partners should not be confused with sexual compulsion or addiction (Carnes 1983). Only when sexual behavior interferes with the activities and goals of an individual should they be seen as a problematic addiction (Goleman 1984).

Acceptable alternatives for promoting AIDS prevention could vary considerably. If rigorously adhering to safe sex guidelines during mutual masturbation with people with even AIDS or ARC is entirely risk-free, then the number of different partners need not be delimited at all. Private sex clubs have emerged in 1983 and 1984 in New York City and elsewhere at which "fluid patrols" ensure that safe sex rules are strictly enforced. Although mutual masturbation alone probably could not result in LAV/HTLV-III transmission between individuals, such transmission has not yet been proven absolutely impossible. Prudence, therefore, dictates a limit to one's number of sexual contacts, even when one engages only in mutual masturbation, until additional epidemiological data become available.

To sum up, a gay man could reduce his risk of contracting AIDS by reducing the number of his sexual partners, completely avoiding the exchange of bodily fluids, and practicing safe sex rules as closely as possible. With a median of 24.5 months between infection and onset of illness (Curran et al. 1984) and an estimated latency period ranging up to seven years (Lawrence 1984), only exclusive monogamy with a partner or lover of more than seven years, or total celibacy, could ensure freedom from AIDS for an otherwise risk-free gay man.

RESEARCH METHODS

During the period of August 1982 through April 1983, a study was conducted in New York City in an attempt to measure the impact that the growing AIDS epidemic was having on the gay male community.[6] A two-page questionnaire was designed, pretested, revised, and distributed to homosexual and bisexual men at a wide variety of gay organizations, churches, bars, professional and medical services, and at the corner of

---

[5]Meredith (1984) indicates that the medians of two studies of lifetime sexual partners of healthy gay men are 550 partners and 685 partners.

[6]A smaller Pittsburgh sample ($n = 39$) has been surveyed, but a comparison of the frequencies of the independent variables from the two cities indicates statistically significant noncomparability of the data (Feldman 1983).

Hudson and Christopher Streets (a major crossroad within the New York City gay community). The frequency distribution of the sample ($n = 403$), although nonrandom, appears to be a close representation of the openly gay, male population of Manhattan.

Questions were asked about the mean number of sexual partners per month before the respondent heard about AIDS, the mean number of sexual partners per month at the time of the study, the change in the frequency of visiting all-male movie theaters or gay bars with a backroom for anonymous sexual activity, the change in the patterns of sexual activity, the change in the frequency of nitrite-drug usage, whether or not the respondent had had any test or indicator for immunodeficiency, whether or not the respondent felt that he may have an immune problem, and familiarity with the symptoms of AIDS.

Each respondent was also asked to reveal his age, race, ethnicity, income level, educational level, and sexual orientation (i.e., homosexual or bisexual). The study was divided into two time frames (i.e., early and late). The type of organization or establishment in which the questionnaire was distributed was noted. Since April 1983, additional data have been collected through an ongoing ethnographic study (entailing both direct observation and informal interviewing of gay males in New York City).

RESULTS

The respondents self-report a decline in the mean number of sexual partners per month from 6.8 before they heard of AIDS to 3.6 at the time of the study (see Table 8.1; cf. Feldman 1984, 1985b for more detailed analyses). Half of the respondents indicated that they altered their sexual behaviors, usually decreasing the frequencies of insertive and receptive oral sex, insertive and receptive anal sex, and kissing; stopping completely analingus, gantizing ("fisting"), and swallowing semen; and increasing the frequencies of masturbation and mutual masturbation.

Of those who occasionally or regularly visited gay bathhouses, all-male movie theaters, or gay bars with a backroom for anonymous sexual activity, most reported that they either decreased the frequency of attending these establishments or stopped going completely. Of those utilizing amyl nitrite, isobutyl nitrite, and butyl nitrite (drugs widely used as an aphrodisiac within the gay community and collectively referred to as "poppers"), most said that they either decreased or terminated usage. Only 16.5% of the sample indicated that they had received any test for immunodeficiency.[7] One in ten said that he felt that he may have an "immune problem."

---

[7]The most common test among the respondents who specified one was a white-blood-cell count.

TABLE 8.1. Study Results (Frequency Percentages)

Number of Sexual Partners Per Month Before Hearing of AIDS:
   Mean = 6.8   (n = 391)

Number of Sexual Partners per Month at Time of the Study:
   Mean = 3.6   (n = 383)

Bathhouses (n = 374)
   Going More Often   2.1%
   Going as Often as Before   10.7%
   Going Less Often   21.1%
   Stopped Going Completely   19.0%
   Never or Rarely Went   47.1%

Backroom Bars and All-Male Theaters (n = 377)
   Going More Often   0.8%
   Going as Often as Before   11.1%
   Going Less Often   20.4%
   Stopped Going Completely   14.3%
   Never or Rarely Went   53.3%

General Change in Sexual Activity (n = 403)
   Increased   1.0%
   No Change   49.6%
   Decreased   46.5%
   Celibacy   3.0%

Primary Specific Changes in Sexual Activity
   Insertive Oral Sex: Cut Down   67.7%   (n = 65)
   Receptive Oral Sex: Cut Down   56.8%   (n = 44)
   Insertive Anal Sex: Cut Down   58.0%   (n = 69)
   Receptive Anal Sex: Cut Down   55.7%   (n = 70)
   Analingus: Stopped   61.8%   (n = 89)
   Masturbation: Increased   48.3%   (n = 58)
   Kissing: Cut Down   69.2%   (n = 39)
   "Fisting": Stopped   66.7%   (n = 18)
   Swallowing Semen: Stopped   58.3%   (n = 12)

Nitrite Drug Usage (n = 388)
   Started Using   1.8%
   Using More Often   1.0%
   Using as Much as Before   8.2%
   Using Less Often   27.1%
   Stopped Using   11.3%
   Never or Rarely Used   50.5%

Saw Physician for Laboratory Test (n = 389)
            Yes   16.5%   No   83.5%

Feel They May Have an "Immune Problem" (n = 374)
            Yes   9.6%   No   90.4%

Although 403 copies of the questionnaire were returned, not all respondents answered every question. Thus, the n varies for each question.

150

Respondents were asked whether or not they were familiar with the symptoms of AIDS. The study was conducted during a transitional period prior to the considerable AIDS publicity in the media during May and June 1983. However, since June 1981, the gay press (e.g., the *New York Native*, the *Advocate*, the *Connection*) has frequently reported at length on the growing AIDS epidemic. The gay press, I would like to note, is probably read predominantly by white, better-educated, upper middle-class, gay men and women over thirty.

Most (61.0%) of the respondents said that they were familiar with the symptoms of AIDS (see Table 8.2). However, AIDS health information, which was probably communicated verbally through informal social networks, has not proceeded uniformly. Respondents in their thirties, which not so incidentally corresponds with the highest risk cohort for contracting AIDS, were most likely to be familiar with the symptoms, whereas those under 25 were least likely to be familiar. Black-American and Hispanic-American men were least familiar, whereas Irish-American and Jewish-American men were most familiar.

Lower income respondents were less familiar with the symptoms than were wealthier respondents. Those individuals who completed and returned the questionnaire earlier during the study (from August 1, 1982 to February 14, 1983) were less familiar with the symptoms than were those who participated in the study later (from February 15, 1983 to April 30, 1983); this fact apparently indicates an increase in awareness and knowledge of AIDS symptoms during this transitional period.

Individuals with some college or less education stated that they were not as familiar with the symptoms of AIDS as were those with a higher educational background. Analogously, a correlation exists between the rate of decrease in the frequency of sexual partners per month after hearing about AIDS and higher educational level. The means range from 8.9 partners per month for high school graduates to 5.8 for individuals with graduate degrees (see Figure 8.1). The less formally educated gay men were more likely to say, in this sample, that they had sex with different men more often (prior to the advent of AIDS) than did the more formally educated gay men.

Respondents who were more sexually active with multiple partners[8] (i.e., those respondents correlating with a lower educational level) decreased their total number of monthly partners by *less* than the respondents who were less sexually active with multiple partners (i.e., those respondents correlating with a higher educational level). The range varied from a mean

---

[8]The term "promiscuous" is a negatively value-laden one: it implies that exclusive monogamy is intrinsically superior. Because this orthodox heterosexual view is sexual-orientation specific, the term will not be used in this chapter.

TABLE 8.2.   Self-Reported Familiarity with AIDS Symptoms among Gay Men in New York City, 1982–83

Familiar with AIDS Symptoms (n = 400)
            Yes   61.0%   No   39.0%

		n	Percentage
Age (p < .05)	Under 25	44	45.5%
	25–29	82	57.3%
	30–39	186	69.9%
	40–49	59	55.9%
	50 or Over	25	52.0%
		n = 396	
Income (p < .0001)	Under $25,000	230	52.6%
	$25,000 or Over	159	74.8%
		n = 389	
Educational Level (p < .0001)	Some College or Less	132	40.9%
	College Graduate or More	267	71.2%
		n = 399	
Ethnic Group (p < .001)	Black-Americans	24	41.7%
	English-Americans	50	62.0%
	Hispanic-Americans	30	23.3%
	Irish-Americans	35	74.3%
	Italian-Americans	36	66.7%
	Jewish-Americans	70	74.3%
	Multiple Ethnicity	74	64.9%
	Other	76	56.6%
		n = 395	
Time Period (p < .0001)	Early	179	45.8%
	Late	221	73.3%
		n = 400	

Although 403 copies of the questionnaire were returned, three respondents did not respond to the "Familiar with AIDS Symptoms" items. The sample size is smaller than 400 for Age, Income, Educational Level, and Ethnic Group, because not all respondents provided this information.

Figure 8.1. Educational Level and the Number of Sexual Partners per Month

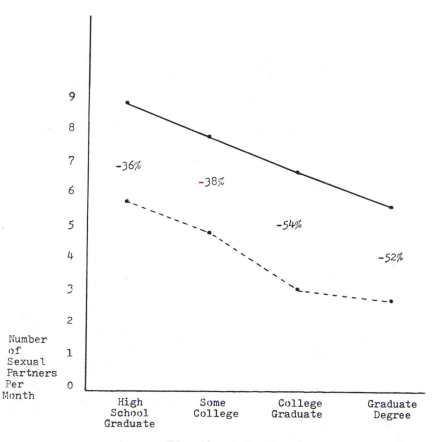

of 5.7 partners per month for high school graduates, a 36% decrease, to a mean of 2.8 for respondents with graduate degrees, a 52% decrease. The respondents with a higher educational background were more knowledgeable about the symptoms of AIDS; this greater awareness may have contributed to their greater likelihood of cutting down further on their number of different same-sex partners.[9]

DISCUSSION

The desired change for the gay community during the course of the AIDS epidemic would be to lower or eliminate the risk for contracting AIDS. Caiazza (1984) estimates that over 60% of the healthy gay men in New York City would test positive for LAV/HTLV-III, and seropositivity for antibody to LAV/HTLV-III was 66% in a San Francisco gay male sample (D'Eramo 1984). Thus, most gay men in these two cities do not need to worry about becoming exposed to LAV/HTLV-III, because they have already been exposed.

The critical question is: What cofactor(s) will trigger the retrovirus to produce AIDS? Because a second sexually transmissible infectious agent may be a cofactor, until research in this area is carried out, gay men are well advised to restrict their sexual contacts and/or follow absolutely strict safe-sex guidelines, even if they test positive for LAV/HTLV-III.

With such a large proportion of gay men having already been exposed to the so-called "AIDS virus," any program for AIDS health promotion should include a plan not only for encouraging changes in sexual behavior, but also for altering potentially immunosuppressive social behavior (i.e., avoiding recreational drugs, excessive alcohol, poor nutrition, lack of exercise, inadequate sleep, debilitating stress). This program for advocating a complete state of wellness and limiting the kind of sexual behavior practiced to mutual masturbation, without exchanging saliva or other bodily fluids, with a finite number of partners should eliminate the possibility of contracting AIDS for those gay men who have not yet been infected with LAV/HTLV-III. It may also significantly reduce the risk of acquiring AIDS to those gay men who would already test positive for antibody to LAV/HTLV-III. Such a comprehensive program, if successfully implemented, would not only reduce future AIDS morbidity and mortality from projected levels (see estimate in the Introduction of this book), but

---

[9]I should like to caution the reader that these conclusions are based upon self-reported data rather than upon direct observation. Independent research should be conducted to ascertain whether or not this negative correlation between educational level and sexual activity exists among gay men in other cities.

would enhance the general state of health for the gay male community as a whole.

Returning to the model of personal health behavior, specific obstacles to an anticipated beneficial behavioral change (i.e., substituting same-sex behaviors that involve the exchange of semen, saliva, and—occassionally—urine and feces for same-sex behaviors that do not) can be analyzed.

Motivation

Recent ethnographic research within the New York City gay community (Feldman 1985c) indicates that health reasons are an important motivating force for ceasing unsafe sexual activity. Gay men, of course, do not want to contract AIDS; yet sex is an extremely pleasurable interpersonal activity. If clinically applied anthropologists and health educators could convince gay men that safe sex is potentially as enjoyable as unsafe sex, then major obstacles to or ambivalence concerning motivation should be eliminated.

Perception of the Threat

Although the awareness of the AIDS threat is generally strong within the gay community, it is likely that gay men who do not regularly read the gay press tend to avoid informational programming in the media, have weak or nonexistent social networks within the gay community, or have social networks primarily with those who also neither read the gay press nor seek out informational programming in the media, will fail to strongly perceive AIDS as a threat. In the research study, as discussed previously, respondents with less formal education admitted to being less familiar with AIDS symptoms and were less likely to modify their level of sexual activity as a response to AIDS. Any program for health promotion would need to locate those gay men who are poorly informed about the risks of AIDS.

For some gay men, not inadequate knowledge about AIDS, but denial of the epidemic has prevented behavioral change. They may see the risk for contracting AIDS as relatively small. They have taken their chances with syphilis, gonorrhea, amebiasis, hepatitis B, and antigay violence. AIDS is seen as simply one more risk for being gay. Others may rationalize that if they have not contracted the disease yet, they may be immune to it. And others hold a fatalistic view that if they should develop AIDS, then it was predestined.

Comparison of the cigarette smoking literature with some of the findings of the AIDS research study on behavior change among the young is an interesting endeavor. The literature on cigarette smoking clearly indicates that teenagers and young adults are unlikely to cease cigarette smoking for health reasons (e.g., Lotecka and MacWhinney 1983; Mittelmark et al. 1982; Newman et al. 1982; Warner and Murt 1983). One should, therefore, expect that younger gay men would be less likely to change their behavior because of fear of dying from AIDS than would older gay men. However, no statistically significant relationship between younger and older respondents can be determined from any of the variables in the study that would indicate behavioral change.

The difference between the results that were found in the AIDS study and those found for cigarette smoking may be a function of the immediacy of the perceived health threat. Emphysema and lung cancer to people under 25 are often seen as something that might eventually affect them, if they should smoke, when they get old. But AIDS is seen as a disease that could affect them at any time, especially if they are relatively young.

Alternative Psychological Mechanisms

Modifying sexual behavior requires not only a change in the patterns of sexual activity, but also a change in the way in which an individual thinks and feels about sex. For many gay men, "cruising" (i.e., establishing eye contact with a stranger in a variety of locations for the possible purpose of initiating a sexual or sexual and romantic liaison) is psychologically gratifying as an adventure sui generis. Today, cruising often creates feelings of ambivalence. If a man should cruise back, does that suggest that he is sexually active with multiple partners, at higher risk for AIDS, less fearful about AIDS, and—subsequently—less likely to be willing to follow safe sex guidelines? If so, why should one bother to cruise at all? Certainly, if a comprehensive program for health promotion is to be implemented successfully, then the psychological assumptions of cruising should include safe sex guideline adherence. Cruising and its aftermath would then become safe.

Reinforcement of the Modified Behavior

Making sex safe is a process, not an event. Sociocultural and interpersonal forces play crucial roles in reinforcing modified sexual behavior. Gay organizations and businesses need to foster the kind of social climate in which unsafe sex is no longer the normative behavior. This is beginning to occur. Some locales at which anonymous sexual activity takes place now post safe sex guidelines. Private clubs that strictly monitor these guidelines among their guests are flourishing. Personal advertisements in the gay press that state an interest in "healthy sex" only or a monogamous relationship are increasing in number. Commercial telephone sex, in which for a fee participants engage in erotic conversation, is a growing phenomenon. The sexual intensity of some cruise bars seems to be lessening.

The gay community does not function within a vacuum. Television, radio, and newspaper reports about AIDS have had a profound effect upon gay men. Misinformation also does occur. When the LAV/HTLV-III virus was reported by the media in the spring of 1984, many gay men confused the discovery of this probable causal agent with a cure for AIDS.[10]

In general, AIDS health promotion and education within the gay community (and among the other high-risk groups) should not be almost entirely the burden of self-help organizations. Comprehensive health promotion programs should be developed to focus upon lowering the risk of contacting AIDS among gay men, especially among those who are least likely to read about AIDS in the gay media and who are at locations in which anonymous sex is readily available.

Unfortunately, the AIDS epidemic continues, with ever-worsening consequences for our entire society. One gay man recently said in an interview of the increasing AIDS morbidity and mortality,

> It's like a tightening circle of fear and death. At first, I knew only people who had acquaintances who had died of AIDS. Now, two of my closest friends have AIDS. What can I tell them? When is it all going to stop? I haven't been feeling too well myself lately.

Sociomedial research urgently needs to be undertaken by medical social scientists and social epidemiologists. Comprehensive health programs must be implemented speedily by clinically applied anthropologists and health educators.

ACKNOWLEDGMENTS

I would like to express my sincere appreciation to Dr. Don des Jarlais, Dr. Sam Friedman, and Dr. Thomas Johnson for their comments on an earlier version of this chapter. I wish to also express my thanks to the following individuals for their assistance in the completion of the study: Dr. Dan Brook, Prof. Anne Buddenhagen, Dr. William Darrow, Dr. James D'Eramo, the late Dr. Scott Francher, Mr. Tony Gambino, Dr. Leon H. Gellman, Dr. Elizabeth Hegeman, Dr. N. Patrick Hennessey, Mr. John Emery Istvan, Dr. Martin Levine, Dr. William Lewis, Dr. G. Alexander Moore, Dr. Serena Nanda, Mr. Michael O'Grady, Dr. Kevin O'Reilly, Dr. Dennis V. Passer, Dr. Marc Rubenstein, Mr. John Stewart (Research Assistant), and the gay male community of New York City.

---

[10]Don Des Jarlais and Samuel Friedman (1985) indicate that this also happened to some IV-drug users.

REFERENCES

Altman, Lawrence K. 1985. Heterosexuals and AIDS: New Data Examined. *New York Times.* January 22: C1, C11.

Beldekas, John C. 1985. Face to Face: the Media and AIDS. *New York Native.* February 15–March 10: 17–19.

Caiazza, Stephen S. 1984. Why You Should Not Be Tested For HTLV-III. *New York Native.* October 8–21.

Carnes, Patrick J. 1983. *Sexual Addiction.* Minneapolis, Minn.: CompCare Publications.

Centers for Disease Control (CDC). 1985. *AIDS Weekly Surveillance Report,* April 15.

Christman, Noel and T. Maretzki. 1982. *Clinically Applied Anthropology: Anthropologists in Health Science Settings.* Hingham, Mass.: D. Reidel.

Curran, James W., D. N. Lawrence, H. Jaffe, J. E. Kaplan, I. D. Zyla, M. Chamberland, R. Weinstein, K. J. Lui, L. B. Schonberger, T. J. Spira, W. J. Alexander, G. Swinger, A. Amman, S. Solomon, D. Auerbach, D. Mildvan, R. Stoneburner, J. M. Jason, H. W. Haverkos, and B. L. Evatt.1984. Acquired Immunodeficiency Syndrome (AIDS) Associated with Tranfusions. *New England Journal of Medicine* 310 (2):69–75, January 12.

D'Eramo, James E. 1984. AIDS Crisis Worse Than Ever: CDC's Curran Explains New Urgency at Doctor's Meeting. *New York Native.* October 8–21.

Des Jarlais, Don and Samuel Friedman. 1985. Personal Communication.

Feldman, Douglas A. 1984. AIDS and Behavioral Change. Unpublished paper read at the Northeastern Anthropological Association, Hartford, Conn., March.

———. 1985a. AIDS, Social Science, and the CDC. *New York Native.* April 4–15: 22–23.

———. 1985b. "AIDS and Social Change" (Human Organization 44(4):343–348.).

———. 1985c. Unpublished data.

Ginsburg, H. M. 1984. Intravenous Drug Users and the Acquired Immune Deficiency Syndrome. *Public Health Reports.* 99(2):206–212.

Goleman, Daniel. 1984. Some Sexual Behavior Viewed As an Addiction. *New York Times.* October 16: C1, C9.

Gregersen, Edgar. 1983. *Sexual Practices.* New York: Franklin Watts.

Horn, Daniel and S. Waingrow. 1966. Some Dimensions of a Model for Smoking Behavior Change. *American Journal of Public Health* 56(12):21–26, December supplement.

Krim, Mathilde. 1984. Personal communication.

Lancet. 1984. Blood Transfusion, Haemophilia, and AIDS. *Lancet* II(8417/8): 1433–1435, December 22, 29.

Lawrence, Dale. 1984. Personal communication.

Lotecka, L. and MacWhinney, M. 1983. Enhancing Decision Behavior in High School "Smokers." *International Journal of the Addictions* 18(4):479–490.

Marmor, M., A. E. Friedman-Kien, L. Lauberstein et al. 1982. Risk Factors for Kaposi's Sarcoma in Homosexual Men. *Lancet* I(8281):1083–1086.

Mayer, Kenneth and J. E. D'Eramo. 1983. Poppers: a Storm Warning. *Christopher Street* 7(6):46–49, July.

Meredith, Nikki. 1984. The Gay Dilemma. *Psychology Today* January: 56–62.

Mittlemark, M. B., D. M. Murray, R. B. Luepker, and T. F. Pechacek. 1982. Cigarette Smoking Among Adolescents: Is the Rate Declining? *Prev. Med.* 11(6):708–712.

Morbidity and Mortality Weekly Report (MMWR). 1981a. Pneumocystis Pneumonia—Los Angeles. *MMWR* 30:250–252. June 5.

_____ . 1981b. Kaposi's sarcoma and Pneumocystis Pneumonia among Homosexual Men—New York City and California. *MMWR* 30:305–308. July 3.

_____ . 1985. Update: Acquired Immunodeficiency Syndrome—Europe. *MMWR* 34:21–31. January 18.

Newman, I. M., G. L. Martin, and R. P. Irwin. 1982. Attitudinal and Normative Factors Associated with Adolescent Cigarette Smoking in Australia and the United States of America: a Methodology to Assist Health Education Planning. *Community Health Stud.* 6(1):47–56.

Oncology Times. 1985. Prostitutes Are Next Big Group to Get AIDS. *Oncology Times* February: 17, 27.

Ortleb, Charles L. 1985. Politics of AIDS. *New York Native.* February 25–March 10: 15.

Phillips, Michael R. 1985. Can "Clinically Applied Anthropology" Survive in Medical Care Settings? *Medical Anthropology Quarterly* 16(2):31–36.

Quadland, Michael. 1984. Psychosexual Issues. Unpublished paper read at "AIDS and Sexuality: a Dialogue," New York University Conference, June 11.

Shore, Abraham, W. R. Mindell, and J. M. Teitel. 1985. Limiting Factor VIII Cryoprecipitate Selection to Female Donors. *Lancet* I(8420):98–99.

Warner, Kenneth E. and H. A. Murt. 1983. Premature Deaths Avoided by the Anti-Smoking Campaign. *American Journal of Public Health* 73(6):672–677.

PART IV
AIDS AND
THE MEDIA

Chapter Nine

Illness and Deviance: The Response of the Press to AIDS

Edward Albert

AIDS has been the subject of considerable press coverage since 1981. AIDS-related material has filled the columns not only of news outlets directly connected to affected groups (e.g., the homosexual [gay] press), but also of general interest publications. The purpose here is to address the AIDS phenomenon as it has been brought to the public in the general circulation, popular magazine press.

The role of the press in reporting AIDS cannot be seen as simply one of an observer on the scene, chronicler of some finite set of events available for anyone to see. Rather, media coverage reveals a selectivity of perspective. For the population at large, those with no direct contact with AIDS or its sufferers, the awareness of this disease is media related. It is to these portrayals that one must turn to help explicate popular reactions to AIDS. Such portrayals can be understood in terms of the larger context of a general confounding in contemporary society of issues of medicine and morality that often results in the stigmatization of the victims of illness.

METHODOLOGY

This paper is based on a content analysis of AIDS-related articles that appeared in national circulation magazines between May 1982 and December 1983. The sample, drawn from the Magazine Index of the Information Access Corporation, begins with the first article listed under a separate AIDS heading and is limited to those articles that appeared in general-interest publications. Articles from science-oriented magazines (e.g.,

Scientific American and *Science*) were excluded. With the exception of several articles appearing in magazines not readily available at the time, the sample represents the population of published magazine treatments on the topic. In total, 57 articles, from forty-four separate issues of 25 different publications were surveyed.[1]

THE THEORETICAL ISSUE OF MORAL VERSUS MEDICAL DECISION MAKING

The production of distinctions that have as their effect the defining of approved and disapproved behavior and the creation of valued and devalued persons is an inescapable feature of social life. The consequences flowing from such distinctions vary from mild expressions of disapproval or praise to the conferring of high or outcast statuses. The magnitude of social response is relative to the nature and centrality of the distinction to the values upon which the society is based. In all cases, however, social distinctions and their implied social judgments have relevance for individual and group identity and ranking within a community. Our interest here is in documenting the production of negative judgments and in observing the creation of disapproved or outcast persons. This process has been variously called stigmatization (Goffman 1963), status degradation, identity transformation (Sarbin 1967), or labeling (Schur 1971).

In all societies, the production of such distinctions is institutionalized; various occupational groups—referred to by Becker (1963) as moral entrepreneurs—function as arbiters of the normal. Parsons (1958) and others have noted the ways by which magicians or priests fulfilled such functions in more undifferentiated societies. As societies become more specialized and differentiated, however, so also do their normative systems. Concomitantly, an increased specialization occurs in the work roles that arbitrate adherence to such complex systems.

The process of social decision making is being transformed from one emphasizing a "moral" accent to one increasingly taking on a technical/secular character. This process, often involving the transformation of perception from a moral cast to one of illness, has been called "medicalization". Conrad and Schneider (1980:28) define medicalization as the finding of "medical solutions for deviant behaviors or conditions." This process can be seen to contain several elements: the focus of decisions is no longer the designation of "crime" or "sin" but "illness"; those designated become "patients" rather than "criminals;" doctors replace police or priests

---

[1]Several articles referred to in this paper were taken from outside of the population defined by the Magazine Index. These occurrences are noted.

as agents of social control; and societal reaction alters from one of punishment to treatment.

Various categories of behaviors can be transformed to a greater or lesser degree by the tendency toward medicalization. When successful, such transformations involve not only the changes noted above, but alterations in perception: new categorical distinctions operating at the institutional level similar to the new identity transformations occurring on the individual level. Behaviors undergoing such alteration from the "deviant" to the "ill" include many now subsumed under the rubric "mental illness" (Foucault 1965; Sarbin 1968a, 1968b; Szasz 1970; Wooten 1959), alcoholism (Robinson 1972), drug abuse, hyperactivity in children (Conrad 1975), child abuse and, perhaps, obesity.

On the individual level the transference of decision making from moral to medical auspices has been consequential. Although, as Wooten (1959) suggested, the medical model of mental illness deemphasized "punitive" reactions and went hand in hand with increasing humanitarianism, this trend did not necessarily result in destigmatization. Illnesses for which victims can be held "accountable" are still condemned. As the brutish world of bacteria decreasingly accounted for illness, lifestyle (over which individual control is viewed as possible) became increasingly important and with it so did the possibility of individual responsibility (Sontag 1977).

In this vein, many taken-for-granted behaviors (e.g., smoking, a sedentary lifestyle, driving without seat belts) have been identified as contributing to morbidity. However, as McKinley (1981) points out, only select behaviors resulting in illness are defined in such a way as to place those who engage in them in the position of risking definition as "deviant" rather than "ill" to the degree that they are made motivationally responsible for their situation. Specifically, behaviors that call into question community moral standards may result in an individual's loss of the illness role and its replacement with the label "deviant."

It has been in this area of the violation of moral standards that, as a society, we have been most reluctant to give up the deviance model for the medical one. Each time a child molester is treated, a John Hinkley hospitalized, or help sought for the drunk driver who commits vehicular homicide, a call goes up for a return to traditional values and a turning away from "permissiveness." Such reactions derive more from the ambiguity attached to such issues in the first place than from a backlash, and such ambiguity is in part explained through the use of Parsons' (1958) typology of deviance. He proposed two variables: the first characterizes the deviant act, which can, in this schema, either be situational or normative; the second characterizes the generality of the deviance, representing a disturbance in the total person or merely in a particular role commitment. Along the first continuum we move from disturbances of role performance (illness) to ones of "character" (sin). On the second, we move from total disturbances over which the individual lacks control to disturbances of particular "volitional" commitments to social expectations. Ambiguity emerges, in the minds of observers, from situations not clearly on one or another pole of these variables. Such ambiguity is consequential, because it carries with it decisiveness in the use of stigmatizing labels with their implications for social identity and life changes.

Sarbin (1967) raises a related issue when he notes that sanctions and their intensity vary on a continuum related to performance of ascribed and achieved role expectations. Toward the achieved role expectation pole, negative labeling is relatively minimal whereas meritorious performance is highly rewarded. On the other hand, no positive reward is attached to ascribed role performance, whereas negative performance is accompanied by strong sanction. With the AIDS/homosexuality connection we have the potential for a confused response to the degree that it becomes unclear whether the sick individual exhibits, on the one hand, deviance (Parsons) and, on the other, role failure (Sarbin). AIDS (as illness) represents situational deviance related to achieved statuses, whereas homosexuality remains normative deviance related to an ascribed status (see Table 9.1). Taken together, we have a bipolarity that may be at the base of situations of evaluative ambiguity wherein those labeled are faced with a structurally induced inability to discern consistent social identities for themselves or, likewise, others for them.

HOMOSEXUALITY: THE MORAL/MEDICAL AMBIGUITY

Observations conducted on AIDS as it is represented in popular magazines document the ambiguity with which we, as a society, view both homosexuality and illness. The nature of the reaction to AIDS as expressed in the media is such that it has, from the very outset, been impossible to separate the disease from the varied contexts of its occurrence. Tied to stigmatized groups (including gays), AIDS has emerged in public perceptions as problematic in that it occurs simultaneously on the two very clearly defined poles of the situational/normative continuum used by Parsons.

TABLE 9.1. Illness versus Moral Evaluations

AIDS (Illness)	Homosexuality (Deviance)
Situational	Normative
Impaired role performance	Sin
Lack of personal control	Individual choice
Achieved role failure	Ascribed role failure

Furthermore, to the extent that AIDS affects homosexuals, it has raised the issue, at least in the eyes of an already unaccepting public, of sexual orientation as a violation of one's ascribed status rather than as a matter of individual choice. The resulting confusion, as we shall discuss, might be understood as the conflict between the increasing hegemony of medical decision making and the remnants of the more undifferentiated patterns of moral decision making that continue in public opinion.

Conrad and Schneider (1980) observe that processes criminalizing and medicalizing homosexuality were both increasing during the late nineteenth century. Medicalizing occurred, perhaps, in reaction to added punitive action taken against homosexuals. Such ambivalence remains. Public opinion surveys continue to document the confusion of illness versus deviance perspectives as they relate to gays. Recent surveys of attitudes toward homosexual behavior indicate predominantly negative reaction. Glen and Weaver (1979) find no significant increase in positive attitudes toward homosexuality during the early to mid-1970s. And, in a recent Gallup Report (1982) survey, a national sample rejected the assertion of homosexuality as an "alternative lifestyle" by 51 to 34%. This is highlighted in the internal battle that occurred in the American Psychiatric Association (APA) over the retention or elimination of homosexuality from its list of disorders in the 1968 revision of its second *Diagnostic and Statistical Manual (DSM II)*. The forces favoring demedicalization of homosexuality won in 1974, and homosexuality was removed from the list of illnesses. From the official perspective of the APA, homosexuality became, by fiat, an alternative lifestyle. However, as noted in Conrad and Schneider (1980), a 1977 study of 2,500 psychiatrists (Leif 1977) showed that 69% still saw homosexuality as "pathological."

The occurrence of AIDS exacerbates this confusion by overlaying an undisputed illness on a highly disputed behavior that carries with it three judgmental options: alternative lifestyle, illness, or deviance. AIDS presents a situation in which the physiological problem occasions the reaffirmation of one of these already-held conceptions concerning the nature of homosexuality.

The media portrayals of AIDS reflect the confusion and ambiguity experienced by the society at large. Further, the media's confusion over the illness/deviance character of people with AIDS has resulted in the raising of issues of personal responsibility in ways that give rise to questions of the degree to which situational difference becomes normative violation.

It is important to note that the perspective here is one that sees the media as reflecting public attitudes rather than producing them. Although this paper will not deal at length with one aspect of the media's AIDS coverage—self-criticism for the re-creation of the stigma attached to homosexuality—it should be remember that the highly publicized liberalization of attitudes toward alternate sexual lifestyles that AIDS coverage is said to have jeopardized did not, in fact, ever really occur.

AIDS: THE MAGAZINE VERSION

The actual portrayal of AIDS in the media, and the groups affected by it, can be seen to focus on several interconnected issues. The themes that emerged cannot be understood as merely the result of reporting on a reality that would be, should anyone wish to look, readily available. Rather, those themes must be seen in the context of the exigencies of news production. We follow a social-constructionist perspective on AIDS coverage, viewing it as, at least in part, related to the problems of getting out the news. Thus, for example, AIDS coverage is slotted into the already extant news categories of "science news" or "lifestyle" sections. Further, such categories appear with a predictable regularity and must be filled whether news is breaking or not.[2] Magazine portrayals have tended to reflect themes of an unfolding, rather than a breaking, character. These are themes congruent with the timing of magazine production. In this way, long-term issues of lifestyle, historic perspective, biography, and rising fear are developed, as opposed to the hit-and-run newspaper presentations of new findings or new categories of sufferers.

On one level, magazine coverage of AIDS appears to be a function of its own attention. The distribution of articles over the period studied is not an accurate reflection of actual increases or decreases in morbidity rates but, rather, appears to follow a "bandwagon effect" generated by media attention in the first place (see Table 9.2). Having uncovered an issue, the media seem to have then set out to fill the need that, at least in part, was its own creation. The upshot, AIDS coverage, is interesting and can be studied not only for the actual issues raised, but for the manner of development.

Particularly curious behavior is usually confined, in the popular press, to the tabloids (e.g., the *Star*, *National Enquirer*, and the *Globe*). Unlike the tabloids, however, other media outlets seem to require a pretext for giving us the nonnormative side of life. For example, a crime like the Manson murders was an opportunity to read about the inside scoop on sex, drugs, and communal living in the 1960s. Jim Jones provided a similar journalistic opportunity to read about a cult that rehearsed mass suicides. AIDS has provided an occasion for such an excursion into a world perceived of as "strange" and "disordered" by the nontabloid media. No in-depth

---

[2]For discussions of the methods utilized by the media to produce the news see Gans, 1979; Molotch and Lester, 1974; Tuchman, 1972, 1973, 1978.

TABLE 9.2. Quarterly Incidence of Surveyed AIDS-Related
Articles and New AIDS Cases

	Quarter	Number of Articles	New AIDS Cases
1982	Jan.–March	0	100
	April–June	1	155
	July–Sept.	2	225
	Oct.–Dec.	3	275
1983	Jan.–March	6	400
	April–June	12	525
	July–Sept.	27	515
	Oct.–Dec.	6	200

exploration of the lifestyles of the members of the American Legion follow-ed reports of Legionnaire's disease or of the U.S. woman in the case of toxic-shock syndrome.

Primarily concerned with homosexual patients, portrayals of AIDS have focused on sociocultural qualities. In this way, gay life has been made to appear to occur in geographic isolation—in bathhouses, on Christopher Street in New York, in San Francisco, at a gay parade, in a prison. This sense of distance is produced in three distinct ways. In the first, gay behavior is made topical in a way that highlights its normative difference. For example:

> Investigators also believe that AIDS is principally a phenomenon of the raunchy subculture in large cities, where bars and bathhouses are literal hotbeds of sexual promiscuity (*Rolling Stone* 1983:19).

> The gays who get AIDS, it turned out, have often had many more sexual contacts (a lifetime average of 1,100 partners) than the controls (500 partners) (*Newsweek* 1983a:76).

> . . . Many of the early cases involved men with vigorous sex lives. Dr. Linda Laubenstein . . . describes the hospital's first patients as having had anywhere from 25 to 500 different sex partners in the course of a year . . . They were also frequent drug users, partial to inhalents like cocaine and marijuana and especially nitrites—amyl, butyl, and isobutyl, popularly known as "poppers," which they used about as frequently as they had sex (*New York* 1982).

> But clearly, urban gay life-style has put many homosexual males at risk. An infectious agent loose in the hothouse environment of a gay bath, where some men have as many as 10 anonymous sexual contacts in one night . . . (*Newsweek* 1983b:80).

> Some gays are attempting to remain celibate . . . Others have set up sexual collectives, usually groups of three to twelve men, who promise to have sex only within the group (*Time* 1983:57).

> Over the next year, Callen pursued his sex life in toilet stalls, referred to as tea rooms . . . . Soon Callen was going to the baths every other day. There were no windows, there were no clocks, there was no music. There was only continuous, impersonal sex, often with men whose early lives had been as tortured as his own (*New York* 1983:26).

> The vast majority of sufferers—75 percent—are homosexual males, many of them highly promiscuous, some with sexual histories involving many hundreds, even thousands of partners (*Macleans* 1983a:34).

Such descriptions began with the early coverage of the illness in the spring of 1982 and seemed to reach a peak in the spring and summer of 1983. Emphasizing non-normative sexual practices, a picture of gay life emerged that was basically and irretrievably at odds with accepted U.S. lifestyles.

Secondly, people with AIDS, especially gay men, are portrayed as experiencing a reign of terror justified by an exponentially increasing death toll. We see a group in panic, its institutions crumbling and its lifestyle becoming increasingly tenuous.

> Believed to be sexually transmitted, AIDS has thrown homosexual communities into near panic (*People* 1983:42).

> According to Gottlieb, homosexuals in the Los Angeles area are aware of AIDS and are frightened by it (*Saturday Evening Post* 1982:26).

> . . . an epidemic of fear is sweeping San Francisco where at least one new case is reported each day (*Macleans* 1983b:6).

> Panic has set in on Greenwich Village streets and in "the Castro," San Francisco's gay quarter (*Time* 1982:55).

> AIDS has struct terror throughout the homosexual population . . . . A frightened gay community is cooperating with public-health officials to track down AIDS victims (*Newsweek* 1982b:63–64).

> . . . the specter of AIDS haunts every member of the homosexual community, especially in the cities where it is most prevalent (*New York Times Magazine* 1983:36).

> As nightmare rumors become fact, fear of contagion prompts a slowing down of life in the fast lane (*Newsweek* 1983b:80).

Perhaps it is here, better than anywhere else, that the distancing of AIDS sufferers can be seen: the "problem group" is detached from the rest of society. In the failure of AIDS to touch the general population and in the face of such massive damage it becomes like a faraway earthquake, a war involving others, or merely a great famine that sweeps across some other place. In short, it becomes something that, due to its lack of effect on "me" and due to its reported serious nature, must be happening somewhere else. In these two ways, media coverage highlights an already present social distance between affected and nonaffected groups.

Such difference is exacerbated in a third way: through the use of characterizations that help produce the very difference that they are seen to report. Regularly, those who ran a higher risk of AIDS were characterized either as belonging to "at-risk groups" or as "victims." Such unfortunates, from the outset, were specifiable in terms of some particular quality: they were homosexual men, Haitians, IV-drug users, or hemophiliacs. In early reports, gay men were variously described as "tinderboxes waiting for an opportunistic disease" (*New York* 1982), "walking time bombs" (*Newsweek* 1982a:101:), or "living playgrounds for infectious agents" (*Time* 1982:55). On the other hand, those not immediately in danger have been left, in large part, to undifferentiated categories reported as the "population at large" or the "general population."

These differences highlight social categories already firmly established. The strength and persistence of such categories lies in the perception that the associated characteristics and/or behaviors place in question the normative grounds for social order. AIDS, because it occurs to "those people," extends a gap and transforms it from a previously moral one to a physiological one.

In this light, one gay man is quoted as expressing the not completely irrational fear that, due to AIDS, homosexuals would all be "shipped off to some leper colony" (*Newsweek* 1983c:20). This is ironic, because gays (and drug users) have always risked isolation. The "Typhoid Marys" associated with these behaviors were teachers, musicians, exposed politicians, and peers.[3] AIDS, as portrayed in the media, has merely helped to transform a

---

[3]It is interesting in this regard to note that the recent Gallup Report (1982) on attitudes toward homosexuality shows a general increase in approval for "equal job opportunities" for homosexuals since the last poll in 1977: 59% in favor in 1982 as compared to 52% in 1977. A full 50% responded favorably to "homosexuals as doctors," 52% to homosexuals in the "armed forces," 70% to homosexuals as "salespersons," but, significantly, only 38% responded favorably to homosexuals in the "clergy" and only 32% to homosexuals as "elementary school teachers." Further, in this context, we might speculate as to the significance of another Gallup finding: that when asked whether homosexuality was innate or acquired, 17% said "born with", 52% said "environment", whereas 13% noted "both." Given the weight placed on environment, the perception of possible "contagion" becomes all the more real not just from AIDS but from homosexuality itself.

metaphorically contagious disease into one concretely so. AIDS concretizes the moral category of homosexuality, and the media—by merging homosexuality with organic disease—very nearly creates a biological distinction between "straights" (heterosexuals) and gays where only normative differences existed before.

The association between lifestyles and disease is such as to become seemingly inseparable.[4] This synthesis has not been made, however, in reports of IV-drug users whose lifestyle also seems linearly related to AIDS. In fact, the lifestyle of the addict seems, for the most part, entirely ignored in the press. We have been willing to see drug addiction as, on the face of it, empirically damaging; however, gay lifestyles have only been assumed to be so. The fact that gays are now dying from disease (as addicts die from overdoses) reaffirms a social difference that lacked twentieth-century evidence (i.e., scientific evidence that one can see, touch, and measure). In the way that psychiatry searches for chemical causes for mental disorders that, if found, prove the appropriateness of the label "illness," so too the finding of physiological consequences of homosexuality—albeit not causal—gives renewed credibility to social distinctions perceived to have been significantly weakened in recent years. Further, although drug addiction has, since the early part of the century, carried a stigma, that stigma is one reflecting violations of conventional norms governing commitment to work and role obligations. The stigma attached to homosexuality reflects a perceived violation of the societal ground for being "human" in the first place: that all individual are clearly of one *or* another gender, and that gender is ascribed at birth (see Raymond 1979 for a discussion of this issue).

AIDS AS THE UNKNOWN: THE "CREEPING" THREAT TO US ALL

That the AIDS epidemic poses no immediate threat to the "population at large" is vouchsafed by a social barrier that, it is taken for granted, preserves a critical separation between populations. However, the barrier *is* permeable. Underlying and fueling the stigmatization of AIDS risk groups is the fear that the social distinctions that protect will be breached, leaving the general population open to the onslaught of fatal infections that AIDS permits. The press in some ways has circled the wagons. Outside are predominantly gay males subject no longer only to opportunistic infections due to disease, but now to an opportunistic morality by which they are held at arm's length. Inside is a population reading about a progressive contagion

---

[4]Not only has AIDS become inextricably tied to homosexuality, but over the course of AIDS coverage, homosexuality's tie to other diseases has been emphasized. References to gays and hepatitis B, syphilis, gonorrhea, herpes, amebiasis, and others are not uncommon.

that moves from homosexual males, IV-drug users, Haitians, and hemophiliacs to health-care workers, children, surgery patients, and heterosexual women (families), with the explicit implication that it will not stop there.

From the perspective of the gay community itself (and from the several media critics who have addressed this issue) the fear of contagion must be seen as a double-edged sword.[5] On the one hand, it is the fear that contributes to the reestablishment of gays as outcasts. On the other, public fear (at least as a reported expression of gay opinion) is perceived to have generated public reaction in the form of research towards a cure.

It cannot be proven that research began in earnest only after the perception that AIDS was—as one article reported—"creeping out of well-defined epidemiological confines." (*Newsweek* 1983a:74). However, a reader of AIDS portrayals would easily become aware of the place and importance of just that fear. Although concern for one's physical well being is at issue, an overriding concern for the spread of disorder and chaos of which gays and other deviant actors can be seen as carriers prevails. Fear of contagion is often, but never clearly, expressed. Beginning as "GRID" (Gay-Related Immune Deficiency), it was given the informal appellation in the press of the "Gay Plague." Although these terms were generally dropped, references to a plague have continued. It is "plague" that conjures up the image of the Dark Ages, of death and disorder against which the modern world lives in fear and must constantly struggle. The hopelessness and disorder of such a world is made available in the descriptions of the people with AIDS.

THE THEME OF BLAME IN MEDIA PORTRAYALS

Perhaps of singular importance to the issue of stigma, and the maintenance of social distance, is the invidious implication of blame and personal responsibility for one's disability that is contained in media coverage. At its most virulent are the reports of accusations that gays are justifiable objects of the righteous punishment of God for sinful behavior. Such condemnations also occasionally arise from within the gay community as expressions of self-doubt and recrimination concerning gay lifestyles. A gay physician is

---

[5]A small number of articles that take a critical stance have appeared in this group. In general, they argue that AIDS has been underfunded due to the stigmatized group that it affects. Further, there is some discussion of the setback that AIDS has given to the movement to normalize alternative sexual lifestyles. (see *Life* 1983; *Ms* 1983; *The Nation* 1983; *National Review* 1983; *The New Leader* 1983; *The New Republic* 1983; *New York* 1983; *Playboy* 1983a, 1983b; *The Progressive* 1983; *Vanity Fair* 1983).

quoted as saying that "perhaps we've needed a situation like this to demonstrate what we've known all along: depravity kills!" (*New York* 1982).

However, of more concern is the implicit use of blame as an indicator of social worth. Three categories of people with AIDS can be documented: the innocent, the suspect, and the guilty. The first category includes hemophiliacs, children, and, more recently, surgery patients. They are portrayed as innocent bystanders who cannot be held responsible for their illness; occupying a valued social position, they thus deserve all the benefits that accrue to any unremarkable sick person. Comparative references such as the following are typical:

> Some of the most tragic victims . . . are . . . children . . . . If the cases among children are the most wrenching . . . (*Newsweek* 1983a:77).

> Among the most tragic victims of the disease are the young children. (*Vanity Fair* 1983:31).

The innocence of children is exemplified in pictures of doctors and others, with benevolent and concerned faces, holding babies suspected of having the disease. Remarkable in such photos is the apparent absence of protective gear (see *Time* 1983:57; *Newsweek* 1982b:63). In other AIDS-contact situations wherein the social characteristics of the victims are suspect, such gear is clearly a mandatory barrier. Thus, a *Newsweek* photograph shows three correctional personnel wearing their protective gear for use in dealing with prisoners suspected of AIDS. Two wear heavy gloves, what appear to be jump suits, and riot helmets with plastic face plates. The third, in a surgical gown, cap, mask, and gloves also carries a walkie-talkie. Other photos show police with special "resuscitation gear" to minimize the chance of contact with a possible at-risk patient (*U.S. News and World Report* 1983:13).

Haitian-Americans who contract AIDS are often seen as closet homosexuals or drug abusers who conceal this fact from medical investigators due to the strong stigma attached to such activities by Haitian society. They are in the second category of the "suspect." Other reports suggest that Haitians prostitute themselves to vacationing gays and so either contract or spread the disease. It might be observed that their reported concealment, even if not actually the case, helps to create a picture of a group who violates a basic assumption associated with illness: the responsibility to cooperate with professional help in one's cure (Parsons 1951).

In this case, they also present pre-existing characteristics of an already non-normative character. They are black, tend to be poor, are recent immigrants, and the association of Haiti with cult-religious practices fuels the current tendency to see deviance in groups at-risk for AIDS.

The third category is, of course, the most invidious: the category of the guilty. Moral spokesmen such as Jerry Falwell aside, the press on its own terms effectively attaches blame to both the homosexual and the drug user. Blame implicitly results in cases in which the attribution of "illness" can be used in situations for which personal responsibility can be seen as both contributory and significant. Such responsibility is an integral part of any illness label that is accompanied by what is seen as a non-normative environment within which the illness was seen to have its origin. Such environments or activities related to at-risk AIDS populations are described in the media as "anonymous sexual contacts," ". . . the paraphernalia of kinky sex . . . ," recreational injection of drugs, "especially with dirty needles . . . ," (*Newsweek* 1983a); the use of "inhalants," a "fast-track" lifestyle (*New York* 1982) or frequently visiting "places of random sex" (*New York* 1983).

It is noteworthy that blame and sanction seem contingent on the finding of a causal link with non-normative behavior. For example, the use of tampons in the case of toxic shock did not result in women being blamed for bringing that upon themselves. Nor was any serious attribution of responsibility assigned for the consequences in women who continued to use tampons.

In a more general context, McKinley (1981:10) notes that:

> Indeed one can argue that certain at-risk behaviors have become so inextricably intertwined with our dominant cultural system (perhaps even symbolic of it), that the routine public display of such behaviors almost signifies membership in this society.

Further, he contends, that to then ask persons to give up such behaviors is tantamount to asking them to abandon their culture. With this in mind then, blame is not so much related to at-risk behaviors per se, but to non-normative at-risk behaviors; sex is sanctionable, smoking is not. In fact, industrialized societies have raised the hazardous lifestyle to heroic proportions insofar as such lifestyles affirm valued cultural traits like machismo or the achieving of worldly goals in the face of adversity. Statistically, however, more deaths result from participation in hazardous sports than from participation in hazardous sex.

CONCLUSION

Although media coverage of AIDS does not appear, for the most part, to have been intentionally stigmatizing, it can, in fact, be seen to have approached the story in ways that have appeared to reaffirm the outcast status of at-risk groups, especially homosexual men. This consequence, however regrettable, is not altogether surprising. The issues surrounding homosexuality, its unclear relationship to illness and medical decision making, and the consequent questions of personal responsibility for deviance all can be seen as problematic in contemporary U.S. society. Media coverage reflects the ambiguity and ambivalence already associated with these issues.

In a larger context, the role of the media in the perception of illness has yet to be addressed in any systematic manner. Its obvious impact in the present context merely serves to point out the necessity for such research if any complete understanding of the experience of illness is to be produced.

REFERENCES

Becker, Howard S. 1963. *Outsiders: Studies in the Sociology of Deviance.* New York. Free Press of Glencoe.

Conrad, Peter. 1975. The Discovery of Hyperkinesis: Notes on the Medicalization of Deviant Behavior. *Social Problems* 23 (October): 12–21.

Conrad, Peter and Joseph W. Schneider. 1980. *Deviance and Medicalization: From Badness to Sickness.* St. Louis: C.V. Mosby.

Foucault, Michel. 1965. *Madness and Civilization: A History of Insanity in the Age of Reason.* New York: Random House.

Gallup Report. 1982. American Pro Equal Rights for Gays . . . but Hedge in Some Areas. *Gallup Report Number* 205 (October): 3–19.

Gans, Herbert. 1979. *Deciding What's News.* New York: Pantheon Books.

Glen, Norval and Charles Weaver. 1979. Attitudes toward Premarital, Extramarital, and Homosexual Relations in the U.S. in the 1970's. *Journal of Sex Research* 15 (May):108–118.

Goffman, Erving. 1963. *Stigma: Notes on the Management of a Spoiled Identity.* Englewood Cliffs, N.J.: Prentice-Hall.

Leif, M. I. 1977. Sexual Survey: #4 Current Thinking on Homosexuality. *Medical Aspects of Human Sexuality* 11:110–111.

Life. 1983. The View from Here. *Life* 6(July):6–7.

Macleans. 1983a. The Growing Canadian AIDS Alarm. *Macleans* 96(July 11):34–35.

Macleans. 1983b. A Crisis of Mounting AIDS Hysteria. *Macleans* 96(August 1): 6–8.

McKinley, John B. 1981. A Case for Refocusing Upstream: The Political Economy of Illness. In *The Sociology of Health and Illness,* pp. 613–633. Peter Conrad and Rochelle Kern, eds., New York: St. Martin's Press.

Molotch, Harvey and Marilyn Lester. 1974. News as Purposive Behavior: On the Strategic Use of Routine Events, Accidents, and Scandals. *American Sociological Review* 39:101–112.

Ms. 1983. The Politics of AIDS. *Ms.* (May):103.

The Nation. 1983. AIDS Neglect. *The Nation.* (May 21):627.

National Review. 1983. AIDS and Public Policy. *National Review* 35(July 8):796.

The New Leader. 1983. AIDS and the Moral Majority. *The New Leader* 66(July 11):12.

The New Republic. 1983. The Politics of a Plague. *New Republic* (August 1):18–21.

Newsweek. 1982a. Homosexual Plague Strikes New Victims. *Newsweek* 100 (August 23):10.

_____ . 1982b. AIDS: A Lethal Mystery Story. *Newsweek* 100(December 27): 63–64.

_____ . 1983a. The AIDS Epidemic: the Search for a Cure.*Newsweek* 101(April 18):74–79.

_____ . 1983b. The Change in Gay Life-Style. *Newsweek* 101(April 18):80.

_____ . 1983c. The Panic Over AIDS. *Newsweek* 101(July 4):20–21.

New York. 1982. The Gay Plague. *New York* 15(May 31):52–61.

_____ . 1983. AIDS Anxiety. *New York* 16(June 20):24–29.

New York Times Magazine. 1983. A New Disease's Deadly Odyssey. *New York Times Magazine* (February 6):28–44.

Parsons, Talcott. 1951. *The Social System*. Glencoe, Ill.: Free Press.

_____ . 1958. Definitions of Health and Illness in the Light of American Values and Social Structure. In *Patients, Physicians and Illness*, E. Gartly Jaco, ed. New York: The Free Press.

People. 1983. AIDS, A Mysterious Disease, Plagues Homosexual Men from New York to California. *People* 19(February 14):42–44.

Playboy. 1983a. AIDS: Journalism in a Plague Year. *Playboy* 30(October): 35–36.

_____ . 1983b. The Desexing of America *Playboy* 30(December):109.

Progressive. 1983. Everybody Out of the Pool. *Progessive* 47(September):11–12.

Raymond, Janice G. 1979. *The Transsexual Empire: The Making of the She-Male*. Boston: Beacon Press.

Robinson, D. 1972. The Alcohologist's Addiction—Some Implications of Having Lost Control over the Disease Concept of Alcoholism. *Quarterly Journal of Studies in Alcoholism* 33:1028–1042.

Rolling Stone. 1983. Is There Death after Sex? *Rolling Stone* (February 3):17ff.

Sarbin, T. R. 1967. The Dangerous Individual: An Outcome of Social Identity Transformation. *British Journal of Criminology* 7:285–295.

_____ . 1968a. Ontology Recapitulates Philogy: The Mythic Nature of Anxiety. *American Psychologist* 23:411–418.

_____ . 1968b. The Transformation of Social Identity: A New Metaphor for the Helping Professions. In *Comprehensive Mental Health*, Leigh M. Roberts, Norman S. Greenfield, and Milton H. Miller, eds., pp. 97–115. Madison: University of Wisconsin Press.

Saturday Evening Post. 1982. Being Gay Is a Health Hazard. *Saturday Evening Post* 254(October):26.

Schur, Edwin M. 1971. *Labeling Deviant Behavior*. New York: Harper & Row.

Sontag, Susan. 1977. *Illness as Metaphor*. New York: Farrar, Straus & Giroux.

Szasz, Thomas. 1970. *The Manufacture of Madness*. New York: Harper & Row.

Time. 1982. The Deadly Spread of AIDS. *Time* 120(September 6):55.

_____ . 1983. The Real Epidemic: Fear and Despair. *Time* 121(July):56–58.

Tuchman, Gaye. 1972. Objectivity as Strategic Ritual: An Examination of Newsmen's Notions of Objectivity. *American Journal of Sociology* 77(January):660–679.

———. 1973. Making News by Doing Work: Routinizing the Unexpected. *American Journal of Sociology* 79(July):110–131.

———. 1978. *Making News: A Study in the Construction of Reality.* New York: The Free Press.

U.S. News and World Report. 1983. Fear of AIDS Infects the Nation. *U.S. News and World Report* 94(June 27):13.

Vanity Fair. 1983. A Moral Epidemic. *Vanity Fair* 46(September):130–132.

Wooton, Barbara. 1959. *Social Science and Social Pathology.* London: George Allen Unwin.

Chapter Ten

The Portrayal of AIDS in the Media: An Analysis of Articles in the *New York Times*

Andrea J. Baker

AIDS can certainly be called a "social problem" or public issue, as opposed to a "private trouble" affecting isolated individuals (Mills 1959:8). Presumably, the exposure of the phenomenon in the mass media contributed to an awareness of AIDS among 91% of all people in the United States polled by *Newsweek* in July 1983 (Morganthau 1983:33). However, after initially reporting the discovery of the serious, often lethal, disease in 1981, the press printed very few stories about AIDS, neglecting the topic for almost two years. This study is an effort to determine the reasons why the lag between the original identification of AIDS and the eventual rise in coverage occurred.

The role of the media in affecting public recognition and response to a social problem remains unclear to sociologists. Research has shown that people gain much of their information and ideas about particular social issues from newspapers, magazines, and television (Mauss 1975; Schoenfeld et al. 1979). Influenced by media content, they form impressions about characteristics of types of individuals and groups (Tuchman et al. 1978). Writers of texts on social problems and social movements have recently claimed that without access to the resources of the mass media, change agents forfeit the power to convince others to attend to their grievances (Schur 1980).

In *The Politics of Deviance*, Edwin Schur (1980) describes the ways by which the "kinds of people" participating in struggles for public recognition can sway outcomes toward success or failure. "Stigma contests" (1980:140–146) pit groups striving for legitimate minority status against opponents who try to define the initiating groups as undesirable people voicing specious complaints. Most people with AIDS may have been characterized as "deviants," perceived as people unworthy of sympathy or concerted action. Those who are stigmatized need public support to ensure the recognition of their problem. Was the early dearth of media attention, research, and political action at all tied to the stigmatized status of most of the people with AIDS? What role did pressure from homosexual (gay) people and other concerned citizens in the United States play in the checkered chronology of the search for biomedical and epidemiological knowledge and for resources to aid the ailing patients?

SOCIAL PROBLEMS THEORY AND AIDS

Sociologists have debated the merits of the "objective" (Manis 1974) versus the "subjective" approaches (Spector and Kitsuse 1977) to social problems. They ask whether responses by policy makers to particular historical circumstances are based mainly upon empirical data or upon intuitive perceptions about which issues should currently receive attention. Promoting a subtype of the subjective school, Spector and Kitsuse (1977) call "claims-making" activities the crucial component in setting national agendas. They assert that social problems can be defined as the "grievances and assertions" of groups and individuals trying to ameliorate conditions that they consider harmful, along with those who oppose such changes. Therefore, rather than studying the available data about the actual condition, scholars should monitor activities of the involved parties. In this view, there are no absolute "facts," because each side will bend data to impress policy makers (Wisemen 1979). Others insist that sociologists can utilize facts—verifiable information gathered by specialists—to formulate specific, objective criteria for recognizing and analyzing social problems (Manis 1974).

Choice of the media as the primary data source would seem to follow the subjectivist perspective. After all, editors of newspapers slant reality through selection of reported topics, amount of coverage, and appeals to interests of advertisers and readers (Hastings 1979). On the other hand, most writers agree that without some set of observable conditions and "social causations" (Schneider et al. 1981), a social problem would not exist. In the case of AIDS, the media reported the "facts" about the first cases, relating the causes to intimate interactions among gay men with multiple partners. The news coverage alerted social scientists to the possibility of a new social problem in the objective sense, but the absence of articles followed by a rather abrupt increase require an explanation from the subjectivist perspective.

Because of the two competing orientations among sociologists, universal definitions of a social problem exist. Schneider et al. (1981) describe five characteristics necessary for classifying social problems. A condition must: 1) have a social rather than a natural causation; 2) be evaluated as a social problem; 3) arouse a substantial degree of "general citizen concern"; 4) affect nonsuffering others who are "not directly involved as victims"; and 5) elicit social actions, which are organized attempts to contain or alleviate the effects of the problem.[1] In particular, the fourth step may be especially important in gauging reactions to AIDS, in that some of the victims' lifestyles are far removed from the U.S. mainstream. For the effective mobilization of action against AIDS, the final step, media personnel had to publicize the responses of nondeviant groups as well as those of victims (Schur 1980). The complaints and countercomplaints of people with AIDS, their advocates, doctors, researchers, and public officials reported by the media may have affected the timing of actions taken to remedy the problem.

METHODOLOGY: USING MEDIA

Using the news as data, documents the twists and turns presented to the U.S. public from the first reports of medical research through the panic over the uncertainties about the causes of AIDS and modes of transmission to the funding decisions of governmental officials. Sidestepping the question of the media's ability to influence changing public opinion as opposed to its tendency to reflect prevailing social norms, evidence will be presented here that the types of actual events reported seemed to foster further lines of development in reality and in print. Also, the frequency of treatment of an issue by the media can be assumed to trace the kind of general interest generated by a problem over time (Schwartz and Leitko 1977).

To check media coverage, *The New York Times Index* with corresponding articles was the primary source employed.[2] Although the concentration on one newspaper poses obvious limitations, it can be partly justified by the fact that 42% of the total number of people with AIDS reported to the Centers for Disease Control in Atlanta from 1981 through March 1984 resided in New York State (*Morbidity and Mortality Weekly Report* 1984). Furthermore, people throughout the United States read the paper, and respect its accuracy and inclusiveness of national news.

---

[1] These five elements of a social problem are "stages" only in the sense that some believe that each precedes the other in time. This author would agree that the first element of social causation tends to come first, and that the element of social action tends to occur last, but believes that the other stages have less-clear temporal order. Actually, all five stages probably overlap considerably.

[2] The choice of *The New York Times* was based partly upon accessibility. Also, *The Reader's Guide to Periodical Literature* was consulted for similar reasons (see Troyer and Markle 1984). In addition to the *Times*, all sixteen articles in *Newsweek* and *Time* magazines were examined for the study period.

Each article in the index was counted and coded into a set of categories designed to summarize its main themes (see Krippendorff 1980). Coded categories included groups thought to be affected by the syndrome, reports of research findings, effects on gay and heterosexual lifestyles, protests and critiques of governmental and medical policies, political acts by state, local and federal officials, and public reactions, including responses of service professionals who had contact with the victims. Some articles were coded in more than one category, depending mainly upon their length and the variety of topics addressed. Both quantitative information derived from the coding and qualitative descriptions from the articles are employed for the analysis below. In addition, over fifty articles examined in depth provided a validity measure of the fit between the abstract in the index and the entire piece as it actually appeared in the final edition of the newspaper. The fit was surprisingly good: the index very rarely omitted relevant data.

The establishment of new major headings in indexes to periodicals can herald a change in thinking about a particular issue (Spector and Kitsuse 1977). Until 1983, articles on AIDS could be located under the listing of "Homosexuality" in the *Times Index* and also in the *The Reader's Guide to Periodical Literature*. In 1981, the subtopics of "virus" and "cancer" below "Homosexuality" pointed to articles about the then-unnamed disease. "AIDS" was added as a separate topic at the beginning of 1983, signaling medical legitimization of its importance.

To briefly describe the placement and frequency of AIDS reportage in the *Times*, only two articles throughout the three-and-one-quarter-year period studied (1981 through March 1984) ever made the front page: the announcement by the Secretary of the Department of Health and Human Services that AIDS must be the number one priority among public health problems (Pear 1983a) and the isolation by scientists of a believable cause of the syndrome (Altman 1984b). The frequency of articles climbed from a low of three per year in both 1981 and 1982 up to a high of 52 for the three-month period between April and June of 1983; the total number of articles for 1983 was 128.

Two working hypotheses emerged from the concurrent development of a social-problems perspective and initial observations of the data to test the reasons for fluctuation in the frequency of media accounts:

1. The media virtually ignored the problem of AIDS until research showed that populations outside the gay world could contract the disease; and
2. Pressure from gays and others hastened governmental and scientific interest, thus increasing media reporting of "claims-making" efforts.

POPULATIONS SUSCEPTIBLE TO AIDS

A dimension of the definition of a social problem is that a significant number of people must be affected and concerned about an issue. However large or small a proportion "significant" may be, some people outside of the affected population must also feel the brunt of the negative condition. In the case of AIDS, people of these two types, those directly affected and those concerned, have been hard to characterize. As soon as the disease seemed to be the product of both social and biological causes, epidemiological work was needed to track different routes of transmission.

So, although the "social causation" element of a problem surfaced early, the number and types of people directly or indirectly involved remained puzzling. The "evaluation" component weaved its way through the entire course of media reporting and, indeed, could best be identified after some social action had transpired. Nevertheless, the thesis here states that the general public, the media, and federal, state, and local governments failed to evaluate AIDS as a social problem until nonstigmatized populations began to worry about their own susceptibility. Neither the media nor the public appeared to focus on AIDS with much frequency until the identification and publication of "at-risk" groups in addition to gays and IV-drug users. Such a finding would lend credence to those (e.g., Cahill 1983a; Cahill 1983b; Van Gelder 1983) who have claimed that AIDS elicited slower responses than other epidemics due to the original and continual predominance among those afflicted of people who still constitute nearly three-quarters of reported cases (*Morbidity and Mortality Weekly Review* 1984: 338). Figure 10.1 depicts the number of stories in the *Times* between 1981 and the first quarter of 1984.[3] It also lists the time periods associated with each revelation of a new group "at risk."[4] The first two articles stressed the almost exclusively male, homosexual connection to AIDS. The third article ever published had a minor reference to a small number of male and female heterosexual patients (*New York Times* 1981). The next article added the speculation that most of the unspecified proportion of hetrosexuals were drug abusers and that bisexual as well as homosexual men had been afflicted (Altman 1982b). Still, nearly all cases discovered initially were among sexually active gay men. In fact, for a short time the disease was called "GRID" (gay-related immune deficiency) (Altman 1982a) until gay medical personnel quickly lobbied for a more accurate label[5] (Van Gelder 1983).

[3]The articles in the *San Francisco Chronicle* followed a very similiar pattern for 1983 (Nathan and Thomas 1984). June 1983 showed the greatest number of articles in both papers, as did the entire second quarter of that year.

[4]Each article in 1981 and 1982 was checked for populations listed. Throughout 1983 and the beginning of 1984, only the *Index* items were coded unless information there led to questions that could be answered by referring to the articles.

[5]In her *Ms.* editorial, Van Gelder (1983: 103) blames "Homophopia" for the GRID label. Though unstated in the article, she may have reasoned that the GRID acronym inappropriately failed to include the already diagnosed heterosexual patients and that it neglected to exclude female gays and celibate or monogamous gay men.

Figure 10.1. Types of AIDS Cases First Appearing and the Number of *New York Times* Articles Over Time.

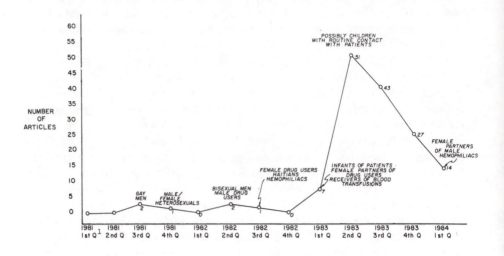

[1]Q = a quarter of a calendar year (three months). Thus, 1st Q = January through March, 2nd Q = April through June, 3rd Q = July through September, and 4th Q = October through December.

[2]Label locations indicate time at which the type *first* appeared. They are not repeated if included with other categories at a later time. For example, gay men were mentioned as patients in every time period, but are only depicted here once.

Additional information about which kinds of heterosexuals had AIDS was revealed in the third quarter of 1982, with the statement that of the more than 500 cases, 60 nongay people used intravenous needles (Herman 1982). The same article warned that thirty heterosexual Haitians of both sexes and "some" hemophiliacs requiring blood products were included in the total caseload. No articles came out during the latter part of 1982, implying that the new populations at risk created no immediate alarm.

The first quarter of 1983 witnessed the additions of three categories of people at risk, a fact that may have contributed to the peak reportage period immediately thereafter: 1) an extension of the female heterosexual drug user group to female partners of male drug using patients; 2) perhaps receivers of blood transfusions aside from hemophiliacs; and 3) infants and children born to females with AIDS (Henig 1983). These three types were "innocent victims" of circumstances in that no direct actions on their parts caused the disease. The blood link prompted the Red Cross during this period to warn people in risk categories to refrain from donating blood. And, of course, the horror of babies born with a lethal disease conjured up images of tragedy in the classical sense. The implication that heterosexual females who are having sexual contact with AIDS patients could contract AIDS frightened those who feared that patients might conceal information from their potential or actual partners.

Early 1983 also marked the publication of the fact that people could be "carriers" of AIDS without showing signs of the syndrome. Another complication was the preliminary finding at that time that overt symptoms might not emerge for an average of between six months and two years after contraction. Thus, ignorance of one's own symptoms could supplement deceit to trigger an even larger epidemic among sexual partners of carriers or unaware victims. The second quarter of 1983 brought evidence of no new types of people at risk, indeed no added groups arose anytime after February 1983 in the *Times*, but two articles in May 1983 publicized studies of women and children (See Figure 10.1). Females who had monogamous, regular sexual activity with male drug users, but who did not use intravenous drugs themselves, were also shown to be at risk (Altman 1983). The *Times* documented that the heterosexual connection sufficed for AIDS by itself, with not active participation in the "deviant" lifestyles of the homosexual and drug addict.[6] Perhaps the most shocking article presented new data on children who seemed to "catch" the disease from "routine" contact with their parents with AIDS (*New York Times* 1983c).

Before the announcement by the Department of Health and Human Services (DHHS) naming AIDS as the number one public health priority, writers in the *Times* accused federal officials of bias. A New York City doctor said that the kinds of people at high risk for AIDS, particularly their "sexual orientation," caused federal politicians to evade the problem by turning it back to local domains (Cahill 1983b).[7] He insisted that until the blood transfusions category implied the spread of the disease to the general population, "organized medicine" was silent about AIDS. An unsigned editorial commended the Centers for Disease Control for its prompt

---

[6]An expansion of the danger for female, heterosexual partners of men in the groups at-risk was presented by the *Times* in January 1984. The wife of an elderly hemophiliac who experienced symptoms one year before her husband died received the AIDS diagnosis one month after he had died. Although the discovery that females with AIDS could be both heterosexual and nonusers of intravenous drugs had appeared in the news almost a year before (see Figure 10.1), the lifestyle of this monogamous, aged woman seemed even further removed from the deviant subcultures of drugs and male homosexuality.

[7]The author of the *Times* articles also noted that no major research programs were developed when the only known groups at-risk were gay men, drug addicts, and "poor Haitian refugees" (Cahill 1983b). Others have pointed to the factor of "racism" toward Haitians as a contributor to the evasion by officials (see Van Gelder 1983:193).

responses, but chided the NIH for its slow funding of a theoretically interesting topic (*New York Times* 1983b). It characterized the Reagan administration as apathetic, explaining that whether or not AIDS infected one population or many, the syndrome demanded more "compassion," action, and resources for the treatment of its affected individuals. Another critical column (Schanberg 1983) referred to the study of heterosexual transmission and claimed that such revelations, along with the association of blood donations with AIDS, "galvanized" national attention: when AIDS was linked only to homosexuals and drug addicts, attitudes tended toward the "less urgent," wrote the *Times* writer.

On May 25, 1983, Dr. Edward Brandt, Assistant Secretary of Health and Human Services, formally recognized AIDS as the number one priority of the U.S. Public Health Service (Pear 1983a). He recalled the recent research on children and women with AIDS described above, although he cautioned against public anxiety that AIDS may spread through casual contact beyond the four primary groups discovered earlier. In this article, political forces jockeyed to define the situation; the director of the National Gay Task Force (NGTF) accused Dr. Brandt's agency of nonresponse, whereas another spokesperson defended the Public Health Service's dedication all along. The time in which intimate heterosexual contact and casual interaction of children with their parents received prominence in the news as possible causes of AIDS coincided with the peak of political action and reaction during the second quarter of 1983.

POLITICAL ACTIONS AND REACTIONS

The height of both number of total articles printed and the actions and reactions of politicians and other concerned parties reported by the *Times* occurred in June 1983, at the end of the second quarter. Then the coverage declined a bit through the third quarter (see Figure 10.1) and decreased even more for the fourth quarter of 1983. If the evaluation of a social problem has a hallmark, then the proliferation of social action can serve as an indicator of the problem's acceptance. However, various interests continued to compete for media and public favor.

Figure 10.2 represents several types of political response to AIDS. "Positive Political Actions" include any declaration by a federal, state, or local politician or public health official of a push for funding for research or services for people with AIDS. "Gay Actions" refer to benefits, marches, demonstrations, organizations, or conferences clearly sponsored by members of the gay community to address the issue of AIDS. Some gays working for people with AIDS could be accused of mere self-interest, even though they

Figure 10.2. Types of Political Actions in *New York Times* Articles Over Time.

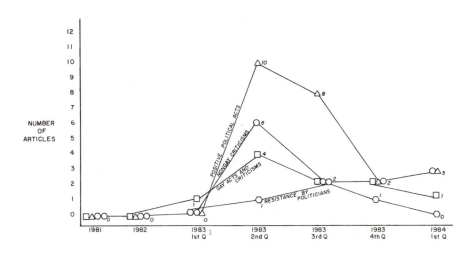

[1]Q = a quarter of a calender year (three months). Thus, 1st Q = January through March, 2nd Q = April through June, 3rd Q = July through September, and 4th Q = October through December.

[2]Key to Types of Political Actions:

□—□ = Gay or primarily gay actions, benefits, demonstrations, and gay criticisms of political action.

△—△ = Positive political actions at the federal, state, and local levels.

◯—◯ = Resistance to action or denial of wrongs by politicians at the federal, state, and local levels.

◯—◯ = Criticisms by nongays of political actions or pressures for political actions.

themselves had little chance of acquiring AIDS.[8] In line with the definition employed here, a ligitimate group of nonsufferers must come forward to fulfill the criteria of a true social problem. As reflected in the *Times'* pages, editorial writers not identified as gay, religious leaders, medical personnel, and politicians pressured the government leaders to pour money into solving the problem. In turn, government representatives occasionally refused to respond or defended their actions or inactions against criticism from gays and nongays.

---

[8]Many gay men prefer a less sexually active lifestyle and confine themselves primarily to either one or no partners. Lesbians had not contracted AIDS, nor had any bisexual women contracted AIDS, according to news reports.

Almost three weeks after Dr. Brandt had committed the DHHS to a major investigative effort, mayors from 11 cities convened in Denver in June 1983 to ask for federal appropriations for AIDS (*New York Times* 1983a); the mayoral task force asked to shift responsibility for research, education, treatment of patients, and training of health professionals to the federal government. Meanwhile, the annual Gay Pride marches in New York City and San Francisco were dedicated to all people with AIDS (McGill 1983). New York's Governor Cuomo reversed himself and decided to recommend larger state revenues for services and community education. Margaret Heckler, Secretary of the DHHS, defended the Reagan's administration's treatment of the AIDS issue at the National Mayor's Conference (Schmidt 1983), and an aide to President Reagan met with gays from the NGTF for the first time at the White House (*New York Times* 1983f). Large grants were made by NIH to research scientists and President Reagan found his response criticized by House representative Ted Weiss (Dem., N.Y.) for lack of an overall, positive policy (Pear 1983b). Mayor Edward I. Koch of New York City promised to prosecute landlords, employers, and others who illegally discriminated against people with AIDS or their associates.

Throughout the summer, Federal officials acted to staff a hotline for free answers to questions about AIDS. But the president of the NGTF and city health personnel kept asking for a greater and more coordinated response. The stigma against gay people became the subject of a long article on the "second epidemic" of fear and panic about AIDS. Feelings toward people with AIDS had led to the denouncing of gay sinners from church pulpits and a refusal to charter a gay and lesbian student organization in Texas (Beauchamp 1983). At the local level, Mayor Koch gave blood to help the public gain confidence and to help assuage temporary blood shortages to cities of the eastern seaboard. By the middle of the third quarter, a *Times* columnist had attacked the media for reporting sensationalized developments on AIDS without restraint or checks on the facts (Winsten 1983).

Less than three weeks later, four scientific journal editors proclaimed a new policy to expedite reviews of research on AIDS, as they had done earlier for studies of Legionnaire's disease and the toxic shock syndrome (*New York Times* 1983a). In return, a professor of medicine criticized the tendency in the United States to overemphasize novel illnesses while virtually ignoring the more commonly known ailments, such as hyperthermia, an often deadly disease affecting many older citizens who lack air conditioners in their homes. (Weissman 1983).

The types of claims and counterclaims of participants interviewed in the *Times* during 1983 can be summarized by a news report in *Science*, a journal read mainly by "hard" researchers of biology, chemistry, physics, and geology. The author (Kolata 1983) credited a surge of research funds from the federal government to the loci of pressure: 1) public fears of a widespread epidemic, which generated "political pressures,"[9] and 2) fears of politicians that homosexual voting blocks could affect the outcome of their reelection attempts. The article said that the NIH had dutifully rushed research awards of a larger-than-usual amount to fund a problem intriguing specialists in cancer, immunology, and infectious disease. Even with the establishing of a newsletter to inform 200 scientists working on AIDS, however, "not everyone" was happy with the NIH funding for AIDS, admitted *Science*. Private foundations have solicited donations from the gay community, and researchers borrowed money or used their own. In its article, *Science* maintained a defensive position against charges of neglecting AIDS as a research problem but quoted distraught researchers who have found the federal funding process too late and lengthy.

By the end of 1983 and the beginning of 1984, federal activity reported by the *Times* reached zero, with only a few positive actions at the state and local levels (see Figure 10.2). Perhaps because of the federal inaction perceived by gays and nongays, a professional lobbyist was hired by homosexual groups to obtain funds from the United States legislature (Shribman 1983). An urgent need for programs to provide psychological and medical training for health professionals treating people with AIDS as well as for special facilities for patients, was mentioned by a cofounder of the Gay Men's Health Crisis (GMHC), a sponsor of the lobbyist. Gerald O'Conner, the lobbyist, stressed the importance of a cooperative, generalized strategy toward the problem. He stated that although he did not deny "the fact that this is a gay issue," a "public health" stance on AIDS would achieve more results than a "gay rights" argument (Shribman 1983). In his view, requests for help from Congress couched in a civil rights framework usually provoked confrontations rather than mutual attempts at workable solutions. The last quarter of 1983 contained a lengthy *Times* article that applauded the endeavors of New York City's GMHC, a volunteer group caring for gay and nongay people with AIDS since 1981 (Dowd 1983). A follow-up item in the medical column praised the volunteers for the scope of their involvement. GMHC workers walked clients' dogs, ran their errands, and even replaced nurses and orderlies afraid to enter rooms of people with AIDS (*New York Times* 1983d).

Politicians continued to vacillate in the *Times* from January through March 1984 as New York Governor Cuomo first refused, then recommended, more money for research and services for people with AIDS. The new year brought another editorial chiding the Reagan administration for its laggardly

---

[9]During the second quarter of 1983, eight articles in the *Times* described panics over the AIDS epidemic. Two of those concentrated on panic within the gay community.

reaction to AIDS (*New York Times* 1984). The anonymous writer traced the initial apathy to feelings of "relief" among people outside the groups of known risk. The writer lamented the two-year lag in the NIH's funding of large and numerous research grants. Using the AIDS case as an example, the writer worried that the United States government could be unpleasantly surprised by the next "epidemic" unless top officials developed a "prompter more coordinated" policy (*New York Times* 1984).

To summarize Figure 10.2, the actions in the *Times* rose from nonexistent throughout 1981 and 1982 to a demonstration led by gays in the first quarter of 1983. As the number of reported gay and, especially, nongay protests rose abruptly in the middle of 1983, the number of local, state, and federal politicians who responded positively to the AIDS crisis grew simultaneously. By the third quarter of 1983, the number of political actions proposed to solve the AIDS problem had declined somewhat in the news, and officials began to resist action advised by others. During the last quarter of 1983 and the first months of 1984, politicians reacted to AIDS much less often than they had during the previous six months, according to the *Times*. As political activity slowed, gay and nongay reactions stabilized; the *Times* printed only two instances of positive actions by public officials, along with two protests by gays and two by nongays. At the end of the study period, publicized gay response to AIDS had dropped back to the 1982 level. Nongays were portrayed in the *Times* as slightly more critical of the reduced rate of official reaction.

CONCLUSIONS: STIGMA, AIDS AND THE MEDIA

Looking at a major newspaper is one way to chart the progress of an issue from a minor concern to a major social problem. Stigma attached to the carriers of the "homosexual plague" (Keerdoja 1982) may have influenced the erratic course of media and political response to the problem. The assignment of the DHHS's priority attention to AIDS could have helped to legitimize the issue to make it an appropriate topic for media coverage and public discussion. Quite probably, the unreplicated report of routine parent/child contact causing AIDS fueled the media's upsurge in coverage (Kaiser 1983). By reviewing the material in *Times* articles and editorials, one can conclude that some published individuals related the sluggish pattern of official action toward AIDS directly to the negatively perceived attributes and habits of a majority of persons with AIDS. The distressed reactions of Haitians in this country and in Haiti after they became an at-risk group certainly indicated their desire to disassociate from an unsavory problem: a disreputable disease.[10] That the subject of AIDS could publicly have been associated with the image of "promiscuous" homosexuals led a gay activist to wonder whether a wave of media interest would "set gays up as a scapegoat" (Kaiser 1983) or whether such focus would spur a search for a cure. From a sample of private U.S. citizens, a *Newsweek* poll documents a decline in the percentage of people who "accept" the gay lifestyle after hearing about AIDS (Morganthau 1983).

Those people who do not suffer from AIDS would seem to play a role in drawing out public support for constituents' troubles. Minority groups engaged in political contests have benefited from assistance of outsiders: for example, in the late 1960s radical black organizations and riots stimulated financial contributions to moderate black organizations from white donors (Haines 1984). Perhaps especially in situations in which they are defined as socially and psychologically deviant, powerless people need help from members of the dominant group who sympathize with their plight (Schur 1980). Theorists and researchers of emerging public issues should more regularly consider the dynamic interrelationships between patients and non-sufferers, particularly when addressing the media's part in the construction of social problems. In the AIDS controversy, the ease of identifying the sexual preferences of spokespeople is hampered by the tendency of many gay people to "pass" as heterosexual (straight) (Byron 1972) in order to become "invisible" (Altman 1982:36). Also, heterosexuals may avoid open alliances with gays for fear of "contamination" by association with negatively labeled people (Adam 1978).

How a stigmatized group frames its complaints in the media can also influence the results of any public contest for power or resources (Cohn and Gallagher 1984; Schur 1980). Although gay leaders quoted in the *Times* claimed that stereotypes about homosexuals temporarily retarded officials' responses, their lobbyist strategized that emphasizing "public health" instead of gay rights would eliminate automatic objections from potential adversaries in Congress who opposed civil rights issues of any kind. In a recent ethnographic case study of the new media's treatment of a gay student organization's activities, Cohn and Gallagher assert that most disputes reported in local newspapers are centered around conflict over definitions of "issue areas" (1984:83). They also imply that news readers agree with positions or ignore claims based upon the ways by which members of each side define the issues in the newspaper.

Theorists and researchers studying the dynamic interplay among social problems, social movements, media, and policy could profit from more

---

[10]In the last two quarters of 1983, the enigma of the Haitians dominated seven articles. Some Haitians in treatment first admitted in October 1983 to homosexual behavior, thereby squelching the spate of articles about the humiliating stigma experienced by supposedly heterosexual Haitians in Haiti and in the U.S.

detailed reports of specific, evolving controversies that successfully combine explicit theoretical concepts with precise histories of events. A weakness of this study is the absence of interview and observational data from people and groups included (and excluded) in the news reports. How did they decide to press their claims and counterclaims and, more crucially, how did they achieve access and entrée to the pages of the *New York Times*?

Unresolved problems for researchers include: 1) how to arrive at a definition of "a social problem" that accounts for the role of the media; 2) how to analyze conflicting political acts, reported in the mass media or not, to calculate the likely effects upon both the public and powerful administrators; and 3) when to weigh types of media portrayals heavily enough to equate their contents with the state of public opinion. The data from the *Times* coverage of AIDS discussed above provide some support for the idea that journalists can influence the course of the emergence and outcome of a social problem.

ACKNOWLEDGMENTS

My thanks to William Milbaugh and the staff of the Ohio University—Lancaster library for research assistance and to Roseanne Kalister and the editors for help in revising earlier drafts.

REFERENCES

Adam, Barry D. 1978. *The Survival of Domination.* New York: Elsevier North Holland.

Altman, Dennis. 1982. *The Homosexualization of America.* Boston: Beacon.

Altman, Lawrence K. 1982a. Clue Found on Homosexuals' Precancer Syndrome. *New York Times.* June 18, II 8:4.

———. 1982b. New Homosexual Disorder Worries Health Officials. *New York Times.* May 11, III, 1:2.

———. 1983 Research Traces AIDS in 6 of 7 Female Partners. *New York Times.* May 19, II 4:5.

———. 1984a. New Cases Widen Views About AIDS. *New York Times.* January 5, I, 20:1.

———. 1984b. New-Found Virus Shown to Cause AIDS-Like Illness in Lab Monkeys. *New York Times.* March 1, 1:5.

Beauchamp, William. 1983. A Second AIDS Epidemic. *New York Times.* August 7, IV, 21:1.

Cahill, Kevin M., ed. 1983a. *The AIDS Epidemic.* New York: St. Martin's.

———. 1983b. Conquering AIDS. *New York Times.* April 22, I, 31:3.

Cohn, Steven F. and James E. Gallagher. 1984. Gay Movements and Legal Change: Some Aspects of the Dynamics of a Social Problem. *Social Problems.* 32:72–86.

Dowd, Maureen. 1983. For Victims of AIDS, Support in a Lonely Siege. *New York Times.* December 5, II, 1:1

Haines, Herbert F. 1984. Black Radicalization and the Funding of Civil Rights: 1957–1970. *Social Problems* 32:31–43.

Hastings, William M. 1979. *How to Think About Social Problems.* New York: Oxford.

Henig, Robin M. 1983. AIDS: A New Disease's Deadly Odyssey. *The New York Times Magazine.* February 6, VI: 28–31.

Herman Robin. 1982. A Disease's Spread Provokes Anxiety. *New York Times.* August 8, 31:1

Kaiser, Charles. 1983. The Media and the Scare. *Newsweek.* July 4:21.

Keerdoja, Eileen. 1982. "Homosexual Plague" Strikes New Victims. *Newsweek.* August 23:10.

Kolata, Gina. 1983. Congress, NIH Open Coffers for AIDS. *Science* 221:436–438.

Krippendorff, Klaus. 1980. *Content Analysis: An Introduction to Its Methodology.* Beverly Hills: Sage.

Manis, Jerome. 1974. Assessing the Seriousness of Social Problems. *Social Problems* 22:1–15.

Mauss, Arnold L. 1975. *Social Problems as Social Movements.* Philadelphia: J.B. Lippencott.

McGill, Douglas C. 1983. Homosexuals' Parade Dedicated to AIDS Victims. *New York Times.* June 27, II, 3:3.

Mills, C. Wright. 1959. *The Sociological Imagination.* New York: Oxford University Press.

Morbidity and Mortality Weekly Report (MMWR). 1984. Update: Acquired Immunodeficiency Syndrome (AIDS)—United States. *MMWR* 33:337–339.

Morganthau, Tom. 1983. Gay America in Transition. *Newsweek.* August 8:30–36.

Nathan, Laura E. and Ted E. Thomas. 1984. Cross-Cultural Media Responses: The Case of AIDS. Unpublished paper presented at the annual meetings of the Western Social Science Association.

New York Times. 1981. Homosexuals Found Particularly Liable to Common Viruses. *New York Times* December 10, IV, 24:1.

_____ . 1983a. AIDS Articles to Be Speeded. *New York Times* August 8, II, 7:1.

_____ . 1983b. The Scourge of a New Disease. Editorial. *New York Times* May 15, IV, 20:1.

_____ . 1983c. Family Contact Studied in Transmitting AIDS. *New York Times* May 6, I, 21:4.

_____ . 1983d. Medicine, False and True: Aids for AIDS. *New York Times* December 11, IV, 20:20.

_____ . 1983e. Mayor's Group Urges Research for AIDS Cure. *New York Times* June 13, I, 12:6.

_____ . 1983f. Seeking Answers for AIDS. *New York Times* June 22, I, 22:1.

_____ . 1984. The Slow Response to AIDS. Editorial. *New York Times* January 9, I, 16:1.

Pear, Robert. 1983a. Health Chief Calls AIDS Battles 'No. 1 Priority'. *New York Times* May 25, I, 1:3ff.

————. 1983b. House Panel in Dispute Over AIDS Research Data. *New York Times* June 5, I, 26:1.

Schanberg, Sydney H. 1983. A Baffling Epidemic. *New York Times.* May 24, I, 25:1.

Schmidt, William E. 1983. Mrs. Heckler Lists Added AIDS Funds. *New York Times.* June 15, I, 18:1.

Schneider, Louis, Cookie White Stephan, Louis A. Zurcher, and Sheldon R. Ekland-Olson. 1981. *Human Responses to Social Problems.* Homewood, Ill: Dorsey.

Schoenfeld, A. Clay, Robert F. Meir, and Robert J. Griffin. 1979. Constructing a Social Problem: The Press and the Environment. *Social Problems* 27:38–61.

Schribman, David. 1983. Seeking Research Funds for AIDS. *New York Times.* December 27, II, 6:4.

Schur, Edwin. 1980. *The Politics of Deviance: Stigma Contests and the Use of Power.* Englewood Cliffs, N.J.: Prentice-Hall.

Schwartz, J.P. and Thomas Leitko. 1977. The Rise of Social Problems: Newspapers as "Thermometers." In *This Land of Promises*, Armaund L. Mauss and Julie Camile Wolfe, eds., pp. 427–436. Philadelphia: Lippincott.

Spector, Malcolm and John I. Kitsuse. 1977. *Constructing Social Problems.* Menlo Park, Cal.: Cummings.

Troyer, J. Ronald and Gerlad E. Markle. 1984. Coffee Drinking: An Emerging Social Problem? *Social Problems* 31:403–416.

Tuchman, Gaye, Arlene K. Daniels, and James Benet, eds. 1978. *Hearth and Home: Images of Women in the Mass Media.* New York: Oxford University Press.

Van Gelder, Lindsey. 1983. AIDS. *Ms.* May:103.

Weissman, Gerald. 1983. AIDS and Heat. *New York Times* September 28, I, 27:1.

Winsten, Jay. 1983. Fighting Panic on AIDS. *New York Times* July 26, I, 21:1.

Wiseman, Jacqueline P. 1979. Toward a Theory of Policy Intervention in Social Problems. *Social Problems* 27:3–18.

Wright, Burton and John P. Weiss. 1980. *Social Problems.* Boston: Little, Brown.

PART V
HEALTH BELIEFS
AND BEHAVIOR

Chapter Eleven

AIDS: A Psychosocial Perspective

Virginia Casper

This paper approaches AIDS from emic and etic viewpoints (i.e., from the points of view of both gay[1] men and Haitians who are most likely to experience it directly, and from the point of view of other segments of society). It will try to explain the role of the gay subculture in particular, in the very definition, construction, and treatment of the illness, and the ways in which the illness has impact on its communities. AIDS, a syndrome that is transmitted through bodily secretions and blood products and the cure for which is possibly years away, appears to be construed differently by various sectors of society. It has, nonetheless, elicited strong emotional responses in almost everyone. It is important, therefore, that the roots of these responses be explored, understood and explained.

CONCEPTS OF DISEASE

Every culture has an ideological system that explains illness, and within the

---

[1]The term "gay," as well as homosexual, will be used throughout this paper, although gay had not yet been fully accepted in scholarly circles. There are a number of arguments that may be given for its use. 1) It is generally preferred by the gay community; 2) it has a wider application than does "homosexual," because "gay" refers to a total lifestyle, rather than sexuality, which seems to be particularly relevant to the current reexamination of values in this community; 3) it is now being used widely in French (from "gai"), Dutch, Japanese, and Swedish to designate, among other things, people preferring erotic contact with their own gender; and 4) lastly, the term "gay," according to Boswell (1980), actually predates the term "homosexual" by at least several centuries. The latter term was coined in the late nineteenth century by German psychologists. Although the full etymology of "gai" has not been researched, evidence exists of its use as early as the thirteenth century in France, where it referred to courtly love in the south, where homosexuality and heretical movements were closely aligned (Boswell 1980).

explanation is often embedded the type of treatment that is required for its cure (Kleinman 1980). For many folk cultures, "dis-ease" means being out of balance. One's health is seen as a reflection either of the group's well being in the eyes of God or other deities or of their place in the cosmos. In traditional Chinese theory, for instance, multiple forces (e.g., hot/cold, wet/dry, body meridians) must be in balance themselves and with each other. In the Western world, beliefs regarding hot and cold balances may be traced back to ancient Greece and remain prevalent in circum-Mediterranean-derived folk cultures around the world today. In many such cultures, illness is a reflection of moral transgressions: a total violation of a cultural system and a way of being. As Diamond (1963) has put it, nonliterate cultures are holistic and moral, but not moralistic in a judgmental sense, primarily because all social relations in these societies are of a "kin" nature.

In our "modern" world, with medical explanations for illness, this moral view usually does not openly prevail. With certain diseases, however (in recent history cancer and tuberculosis [Sontag 1978]), the moral construction of causality reappears, as it has with AIDS. It returns, however, as an incomplete system lacking the integration of self and community and the full cultural context from which it has been extracted over the centuries. We are left with the worst of both worlds: the moralistic underpinnings remain, but without a holistic understanding of how our health and well being are tied to other aspects of our existence.

As of November, 1984, the Centers for Disease Control (CDC) cited 6,993 cases of AIDS reported since 1981 (Webster 1984). Any disease that is often fatal and that spreads so rapidly will evoke fear in vulnerable groups. With AIDS, this is particularly true, because the syndrome has limited itself primarily to certain segments of the population, creating a mysteriousness that has made it all the more treacherous for those at risk. In the United States, the risk groups have crosscut seemingly incongruous geographical and social boundaries and include gay men, IV-drug users, hemophiliacs, recipients of blood transfusions, sexual partners of people with AIDS, Haitian immigrants, and children of mothers at risk for AIDS. Given the social and ethnic diversity of people who are affected, it has been an epidemiological challenge to unravel.

HAITIANS

As of November 1984, the CDC reported that 4% of the total number of reported people with AIDS in the United States were Haitians (CDC 1984). Haitian patients, physicians, and researchers have all felt stigmatized. At one point, Haitian physicians in this country threatened to instruct their patients to refuse cooperation with medical researchers and the CDC unless Haitian medical scientists were allowed to play a greater role in ongoing research.

Haiti has suffered as well. In a country that has been known to be the poorest in the Western hemisphere and in which tourism provides the largest source of foreign income, AIDS has become a financial as well as a medical catastrophe (Simons 1983). Once the syndrome appeared, it spread quickly. One method of transfer appears to be from injections, the preferred route of administration of medication in Haiti (LaGuerre 1981). Medications of many types are administered in this way, by self-injections, or, more commonly, from *picturistes*, who are one of the many types of folk healers in Haiti. They offer their services at home or in the back rooms of pharmacies, in which needles are said to be reused often without sterilization (Baum 1983).

Another means of transmission is said to be through male homosexual prostitution (Baum 1983). For months, epidemiologists were confused as Haitian people with AIDS categorically denied being homosexual. There appear to be two related explanations for this. First, as one Haitian put it,

> In Haiti, everyone puts the homosexual down at the bottom of the ladder. If you put a gun to his head, he'll tell you he's not gay (Schear 1983:57).

Secondly, many of the Haitian men with AIDS claim to be heterosexual, for either the reason stated above or for financial considerations only. Many of the Haitian *Massisi* (the Haitian term for homosexual) are married and have prostituted themselves to other men for economic survival in a country in which the average per capita yearly income is under three hundred dollars (Fettner and Check 1984). Regardless of the reasons, homosexuality as the only risk factor appears to be ruled out by the fact that one-quarter to one-third of Haitians with AIDS are women. Lastly, AIDS seems to spread more quickly in Haiti due to the generally weakened condition of the people, caused by poor nutrition, traditional infections, and parasites (cf. Moore and Le Baron in this volume, Chapter Four).

An awareness of the health profile of the Haitian-American community is very important but will not solve all the data collection or treatment problems. Communication is complicated not only by language differences, but also because of Haitian use of symbolic and metaphoric language to describe symptoms or parts of the body (LaGuerre 1981). Additionally, Haitians are generally known for their late presentation of illness to physicians, with whom they will usually consult only when in great pain. This has particularly negative ramifications for AIDS, which often manifests itself intermittently and at first with relatively minor symptoms such as swollen lymph nodes, fever, sore throat, sweating at night, weight loss, and general lethargy. Diagnosis is further complicated because many conditions such as anemia and parasites are endemic to Haiti, are present in immigrants from Haiti, and are symptoms of AIDS itself.

Haitian concepts of illness recognize both natural and supernatural forces. Natural illnesses tend to have commonplace symptoms, are usually brief, and are thought to be brought about by God. Supernaturally induced illnesses appear suddenly, are often thought to be caused by angry voodoo spirits and, if not treated, are thought to spread throughout the body. Although voodoo is a belief system complex beyond the scope of this paper, health in the total sense is maintained through a relationship and contract between a person and his or her "spirit protector." Supernatural illnesses then, are thought to be the result of a breach of this contract. AIDS would appear to have such a supernatural etiology in Haitian folk culture.

Probably more relevant to AIDS than voodoo, however, is the complex belief system surrounding blood, which forms the core of Haitian conceptualizations of bodily functioning and disease. Irregularities of the blood are thought to be connected to the most serious diseases. Blood is categorized into hot or cold, thick or thin, and various colors. Spoiled and dirty blood is associated with sexually transmitted diseases, with which much shame is also attached (LaGuerre 1981).

An analysis of AIDS as viewed from a Haitian emic perspective has not yet appeared in the U.S. literature, but it can be hypothesized from the material reviewed that it is associated with shame in a different and perhaps more powerful manner than it is in the United States. Initial anthropological inquiry into Haitian culture suggests that interpretations of sexual behavior vary somewhat from those in the U.S. gay community. Specifically, self-identification as a homosexual appears to be entirely avoided. Anal or vaginal penetration is seen as a "masculine" role, regardless of the partner's gender (Fettner and Check 1984). Fettner and Check have also noted that people from the United States tend to be more concerned than Haitians are with the morals of the act, and Haitians with what they believe are the penetrative aspects of the masculine role.

Given the distinct cultural differences from U.S. gay men and biases against homosexuality, one should not be surprised to find that Haitians with AIDS have kept themselves more or less separate from the gay community and have not used many of the free services available to them, much less joining in coalitions for funding. Funds for specifically Haitian-controlled or Haitian-oriented medical and psychological services are substantially fewer than are those for gay men.

For Haitian-Americans, AIDS has meant loss of jobs and increased stigmatization beyond that that they have already faced by being black and part of the last wave of Latin American and Caribbean immigrants. A Haitian man without AIDS states:

> People avoid shaking my hand when they know I'm Haitian. And my wife and I won't speak Haitian at the laundromat because other people are afraid to use the same machine as us. We can pass as Jamaican (Schear 1983:57).

GAY MEN

Gay men with AIDS appear to be in double jeopardy, in that they make up a stigmatized subculture and have also contracted an illness that has become further stigmatized as a result of being associated with this subculture. This stigmatization that gay men have faced has been well documented in the press and repeatedly comes back to the notion of contagion as well as to an underlying prejudice against homosexuality. What makes for greater difficulty is the fact that when dealing with people with AIDS precautions must be taken, but, in fact, the people who need the most protection are those with depressed immune systems. Once diagnosed, the stigma remains, as it has been known to do with other diseases such as cancer (Waxler 1981).

Definition of the Community

In this paper, homosexuals are collectively treated as a subculture within the larger culture. As such, they reflect one particular segment within the broad range of normal, human sexual expressions and lifestyles. Conflict remains as to whether gay people constitute a minority group (Paul 1982), but, as a group, they have distinct differences that separate them from ethnic and racial minorities that share common bonds of culture and genetics. Gay people are found in all walks of life, from all races and religions, and, on the whole, are usually not visibly distinguishable from the nongay population.

Stress and Internalized Homophobia

The stresses of having AIDS have been well documented (Morin et al. 1984; Fisher 1983). What is less well known and more open to dispute is the role stress plays in contracting AIDS. One perspective posits that individuals with low stress tolerance are more vulnerable than individuals who better handle stress. Specifically, Kooden (1983) has argued that individuals who have internalized homophobic ideas are more at risk. This is, in a sense, turning the "sin/sickness" approach (Erickson 1982) on its head by suggesting that the act itself is not immoral but internalizing the belief that it is wrong can help make people sick or can increase stress. This particular approach does not minimize the medical risk of multiple sexual contact for infection by a virus, but implies that the interaction with internalized homophobia may be the dangerous thing.

Whatever validity there is to this, the view expressed by the gay community (as seen in the gay press) is that a positive self-image is crucial ("taking control of your life" seems to be the current phrase). Good nutrition, adequate sleep, exercise, and self-respect are the often-mentioned components of prevention, along with "safe-sex" guidelines. Debates continue to rage within the community, however, as to whether or not lifestyles have moved in the direction of monogamy and if, in fact, they should. Thus, gay men are readdressing the ongoing problems of what it means to be male in this society, albeit somewhat ironically, for gay men undertook the lead in initiating this debate in the early 1970s.

Doctor-Patient Relations

Within the gay community a renewed questioning of traditional doctor-patient relations has appeared. This relationship is an important aspect of the treatment of any serious disease, and physician communication with gay men with AIDS has been reported to be generally poor, even outside of hospitals (Kooden 1983). Unless the patient has gone out of his way to choose a physician from his own community, of which there is a limited supply, gay patients usually face a cultural gap between themselves and the physician. Although different than the ethnic or language barriers that Haitian patients must face, the barrier exists nonetheless. For some, having AIDS may mean premature disclosure of sexual orientation; for others it may mean remaining closeted (i.e., not self-identified publicly as gay). Secrecy about homosexuality (for self-protective purposes) has been generally diminishing over the years, but continues to be necessary and has been a well-established fact ever since a stigma was attached to homosexuality (Goffman 1963).

In the context of a reportable disease like AIDS, however, the sense of secrecy is also related to confidentiality of medical records. For gay men, with or without AIDS, this has raised questions not only about physician-patient trust, but about the patient's role as a research subject. Recently, as blood tests for antibodies (LAV/HTLV-III) have been developed, this has become an issue entangled with complex ethical, legal, and political implications. Research is so obviously needed, yet at what personal cost to subjects? How can gay men feel secure that personal information about them, their lives, and their states of health will be used productively, especially in a political climate that rejects homosexuality as a basic human right? In fact, almost all the risk groups are vulnerable in some social, political, or economic way.

Physicians do not help to create trust when they moralize about lifestyles, and language in medical practice in particular becomes important. For example, one psychologist with a predominantly gay group of clients has suggested the term "multiple partnering" to replace the term "promiscuity" during the medical interview (Kooden 1983), because inducing guilt does not appear to be the best technique for changing such patterns. The physician faces many of the issues that are faced by any physician of patients with life-threatening diseases (e.g., how to communicate a poor prognosis to the patient). How this particular task is handled surely must have an impact on the ways in which people with the syndrome see themselves and their illness from that point on. In an interview with a young man with AIDS-related complex (ARC), the patient tells of his first and second diagnostic experiences (Futterman 1983:8):

> After the physical exam the doctor asked me into the office whereupon he sat with his head in his hands without looking at me, and told me to come back next week, because he wasn't sure what was happening and wanted someone else to see me. I walked out of the office in a daze, and although the doctor didn't tell me anything, I knew what was on his mind.

He tried not to get more upset than he already was, and went for a second opinion:

> This doctor gave me a number of tests and proceeded to tell me that I had an immune deficiency, but that I didn't have an opportunistic infection yet, and probably had as good a chance to recover as anyone did, although she couldn't promise. She then proceeded to discuss the importance of a good diet, safe sex, and how to take better care of myself in general.

The gay men who are reexamining the structure of doctor-patient relations fit into the group described by Haug and Lavin (1981) as those who are likely to be young, who feel that errors have been made in their diagnosis or care, and who question physician competence. The urban gay man also tend to fall within the wide range of middle and working classes, possibly also fitting into Haug and Lavin's further classification as a knowledgeable and consumer-oriented individual.

According to their model, a negotiation process occurs in which the physician is not in full control, but both parties come to the encounter closer to being equals and try to work out a program of treatment. Katon and Kleinman (1981) place this issue within a broader context of the

Western social crisis of autonomy and the questioning of all authority. Whatever the cause, this changing doctor-patient relationship is intensified by AIDS, a syndrome that the medical community does not yet fully understand or have an adequate treatment for.

Social Labels

According to Waxler (1981), a patient's diagnosis, not ethnic group or lifestyle, should determine his or her treatment. This has become especially difficult for people with AIDS, because, as the everyday terminology instructs us, they are no longer "people with AIDS," but have become "AIDS patients." AIDS, in the public's eyes, is the "gay disease." In fact, when AIDS first surfaced in 1981, it was dubbed "GRID," for "Gay-Related Immune Deficiency." A linguistic and social labeling analysis of AIDS demonstrates the potent process of language, especially through labels, serving to further a construct and entrench it in the culture ever more deeply. Homosexuality itself seems to be such a construct, with society's labels serving to maintain its devalued status.

At present, against a backdrop of a stigmatized and alienated subculture, AIDS has become synonymous with death, an association not always true. Within the last two years, many people with AIDS and ARC have begun to resist death as an inevitable outcome. This may have been facilitated by the knowledge that ARC may not necessarily develop into AIDS with its opportunistic infections, Kaposi's sarcoma, and death. New medical questions have also arisen. Recent blood tests of healthy gay men in San Francisco revealed that 55% showed positive LAV/HTLV-III antibodies (Curran 1984). Exactly what this means, however, is not at all clear, although such men may have been exposed to the virus but are now showing some form of immunity.

All these factors have fostered some new hope, and, for some, changes in attitudes and lives. For many, one big effect of AIDS has meant a new or second "coming out," especially on an occupational level. Contrary to the effect on the Haitian community, the gay community appears to be experiencing a new "gay pride."

This, in turn, has had additional effects on the actual illness. Healing can take place more easily in an environment of acceptance. Thus, the negativity and fear that has been expressed by the "public" reaction appears to be somewhat counterbalanced by the response from the gay community itself. When epidemics have developed in our society in the past, the public tended to show alarm and to pitch in, as was seen with the polio epidemic and more recently with Legionnaire's disease; public participation in fighting AIDS paled by comparison. Much media coverage has in fact adversely affected motivations to help by instilling the question in people's minds: "What if it spreads to the general population?" This kind of phrasing implies that the syndrome becomes really serious only when it travels beyond the current stigmatized groups. It is yet another way of clearly demarcating an "us" and a "them."

Personality Factors

Over the past ten years certain personality factors have been reported to correlate positively with longer survival rates in patients with serious diseases such as breast cancer (Greer et al. 1979). Norman Cousins (1979) claimed that positive emotions were instrumental in his dramatic and controversial "laughing cure." Evidence with greater scientific backing has come from the field of psychoneuroimmunology, which assesses the role of psychological and environmental stress in relation to diseases that involve the body's immune system (Coates et al. 1984).

AIDS research appears to have much to contribute in the field of patient personality and attitude in relationship to fighting off illness. Jeffrey Mandel and Jeffrey Leiphart have been involved in research to determine whether or not a psychological component to AIDS exists in fighting off the disease. So far they have found that adaptive personalities are not doing as well in warding off the opportunistic infections as are the men who do not "accept their disease, who fight it, who perhaps get even a little rude and tough or bitchy about it . . . ." (Fain 1983:83).

The Sick Role

A more sophisticated and subtle perception of illness has also appeared in the last ten years. On the one hand, the number of syndromes and symptoms that are thought to constitute sickness has increased, prompting Illich (1975) to dub this phenomenon the "medicalization of health." On the other hand, an increased interest in holistic medicine, including diet, exercise, and a sense of responsibility for being healthy or sick, has become popular. This trend may be seen in an intensified way among those healthy gay men who are called the "worried well." A conference on AIDS in New York City sponsored by the Gay Men's Health Crisis (GMHC) (1983) featured workshops concerning macrobiotic cooking, health, and nutrition and spirituality.

For a syndrome like AIDS, for which no known cure exists, the traditional Parsonian sick-role model (Parsons 1958) offers little insight; nor does calling sickness "deviance" solve much. Deviance, as Alexander (1982) argues in her critique of the Parsonian model, applies to someone pretending to be sick for secondary gains. Although no one would accuse a person with AIDS of malingering, a confusion or misuse of terms does appear, because no absolute diagnostic line separating AIDS and ARC has been defined. People with a T-cell ratio reversal and who have mild symptoms without a serious opportunistic infection usually carry on with their lives even with their mild symptoms. They are in a state of limbo, a type of permanent "medical probation." One man with ARC described his situation this way:

> Sometimes I just wish I had KS [Kaposi's sarcoma] or PCP [*Pneumocystis carinii* pneumonia] so that it would just be over or I'd have something concrete to fight against. At times I just feel so fatigued—like an old man, I can hardly walk two blocks without being exhausted. It comes and goes and relapses are very difficult (Futterman 1983:11).

Support Groups

One of the primary ways in which the gay community has marshaled its forces is through networks and self-help groups. An article about the Gay Men's Health Crisis in New York explains their "buddy system" (Dowd 1983). "Buddies" walk dogs, shop, clean house, and may sit and read to the person with AIDS, who usually is no longer able to perform these chores because of the debilitating aspects of AIDS in its later stages. In this sense, the community is reconstituting itself in a new way, taking on the "family" function for each other. In a volunteer's own words:

> I deeply identify with these men. I wanted to offer the support that I would get if I were to come down with it. There is a sense of taking care of one's own (Dowd 1983).

Clearly, the need for a sense of "family," however defined, is tremendous, and support is a basic necessity. The support groups for people with AIDS fulfill Pattison's (1980) criteria for social networks in that they represent a high degree of interaction, or investment, and symmetrical reciprocity whenever possible. To quote a member of such a group:

> In the support group, like AA, we have been able to help each other in a way that no one else can, we know what each other is going through even though we come from such different backgrounds (Futterman 1983:11).

Because a cure for AIDS does not seem imminent, medical and lay people are becoming aware that counseling, support groups, and holistic treatment may be the only help available. This realization is slow in coming; a quick scan of the AIDS literature of the last three years reveals hundreds of medical and lay articles, but only a meager handful of social science ones. The thoughts of a gay writer make this point well:

> For an epidemic with unparalleled overtones of social and political disaster, what AIDS does to the mind could well outstrip the considerable horror it wreaks on the body, both to the individual, and to the community of gay men who are [nearly], three out of four of its victims (Fain 1983:22).

Through avenues such as these, despite the tragedy of AIDS, many men and women are finding new sources of strength, identity, friendship, and community, all of which will, we hope, endure long after this devastating syndrome is gone.

ACKNOWLEDGMENTS

The author wishes to thank Donna Futterman and Dr. Joshua Fishman for their resources, encouragement, and careful review of this paper.

REFERENCES

Alexander, L. 1982. Illness Maintenance and the New American Sick Role. In *Clinically Applied Anthropology: Anthropologists in Health Science Settings*, N. Chrisman and W. Maretzki, eds., pp. 351–367. Boston: Reidel.

Baum, S. 1983. Unpublished paper read at "Research Overview of AIDS: The Disease and its Consequences," forum conducted at Albert Einstein College of Medicine, Bronx, N.Y., October.

Boswell, J. 1980. *Christianity, Social Tolerance and Homosexuality: Gay People in Western Europe from the Beginning of the Christian Era to the Fourteenth Century*. Chicago: University of Chicago Press.

Centers for Disease Control (CDC). 1984. *AIDS Report: Weekly Surveillance for the Week of November 12*. Atlanta: CDC.

Coates, T., L. Temoshok, J. Mandel. 1984. Psychosocial Research Is Essential to Understanding and Treating AIDS. *American Psychologist* 39 (11):1309–1314.

Cousins, N. 1979. *Anatomy of an Illness*. New York: Norton.

Curran, J. 1984. Unpublished paper presented at meeting of New York Physicians for Human Rights, New York City, September 23.

Diamond, S. 1963. The Search for the Primitive. In *Man's Image in Medicine and Anthropology*, J. Goldstone, ed., pp. 62–116. New York: International Universities Press.

Dolce, J. 1983. The Politics of Fear: Haitians and AIDS. *The New York Native* August 1:16–18.

Dowd, M. 1983. For Victims of AIDS, Support in a Lonely Siege. *New York Times*. December 5: B1, B6.

Erickson, R. 1982. Reconsidering Three Dichotomies (Mind/Body, Individual/ Group, Sickness/Sin). *Journal of Religion and Health* 21:115–123.

Fain, N. 1983. AIDS and the Mind. *The Advocate*. October 27, 379:22, 33.

Fettner, A. G. and W. A. Check. 1984. *The Truth About AIDS: Evolution of an Epidemic*. New York: Holt, Rinehart and Winston.

Fisher, K. 1983. Stress: The Unseen Killer in AIDS. *APA Monitor* 14(7):1, 20, 21.

Futterman, D. 1983. AIDS: It's Psychosocial Impact: Interviews with Gay Men with the Disease. Unpublished manuscript: p. 22.

Gay Men's Health Crisis (GMHC). 1983. Meeting the Challenge of AIDS: Professional and Community Response. A conference cosponsored by New York Physicians for Human Rights and Hunter College School of Social Work. New York City, November 5.

Goffman, E. 1963. *Stigma: Notes on the Management of Spoiled Identity*. Englewood Cliffs, N.J.: Prentice-Hall.

Greer, S., T. E. Morris, K. W. Pettingale. 1979. Psychological Response to Breast Cancer: Effect on Outcome. *Lancet* 2:785–787.

Haug, M., and B. Lavin. 1981. Practitioner or Patient—Who's in Charge? *Journal of Health and Social Behavior* 22:212–228.

Illich, I. 1975. The Epidemic of Modern Medicine and the Destruction of Medical Cultures. In *Medical Nemesis: The Expropriation of Health*. London: Calder & Boyars, Marion Boyars.

Katon W. and A. Kleinman. 1981. Doctor-Patient Negotiation and Other Social Science Strategies in Patient Care. In *The Relevance of Social Science to Medicine*, L. Eisenberg and A. Kleinman, eds., pp. 257–279. Boston: Reidel.

Kleinman, A. (ed.). 1980. *Culture, Health Care Systems and Clinical Reality in Patients and Healers in the Context of Culture: An Exploration of the Borderland between Anthropology, Medicine and Psychiatry*. California: University of California Press, pp. 24–70.

Kooden, H. 1983. The Rebirthing of a Community. *New York Native*. June 20, 66:22–23.

LaGuerre, M. 1981. Haitian Americans. In *Ethnicity and Medical Care*, A Harwood, ed., pp. 172–210. Cambridge: Harvard University Press.

Morin, S. F., K. A. Charles, and A. K. Malyon. 1984. The Psychological Impact of AIDS on Gay Men. *The American Psychologist* 39:1288–1293.

Parsons, T. 1958. Definitions of Health and Illness in the Light of American Values and Social Structure. In *Patients, Physicians and Illness*, E. G. Jaco, ed., pp. 120–144. New York: Free Press of Glencoe.

Pattison, E. 1980. Religious Youth Cults: Alternative Healing Social Networks. *Journal of Religion and Health* 19:275–286.

Paul, W. 1982. Minority Status for Gay People: Majority Reaction and Social Context. In *Homosexuality: Social Psychological and Biological Issues*, W. Paul, J. Weinrich, J. Gonsiorek, and M. Hotvedt, eds., pp. 351–369. Beverly Hills: Sage Publications.

Schear, S. 1983. Haitians Protest Classification. *New York Native*. October 10:13, 57.

Simons, M. 1983. For Haiti's Tourism, the Stigma of AIDS Is Fatal. *New York Times*. November 29, A2.

Sontag, S. 1978. *Illness as Metaphor*. New York: Vintage Books.

Waxler, N. 1981. The Social Labeling Perspective on Illness and Medical Practice. In *The Relevance of Social Science for Medicine*, L. Eisenberg and A. Kleinkman, eds., pp. 283–306. Boston: Reidel.

Webster, B. 1984. Increase in AIDS Cases Reported. *New York Times*. November 30, B10.

Chapter Twelve

Explanatory Models for AIDS

Diane Bolognone

Thomas M. Johnson

BACKGROUND

Social sciences in general and anthropology in particular have witnessed a recent emphasis on "popular health culture." The thrust of this interest has been to demonstrate that nonprofessionals, rather than having incoherent or incomplete systems of understanding about health and illness, have ideas about sickness and symptoms that are logically consistent and often elaborate. Indeed, these lay understandings about sickness are believed to have profound effects upon health behavior; they significantly influence the interpretations of symptoms and the interactions between patients and medical professionals. Two major foci of study in the endeavor to better understand the popular view of sickness have been the Health Belief Model (Rosenstock, 1974) in psychology, and the Explanatory Model (EM) approach in anthropology (Kleinman, 1980).

The purpose of this paper is to report on research to better understand the lay explanatory models (EMs) for acquired immune deficiency syndrome (AIDS), a medical condition still incompletely understood by professional investigators, yet having enormous public health and health-education repercussions. In addition, AIDS is deeply enmeshed with classic social science issues such as stigmatization. The study of EMs for AIDS also provides an opportunity heretofore not feasible (with the possible exception of Legionnaire's disease and toxic shock syndrome) to study health beliefs in the lay

This research was funded by a Faculty Seed Grant from Southern Methodist University. The authors wish to acknowledge the assistance of Dr. Campbell Reid, Professor of Statistics, SMU; Harold Dare, Former Director, Oak Lawn Counseling Center; and members of the Dallas Gay Alliance, Dallas, Texas.

public as knowledge diffuses from the scientific community. In short, this research is informative not only about perceptions of AIDS, but also about the formation of EMs, the relationship of EMs to behavior, and the implications of EMs for public health and health education programs.

Explanatory Models are sets of beliefs formed in relation to any illness; these include perspectives on etiology, onset of symptoms, pathophysiology, severity, and treatment (Kleinman 1980). EMs are held by everyone and are related to beliefs passed on during enculturation (as part of the general world view and care-value system) and are learned through formal education, media exposure, and personal experience (Kleinman 1980; Young 1982). Although EMs are held by everyone, lay persons and health care professionals often have different models, much as might individuals from two different cultures. Incongruity of EMs is now recognized as a common impediment in health care delivery when patient and practitioner are from different cultural backgrounds, but incongruity can also exist within a culture, and the interaction of EMs is a central feature of health care delivery in any setting. In short, when a patient seeks care from a practitioner, expectations on the part of each will be conditioned by their respective EMs.

In the United States, lay and professional EMs are seen as quite different: lay EMs reflect an "illness orientation" that emphasizes psychosocial dysfunction; and professional EMs reflect a "disease orientation" that emphasizes biophysiological abnormality (Taussig 1980). This broad difference underlies the tremendous variability associated with membership in distinctive subcultures or idiosyncratic beliefs. Within our own culture, then, patients and professionals bring to the clinical encounter different notions about episodes of sickness and treatment, with the successful resolution of these incongruities thought to be the cornerstone of mutually satisfying patient care. Indeed, EMs have been touted as a promising new tool for medical anthropologists who can elicit both lay and professional perceptions for sickness, assist in the negotiation of differences, and thus increase compliance and satisfaction with health care.

Because EMs are learned and culturally derived (Kleinman 1978; Levin and Idler 1981), they are heavily influenced by cultural dynamics such as isolation, diffusion, and stigmatization. In the case of AIDS, this is particularly true because the homosexual (gay) community has been seen to be the primary cultural group most at risk for AIDS and is a group already stigmatized (Goffman 1963). By stigmatization, society constructs a theory or ideology to account for the "danger" that the stigmatized group represents. A review of recent literature reveals concern over stigma attached to homosexuals in relation to AIDS (Bush 1983; Fain 1983); the issue of stigma cannot be divorced from the EMs of AIDS. In fact, the EMs of both the gay community and larger society should be profoundly influenced by the perceived threat accompanying stigmatization, as beliefs about medical reality of AIDS and the health behavior of actual and potential victims of AIDS is better understood.

Finally, the actual mechanisms for the transmission of EMs is not well documented. Clearly, some aspects of EMs are derivatives of basic cultural patterns (e.g., illness seen as punishment) that are components of a larger world view. Nevertheless, the nature of diffusion of specific ideas about a disease and their incorporation into EMs has only recently been studied (Kleinman 1982). By studying EMs for AIDS, before either professional or lay persepctives are fixed, and by inquiring about patterns of diffusion of information we can better our understanding of the process of EM elaboration and use such knowledge to assist public health education programs related to AIDS.

METHODOLOGY

In this study, EMs were elicited by use of two techniques: 1) the professional EM was constructed by content analysis of professional and popular literature (from 1982–1984), such as the *New England Journal of Medicine* and *Advocate*; and 2) lay EMs were derived through personal, structured interviews (from 1983–1984). Both professional and lay EMs were structured by focusing on perceptions of AIDS etiology, symptoms, pathophysiology (includes definition of AIDS, transmission, and perception of high-risk groups), prognosis, and treatment (See Table 12.1). Data concerning diffusion of information were obtained by questioning lay subjects about their sources of information on AIDS and by content analysis over time of both lay and professional publications. Data about the relationships of stigma to AIDS and about change in individuals' lifestyles were collected by questioning lay informants about the effects of AIDS on their lifestyles.

The goal of this research is to understand lay perceptions of AIDS. Within the lay sector, two study groups emerge: the nongay sector, which is identified as being at low risk for acquiring AIDS, and the gay sector, which is identified as being at high risk for acquiring AIDS. To capture the potential differences in EMs for these two groups, individuals from each group were selected for interviewing. Interview subjects from the gay sector were selected with the assistance of the Dallas Gay Alliance; and the interview subjects from the nongay sector were selected with the assistance of the Dallas Democratic Party. Additional interview subjects were obtained to achieve a total sample of 16 gay and 14 nongay adults matched for the following sociodemographic characteristics: age, gender, and socioeconomic levels.

TABLE 12.1. Interview Outline: Acquired Immunodeficiency Syndrome

Interview Focus	Interview Probes
Demographic Data	
Explanatory Model	
Etiology of AIDS	What is your understanding of AIDS? What do you know about it? Or what causes the disease? Or what is the pathophysiology of AIDS?
Mode of Transfer	How do you get it?
Symptoms	How does it affect the body? What happens when you get the disease? Or how do you known when you have it?
Prognosis	How serious is the disease? How much do you worry about it?
Treatment	How do you get rid of the disease? How do you treat it?
High-Risk Group	Who can get AIDS? Who's at risk for AIDS?
Prevention	How do you avoid getting AIDS?
Sources of Information	From what sources have you heard about AIDS?
Effects on Lifestyle	How has your understanding of this syndrome changed your life?

The personal interview is the chosen method of data collection on popular perceptions of AIDS due to its exploratory nature. Because of the open-ended format, interview subjects were free to elaborate about EM construction. Informants were encouraged to talk about important issues (as defined in an interview outline), about which pertinent data were recorded in the researcher's notes. An average interview took approximately one hour; most were conducted in the homes of respondents.

RESULTS

Homogeneity of sex, gender, and level of education is noted among the individuals sampled. Of the thirty informants, 76% were males, with an almost equal number of gay and nongay males in the sample. Comparability is also demonstrated in both sectors for age: 83% of the respondents were between the ages of 27 and 40 years at the time of the interviews. All individuals surveyed received some form of post–high school education: this training ranged from a technical degree in cosmetology to a doctorate in jurisprudence. Seventy–three percent of the respondents had received at least a baccalaureate degree. A composite for the entire sample is, therefore, a white male citizen of Dallas, between 27 and 40 years of age, with a college degree.

To demonstrate EMs for AIDS, six components of the model were chosen for analysis. Three of the components surveyed—etiology (cause of disease), onset of symptoms, and treatment—correspond to Kleinman's (1980) format for eliciting EMs. Three additional components—transmission, high-risk group, definition of AIDS—were surveyed in this study due to their perceived relationship to "pathophysiology," as well as their perceived relationship to stigma. Because the prognosis for a person with AIDS is considered by 97% of the respondents to be serious/fatal once the disease is established, prognosis was not included as one of the components analyzed. These six components—definition of AIDS, etiology, symptoms, transmission, high-risk groups, and treatment—formed the basic structure for professional and lay EMs for AIDS as defined and analyzed in this study.

Lay perceptions of AIDS vary considerably. One aspect of this variability is demonstrated in the degree of elaboration in EMs: some EMs are simple and truncated, others highly elaborated. Two extremes of this continuum of "degree of elaboration" are represented in Table 12.2. Simple models are incomplete in the number of components defined (Symptoms and Treatment in Table 12.2), as well as lacking in detailed responses (High-Risk Group: "Predominantly gays"). Whereas, in elaborate models, all components are defined and responded to in greater detail (High-Risk Group: Male homosexuals, etc.). Although the two models show considerable variance in elaboration, note that they do demonstrate internal consistency, or compatability in responses between components. This is exemplified in both informants' responses to high-risk groups, transmission, and prevention of AIDS. For example, in the simple model, the informant identifies "Predominantly gays" as the high-risk group that transmits AIDS sexually and, therefore, that should abstain from sexual contact in order to prevent AIDS. In short, the lay informants demonstrate ideas about AIDS that are logically consistent internally, yet, for reasons cited in the remainder of this section, vary considerably in degree of elaboration.

Congruence of Explanatory Models between lay persons and professionals has been cited as a crucial variable in health-care delivery. For example, Kleinman (1982) notes that this incongruence may lead to important conflicts that impinge on health care. The lack of congruence between lay and professional EMs for AIDS is demonstrated in Figure 12.1. This study indicates that there is further variation in EMs, based on sexual preference of lay respondents, when compared to professional EMs. By use of VENN diagrams, Figure 12.1 graphically compares the gay EMs with professional EMs, and the nongay EMs with professional EMs using the six components—definition of AIDS, etiology, symptoms, transmission, high-risk

TABLE 12.2.   Two Types of Explanatory Models for A.I.D.S.

Components	Simple Model Responses	Elaborate Model Responses
Definition	"Acquired Immune Deficiency Syndrome" "Gay's Disease" (sic)	"Immune system dying off and disease taking over"
Etiology	"Something you pick up . . . means immune system will break down"	"Think it's a virus . . . lots of theories . . . system being run down when exposed to it [virus]"
Symptoms	"Don't know"	"Tired all the time" "Weight loss" "Pain in the stomach" "Night sweats" "Low-grade fever" "Cough" "Opportunistic infections—herpes, P.C.P., K.S."
Transmission	"Gays, passed on sexually"	"Blood" "Sexual contact" "Open wounds" "Needles" "Maybe semen"
High-Risk Group	"Predominantly gays"	"Male homosexuals" "Tahitians" (sic) "Hemophiliacs" "I.V.-drug users"
Treatment	"Don't know"	"Very poorly" "Really isn't a treatment for AIDS . . . treat opportunistic infections" "Interferon"
Prevention	"Abstinence" "Gays stay the hell away from each other"	"Change sex habits" "Cut out drugs" "Adequate diet, sleep" "Not sure it can be prevented"

group, and treatment—as the base for the AIDS model. The level of congruence of lay to professional EMs for AIDS can be interpreted by noting the percentage of lay responses corresponding to professional responses (size of broken circles, lay responses, within solid circles—professional responses), and by proximity of lay responses to professional responses (inclusion or exclusion of broken circles within solid circles).

Statistically, the gay and nongay samples can also be seen to differ ($p <$ .05) in their level of congruence with professional EMs for AIDS by comparing the number of correct responses to professional responses as a measure of agreement or congruence. All p values are computed for two-by-two contingency tables using Fisher's Exact Test to adjust for small samples. The gay respondents cite an average of nine correct responses (of a possibility of more than 26 correct responses), whereas the nongay respondents cite an average of six correct responses. Age is also examined for its effect on number of correct responses: the 30-39 year-old age cohort seems slightly best informed. Statistically, sexual preference has the greatest impact on level of congruence with professional EMs for AIDS.

One explanatory model area for AIDS accounting for variation in responses between the two sampled groups is Symptoms. The gay sector varies considerably in number of symptoms they cite (zero to five), whereas most of the nongay subjects identify fewer than two correct symptoms (see Figure 12.2). The "degree of vagueness" in one's responses to symptoms can also be analyzed and shows a trend toward increasing vagueness in responses by the nongay sample. Degree of vagueness scores are calculated by grouping the number of correct responses (the degree factual) with degree of vagueness in responses (see Table 12.3 for the formulation of scores). The following are examples of degree of vagueness responses to symptoms of AIDS:

Degree of Vagueness	Symptoms Cited
Not Vague	"Purple Spots"
Intermediate Vague	"Skin Rash"
Very Vague	"Slow Healing"

Perceptions about AIDS, as witnessed in degree of vagueness and number of correct responses, differ between the gay and nongay sample studied.

From a health education, public health standpoint, identifying sources in the formation of EMs is crucial to understanding and preventing incongruities between lay and professional EMs. Formation of lay health

Figure 12.1. Congruence of Lay and Professional Explanatory Models (EMs) for AIDS[1]

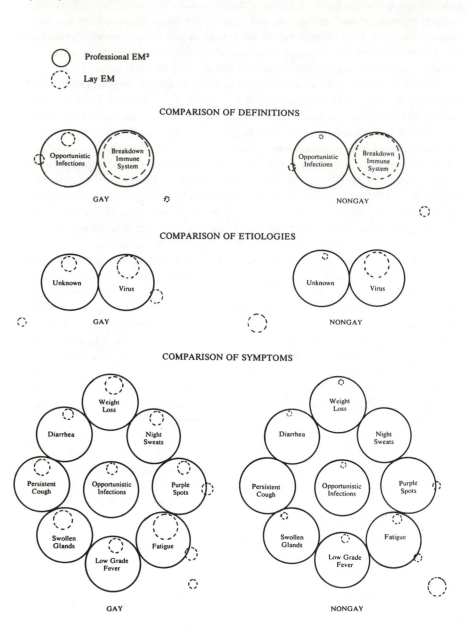

Professional EM[2]

Lay EM

COMPARISON OF DEFINITIONS

GAY — NONGAY

COMPARISON OF ETIOLOGIES

GAY — NONGAY

COMPARISON OF SYMPTOMS

GAY — NONGAY

COMPARISON OF MODES OF TRANSMISSION

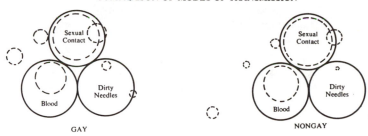

COMPARISON OF GROUPS AT RISK

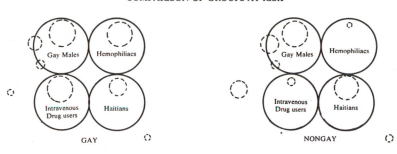

COMPARISON OF TREATMENTS

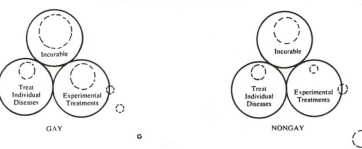

[1]Size of broken circles represents relative percentages of responses both congruent and at variance with professional EMs. Complete agreement (congruence) between lay and professional models would result in broken circles perfectly superimposed over solid circles.

[2]Sources for construction of Professional EMs: (Aledort 1983; D'Eramo 1984; Dowdle 1983; Durack 1981; GMHC 1983: Mildvan 1982).

Figure 12.2. Number of Responses Corresponding to Professional EM for Symptoms

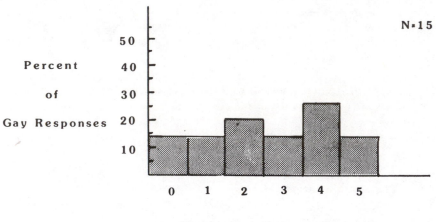

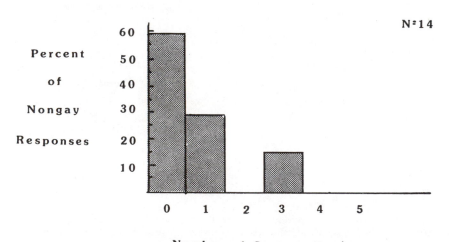

TABLE 12.3.   Degree of Vagueness Score for Symptoms

	Low Factual (0)	Intermediate Factual (1–3)	High Factual (4–5)
Not Vague: (0,0)	2	1	0
Intermediate Vague (1,0), (1,1), (2,2)	3	2	1
Very Vague: (0,1)	4	3	2

Note: Individual scores were calculated by placing them into a category that reflects the number of correct responses to the number of vague responses. A high degree of vagueness score, therefore, corresponds to few or no correct responses for Symptoms and one or more vague responses.

beliefs are believed, in part, to relate to learning and personal experience. This study indicates that the gay sample is more informed than is the nongay sample ($p = .001$). The gay respondents cite a mean of five sources of information, whereas the nongay respondents cite a mean of three sources of information (see Table 12.4 for all sources of information). These averages in sources of information for the two groups mirror the number of correct responses for each group. Yet, although a relationship is noted between number of information sources and number of correct responses in the gay sector (R = 0.478), their correlation in the nongay sector is low (R = 0.186). These findings show that the number of information sources is not a key factor influencing the formation of EMs.

The number of the information sources cited, however, is important in correctness of beliefs about AIDS. A stronger relationship between correctness and information sources is demonstrated by comparing specific information sources to correct responses. For example, *Time* and *Newsweek* are cited by 46.6% of respondents as sources of information; yet these two sources have no relationship to the number of correct responses. Another publication source frequently cited among the gay sample, *The Advocate* magazine, also has a negligible effect on the number of correct responses. The only significant source of information ($p < .05$) in informing gay and nongay respondents about AIDS is physicians (see Table 12.5 for results). Two additional sources of information, friends ($p = .089$) and attendance at Dallas Gay Alliance meetings on AIDS ($p = .107$), show trends toward correctly informing respondents. Nonmedia sources, therefore, rank highest among specific sources in determining congruence of lay EMs to the professional EM: no single publication source has an impact on congruence of responses.

Explanatory models often include notions about prevention or notions that one should alter one's lifestyle in response to either symptoms or the threat of AIDS. Here the impact of AIDS is greater on the gay sample, in

TABLE 12.4. Frequency of Information Sources Cited by Respondents

Sources	Frequency
Media Sources	
Local Newspapers	24
News Magazines	20
Nonspecific Magazines	6
Professional Journals	3
Local Gay Press	16
National Gay Press	10
AIDS Pamphlets	2
Television	19
Radio	5
Nonmedia Sources	
Friends	10
Dallas Gay Alliance Meetings	10
Physician	6
Counselors	2

TABLE 12.5. Comparison of Physician as a Source of Information to Number of Correct Responses

| Physician | Number of Correct Responses (Maximum = 15) | |
	Less than 8	8 or More
Cited	1	5
Not Cited	16	7

which an average of three changes per individual in their lifestyle due to AIDS are cited, although such notions were negligible among the nongay sample. The reason for the negligible effect on the nongay sample is that AIDS is almost uniformly perceived as a disease affecting gay men. For example, one nongay respondent noted, "Candidly I don't think I'll ever be affected by it. . . it's a homosexual disease."

Concern in the low-risk groups (e.g., nongays and gay women) include:

. . . if I knew someone had AIDS, I would not give him a hug or kiss, just like if someone had diphtheria (gay female).

. . . I worry about blood tranfusions (nongay male).

I would be scared and very worried if AIDS flows over to the general public (nongay female).

The range in the number of effects on one's lifestyle as well as reasons cited are greater among the gay sample. One respondent, a gay male with ARC, listed eight changes in his lifestyle since his diagnosis. One change, the number of sexual partners, is frequently but variably noted among the gay sample, with the following rationalizations:

> When I think about sex in general, I think about AIDS. . . . I have reduced number of contacts outside my relationship (gay male).

> One relationship per week before AIDS. . . . almost nothing now. . . . AIDS cannot be treated (gay male).

> No outside relationship for the last year because of AIDS. . . . Guess I had AIDS hysteria (gay male).

> Know three people who have died from AIDS. . . . trick with two or three people steadily. . . . Change what I do sexually (gay male).

> No change in the number of partners. . . . Some people have naturally high immune system like me to fight off disease easily (gay male).

Males citing more sexual partners in the year prior to the interview show a slight trend toward listing more changes in lifestyle due to AIDS ($p = .113$). A stronger relationship is noted between the number of preventive measures cited and number of life changes cited ($p = .01$). The nongay respondents believe that they are not at risk for AIDS, therefore they require little or no change in their lifestyles; the gay respondents vary in the degree to which they feel lifestyle changes are necessary.

CONCLUSIONS

All people, both lay and professional, have understandings about symptoms or sickness, including beliefs about etiology, pathophysiology, prognosis, treatment, and prevention. Convergence of such health beliefs or Explanatory Models (EMs) between patients and practitioners is thought to increase effectiveness and satisfaction in clinical practice. Thus, techniques for measuring and increasing congruence may be of great benefit. This is particularly true for AIDS, for which the lack of understanding by both the lay public and health professionals, coupled with the social stigma associated with the group most at risk, makes the understanding of EMs critical for health education programs.

This study, based on personal interviews with 30 informants (16 gay, 14 nongay) to elicit explanatory models for AIDS, reveals that lay EMs for AIDS vary considerably in both degree of elaboration and congruence with professional EMs.

EMs of gay respondents were both more detailed and more congruent with professional EMs than were those of nongay respondents. Gay EMs are particularly noteworthy for their greater accuracy and the number of symptoms described for AIDS, whereas those of the nongay respondents are more vague. Fewer differences between gay and nongay EMs are found in areas of definition, etiology, and treatment. The level of EM congruence, as measured by the number of lay responses corresponding to professional EMs, is influenced by two factors: 1) sexual preference, and 2) sources of information. Members of the high-risk group cite more responses paralleling professional EMs and list more sources of information than does the nongay sector. A content analysis of gay publications reveals that articles on AIDS are contained in almost every issue, whereas AIDS-related articles are only occasionally found in nongay popular literature. Although the availability of such published information is one factor influencing lay EMs, personal communication, particularly with physicians, appears to be more influential in EM congruence. One variable influencing respondents' recognition of "the physician" as a source of information is clearly the fear of acquiring AIDS. The degree to which one sees oneself at risk for acquiring AIDS, a disease acknowledged to be fatal by most respondents, seems to be very influential for seeking accurate information, which thereby assists in producing a more elaborate, congruent EM.

The relationship of EMs to behavior differs for the gay and nongay groups. The gay sector lists more changes in lifestyle due to AIDS. The number of changes in behavior among gay respondents corresponds to elaborateness of EM and number of sexual partners. In contrast, the nongay respondents list few or no changes in lifestyle due to AIDS. At least three variables influence degree of lifestyle modification due to AIDS: 1) the degree to which one sees oneself at risk, 2) if in a high-risk category, the number of sexual partners, and 3) if in a high-risk category, the level of knowledge about AIDS.

If public health programs for educating the lay public about AIDS are to succeed, this study would indicate that individuals who perceive themselves at greatest risk will seek information, and that the best sources of information are physicians or other health professionals, rather than the print media. Findings from this study reveal that even members of the high-risk group are only aware of 30% of the symptoms of AIDS. Health education efforts, therefore, should be aimed at identifying and informing groups at risk, coupled with continuing education for health practitioners, a process that must be ongoing and continuously revised, because our understanding of AIDS is currently in flux.

REFERENCES

Aledort, Louis. 1983. AIDS: An Update. *Hospital Practice* 18(9):159–171. September.

Bush, Larry. 1983. Coping with a Crisis—Action and Reaction—The Community Responds to a Serious Health Problem. *Advocate* 361:19–54.

D'Eramo, James. 1984. Discovering the Cause of AIDS: An Interview with Dr. Robert C. Gallo. *New York Native* 97:16–19.

Dowdle, Walter. 1983. The Epidemiology of AIDS. *Public Health Reports* 98(4): 308–318.

Durack, David. 1981. Opportunistic Infections and Kaposi's Sarcoma in Homosexual Males. *New England Journal of Medicine* 305(24):1465–1467.

Fain, Nathan. 1983. Coping with a Crisis—AIDS—and the Issues It Raises. *Advocate* 361:15–54.

Gallo, Robert. 1984. Frequent Detection and Isolation of Cytopathic Retroviruses (HTLV-III) from Patients with AIDS and at Risk for AIDS. *Science* 224:500–502.

GMHC (Gay Men's Health Crisis, Inc.). 1983. *AIDS: What You Should Know About Our Health Emergency* (brochure). New York: GMHC.

Goffman, Erving. 1963. *Stigma*. Englewood Cliffs, N.J.: Prentice-Hall.

Kleinman, Arthur, 1978. Culture, Illness, and Care: Clinical Lessons from Anthropologic and Cross-Cultural Research. *Annals of Internal Medicine* 68(2):251–258.

————. 1980. *Patients and Healers in the Context of Culture*. Berkeley and Los Angeles: University of California Press.

————. 1982. Clinically Applied Anthropology on a Psychiatric Consultation-Liaison Service. In *Clinically Applied Anthropology*, N. Chrisman and W. Maretzki, eds., pp. 83–115. Boston: Reidel.

Levin, L. and E. Idler. 1981. *The Hidden Health Care System*. Cambridge: Ballinger, pp. 1–54.

Mildvan, Donna et al. 1982. Opportunistic Infections and Immune Deficiency in Homosexual Men. *Annals of Internal Medicine* 96(6, Part 1): 700–4.

Rosenstock, I. M. 1974. The Health Belief Model and Preventive Health Behavior. *Health Education Monograph* 2(4):354–386.

Taussig, Michael. 1980. Reification and the Consciousness of the Patient. *Social Science and Medicine* 14:3–13.

Young, Allan. 1982. The Anthropology of Illness and Sickness. *Annual Reviews in Anthropology* 11:257–285.

Chapter Thirteen

Fear of AIDS and Its Effects on the Nation's Blood Supply

Peter L. Callero, David V. Baker, Jeannette Carpenter, and Jane Magarigal

In a 1983 meeting of the nation's mayors, Margaret Heckler, the United States Secretary of Health and Human Services, stated that the discovery of the cause and cure of acquired immunodeficiency syndrome (AIDS) is the government's number-one health priority. In the same speech, Secretary Heckler made a very important observation when she noted that this disease has two names: one is AIDS, and the other is *fear*. Although the actual physical symptoms of the disease may touch a relatively small percentage of the population, the psychological effects of fear are far reaching and potentially limitless.

This paper is concerned with one particular consequence of the AIDS fear; namely, its effects on the donation habits of the nation's volunteer blood donors. Although AIDS may be contracted through blood *transfusions*, no evidence exists to show that blood *donors* are susceptible to contracting the disease. This fact, however, is apparently not well known by the general public. A national Roper poll conducted in August 1983 found 26% of the respondents mentioning "blood donation" in response to an open-ended question asking about the cause of AIDS.[1] In terms of blood collection, the implications of such a misconception are great. In fact, blood collection officials are concerned that the mistaken belief that AIDS is linked to blood donation has contributed to recently experienced shortages in the nation's blood supply (Mann 1983).

---

[1]Reported in the *American Red Cross Observer*, October 1, 1983.

If the fear of AIDS is affecting the nation's supply of blood, and short-ages worsen, then hospitals may begin to perform only the most vital types of surgery (Mann 1983:72). No empirical research, however, has been designed to directly examine the question of whether or not fear of AIDS is actually a factor in individual decisions to voluntarily donate blood. The research reported here examines this question for a sample of blood donors who participated in a telephone interview in March of 1984.

METHODOLOGY

The study population consisted of all individuals who were registered as donors at the Riverside, California donation center of the Blood Bank of San Bernardino and Riverside Counties. The Riverside center is the only permanent blood collection facility in the city of Riverside (population 174,000) and resembles any typical donation center. The center averages about 175 donations during the approximately 30 hours per week that it is open. Between January of 1983, when AIDS first began receiving sustained national exposure, and March of 1984, when this study was conducted, of-ficials did not notice any major decline in the rate of donation at the center; however, some slow periods worried officials.

Subjects were selected by taking a systematic random sample of donor records from the donation center files. In order to ensure a large enough sample of subjects who had not donated since January of 1983, the sample was stratified by date of most recent donation. The final sample, excluding ineligibles (i.e., those no longer able to donate and those who had moved outside the region), consisted of 43 subjects who had not donated since January of 1983, 92 subjects whose most recent donation was sometime after January 1983, and 8 subjects who were unsure. Sixty percent of the sample was male, which corresponds to both local and national percen-tages, and two subjects, when contacted by phone, refused to participate, yielding a 99% response rate.

The interview itself was designed to be as brief as possible and con-sisted of seven questions answered in a Yes–No–Don't-Know format.[2] The average interview took five minutes to complete after which all subjects were given full and correct information concerning AIDS.

RESULTS

The distribution of responses to all questions is presented in Table 13.1. As

---

[2]The interview was deliberately designed to be as brief as possible so as to not alienate donors from the donation center.

the table indicates, all subjects responded in the affirmative when asked whether or not they had heard or read about AIDS. Given the massive media exposure and the fact that all donors had recently been required to read a statement describing AIDS and its high-risk groups, this finding is not at all surprising.

TABLE 13.1. Distribution of Responses to All Questions

		Yes	No	Don't Know
1.	Have you heard or read anything at all about the disease called AIDS?	100%	0%	0%
2.	Have you heard or read anything that suggests there is a connection between donating blood and getting AIDS?	47.6%	49%	3.5%
3.	Do you personally believe that you can get AIDS from donating blood?	12.6%	72.7%	14.7%
4.	Think back to the last time you considered giving blood. At that time did you think about the possibility of getting AIDS?	2.1%	97.9%	0%
5.	Now we would like to know if the fear of getting AIDS has caused you to *not give blood* at any time in the past?	2.1%	97.9%	0%
6.	At this time do you plan on donating blood sometime during the next six months?	75.5%	21%	3.5%

What is less expected, however, is that 47.6% of the donors said they had heard or read about a connection between getting AIDS and donating blood. Furthermore, 13% of the donors said that they actually believed that they could get AIDS from donating. Looked at in another way, of the 48% that had heard or read of the connection, 22% said they believed it.

Of the donors who said that they believed in the connection between AIDS and blood donation, none said that they actually thought about AIDS when they last considered whether or not to donate. Similarly, none of the believers said that the fear of AIDS had actually caused them to stop donating. Three donors, or approximately 2% of the total sample, did say, however, that they thought about getting AIDS when last deciding whether or not to donate. Moreover, the same three said that they actually did not donate because of the fear, but none of the three said that they believed in the connection (two said they did not believe in it and one was uncertain).

As a further examination of this issue, a number of contingency table analyses were run to determine if those who had not donated since January 1, 1983, differed on any relevant questions from those who had donated since that date. Results revealed no statistically significant differences between the two groups of donors ($p > .05$). Both groups were just as likely to say that they had heard or read of the AIDS-donation link and were just as likely to say that they believed in it.[3]

As can be seen in Table 13.1, 21% of the sample said that they did not plan to donate blood again within the next six months. Therefore, a second set of contingency table analyses were run to see if these subjects were any more likely to have heard of the connection or to believe in it. Again, however, no statistically significant differences were found.

Finally, a third series of analyses were conducted to determine whether or not men and women differed in their responses to any of the questions. These results also indicated no statistically significant differences. Men and women were just as likely to say they had heard of the AIDS-blood donation link, were equally as unlikely to believe it, and reported having similar future plans.

DISCUSSION

In addition to its catastrophic effects on the health and life of thousands of individuals, AIDS is also having widespread psychosocial effects on the population as a consequence of the fear that it has generated. One particularly troublesome, and potentially devastating, consequence of this fear is the possibility that it is adversely affecting the nation's supply of voluntarily donated blood. Blood collection officials suspect that recent drops in the donation rate are linked to erroneous beliefs that people can contract AIDS through blood donation.

On the face of it, these results seem very encouraging. Although almost 50% of the donors sampled said that they had heard or read that it is possible to get AIDS from donating blood, only 13% believe this to be true, and only 2% said that they refrained from donating because of this possibility. Moreover, donors who had not donated in over a year have apparently not been affected by the AIDS fear, and donors who have no immediate plans to donate are apparently not basing their decisions on a fear of AIDS. Only a very small percentage of donors appear to be refraining because of the belief that they may contract AIDS if they continue to donate.

---

[3]Because only three donors responded in the Yes category to Questions 4 and 5, contingency table analyses involving these two questions are not appropriate. Similarly, because no variation at all exists on Question 1, analyses with this variable would not make any sense.

As a note of caution, however, we emphasize the restricted generalizability of these findings. Although no obvious differences exist between blood donors in Riverside, California, and donors in other regions of the country, we cannot safely generalize outside of the Riverside area. A second limitation that we note is that this study focused only on individuals who had donated at least once before. Although the majority of blood is collected from return donors, new donors must continually be recruited. We cannot say from this study whether or not the AIDS–blood donation misconception is affecting recruitment of new donors. To the degree that recruitment of new donors is hindered, the effects of fear on the blood supply will be larger than this study suggests.

In addition, a very important point that cannot be ignored when discussing the overall influence of AIDS on the nation's blood supply is the fact that individuals who fall into the high-risk categories are being asked to refrain from donating blood. If we assume that individuals in these high-risk groups are distributed in the blood donor population in the same proportions that they are found in the general population, then, a very significant amount of blood can no longer be counted on. Such a loss may be especially large in major metropolitan areas where high-risk groups are more prevalent.

Although the total effect of the fear of AIDS seem to be rather limited now, the potential for a much larger problem remains. That most donors had some sense of uncertainty about the issue became quite clear in post-interview discussions with respondents. Even those donors who said they did not believe that AIDS could be contracted from donating blood were not totally confident of the "accuracy" of their answer. As long as the general public is not informed otherwise, such uncertainty cannot be expected to decrease. In fact, given the general scientific uncertainty that surrounds the disease, ill-founded fears regarding AIDS may likely grow. Although 50% of the donors had not heard of an AIDS–blood donation link at the time of the interview, one can only expect such misinformation to spread. An important question, then, is how many individuals will stop donating when they do hear about an AIDS–blood donation link?

From a sociological point of view, the general uncertainty and fear surrounding AIDS is equivalent to a potential explosion: all the necessary materials for an episode of collective behavior characterized as a "mass fear" are on hand (Lofland 1981). Such collective action is not usually based in crowds but results from collectively held beliefs (in this case, false beliefs), which indicate danger and spread quickly over a rather short time. Mass fear can quite possibly develop around the AIDS–blood donation link. If it does, the behavioral consequences could be devastating. Although such a mass fear would not likely affect the entire U.S. population, certain regional blood collection centers could be hard hit.

In summary, there are two ways in which the nation's blood supply could be affected by the false belief that AIDS may be contracted from donating blood. First by a long-lasting but relatively small loss of donors due to a sustained misconception; this is apparently occurring now. Second is an episode of mass fear. This loss would probably be regionally limited and would not have any long-term consequences; but it would involve a very large percentage of donors.

REFERENCES

Lofland, John F. 1981. Collective Behavior: The Elementary Forms. In *Social Psychology: Social Perspectives*, M. Rosenberg and R. Turner, eds. New York: Basic Books.

Mann, James. 1983. As AIDS Scare Hits Nation's Blood Supply. *U.S. News and World Report* July 25.

PART VI
IMPACT OF AIDS ON HEALTH CARE DELIVERY

Chapter Fourteen

Hospice Staff Response to Fear of AIDS

Sally Geis and Ruth Fuller

INTRODUCTION

A hospice tries to provide a way for people with terminal illness to die with
dignity (Saunders 1983). The hospice movement began as a volunteer
response to the negative aspects of hospital care. Hospice care is directed
toward returning control to the individual who is facing imminent death by
offering choices through teaching and anticipatory guidance for the patient
and family. Care is palliative and is directed toward the relief of symptoms
in order to enable patients to direct their energies toward goals that they
have set and toward achieving a heightened sense of dignity and self-worth.

An interdisciplinary team is responsible for the assessment, intervention, and evaluation of hospice care for each family. The team includes
physicians, primary-care nurses, home health attendants, social workers,
ergy, nutritionists, psychiatric consultants, trained volunteers, and other
lividual therapists as needed. Hospice care is available 24 hours a day,
seven days a week. It provides an alternative for traditional hospital treatment of the terminally ill (Benoliel 1982; Corr and Corr 1983; Hamilton and
Reid 1980; McNulty and Holderby 1983; Rossman 1977).

Some hospices provide a special place in which patients are housed and
receive in-patient care. Other hospices provide care and support services for
patients who want to continue to live at home as long as possible and patients
who want to die at home. All hospices strive to implement the belief that, as
far as they are able to, dying people should be in control of their lives, including their care, treatment, environment, and activities (Wentzel 1981).

People with AIDS have died in hospice care. This report is a description of various hospice staff responses to patients with AIDS. This report does not describe urban areas with large populations of AIDS patients. Rather, it is concerned with communities that are receiving a small but growing number of people with AIDS. The four hospices included are located in Midwestern states with relatively few AIDS cases in June 1984; New York and California accounted for about 65% of all cases in the United States at that time (Centers for Disease Control 1984).

Material was drawn from all four hospices, some of which offer home care and others hospital care. The settings are not described individually; they are treated as a composite, ideal type. This report raises issues about staff fear of contagion that are worthy of consideration by other hospices and community groups that care for people with AIDS. Differences were found among the four hospices, but this paper shall be concerned with their commonalities.

ASSUMPTIONS

ASSUMPTION 1. *Readers will tend to distance themselves from the experiences described here.*

We caution health care personnel not to dismiss this account by saying, "It could not happen here." The hospices that participated in this study are well run. So far as we can ascertain, no person with AIDS or his "family" (biological family or nonsexual [gay] community family) failed to receive competent care. Do not assume that these problems could occur only in a poorly run facility staffed by insensitive people. Because they occurred in well-run facilities they deserve attention.

ASSUMPTION 2. *Individuals and groups of individuals are unique but share some similarities.*

Even though all patients in these four hospices are young, gay men, no two patients are identical. Similarly, no two hospice staff members are exactly alike. Some patients and some hospice staff members may have experiences that are very different from any reported in this data collection. Because people tend to stereotype individuals and groups unfamiliar to them, caution should be used in generalizing too widely from this report. Some hospice personnel reported being affected little, if at all, by the issues discussed here, but most were affected significantly; many were affected deeply.

METHODOLOGY

Data were obtained by both observation and structured interviews. Observations were made at hospice in-service sessions, staffing meetings, and training sessions in all four hospices. A structured interview, lasting one-and-one-half to two hours, was administered to 15 hospice staff members. The observations were conducted from August 1983 to August 1984. The interviews were conducted in one hospice over a four-week period in June and July 1984. Staff members included physicians, gay community representatives, chaplains, social workers, nurses, home health aides, and hospice administrators.

FINDINGS

The admission of people with AIDS caused both fear and confusion for staff members. The fear was a result of the characteristics of the disease itself. At the time of the study the cause of the disease was unknown. The incubation period was long (believed at that time to be perhaps one-and-one-half to two years), the assumption of contagion was real. Finally, and most importantly, the expectation that contracting the disease would be fatal was also real (Conte et al. 1983; Solomon 1984). The fact that no health care worker had yet contracted the disease was not totally reassuring to the staff members assigned to work with a person with AIDS, no matter how thorough were the in-service sessions concerning protocol.

The confusion was caused by the fear. When staff members discovered that they were fearful of contagion and death, they were not comfortable with their feelings. People who work within a hospice are not unduly afraid of the atmosphere that surrounds a terminal illness, but most terminal illnesses with which they work are not contagious.

People, of course, tend to be less afraid of something familiar than of something unknown. Hospice workers have a great deal of experience with dying patients and their families. The intensity of staff involvement varies from patient to patient, but a pervasive feeling of fear is not common among hospice personnel. The smells and sounds of death are familiar. The pains and anxieties experienced by patients and families are stressful but expected by staff members. The final emptiness and/or rage that frequently follows death is also a familiar experience (McNulty and Holderby 1983; Saunders 1983).

An experienced staff was both surprised and disappointed to find that fear and uneasiness began to pervade the work environment after a person with AIDS was accepted. Hospice staff members thought that they had resolved their fear of contagious, fatal diseases, even fatal diseases of unknown cause, before they decided to become a part of the health-care profession. Their individual decisions to become hospice staff members had required further self-examination about their attitudes toward death.

Furthermore, fearfulness is not a professional image that any hospice staff member can publicly project. This strain between ideology and behavior created problems for both administrators and for staff members working directly with patients. Individuals had to cope by negotiating themselves out of this dilemma.

Coping with Fear

One way to cope with an unpleasant reality is to pretend it does not exist (Freud 1966). A number of administrators told us that fear simply did not exist. Interviews with their staff members indicated that it did.

Hospice staff and administrators were asked, Were you comfortable with the medical protocol used? How do you think other people felt about the protocol?

Selected responses are:

> Our medical director assured us that hepatitis B precautions were completely adequate for handling AIDS patients. Our staff is well trained and professional. They are used to handling contagious disease.

> We had specialists from the Centers for Disease Control instruct our staff. There may have been a little concern before those meetings, but after that everyone felt completely reassured.

In response to the same two interview questions, staff members caring for patients admitted being fearful. Some respondents apologized for being afraid or indicated that their fearfulness had been a temporary situation that was no longer a problem.

Selected responses from the staff to the questions asked are:

> I suppose the protocol was all right, but there were still lots of questions I had when I went to see the patient. I was really glad he didn't offer to shake hands with me or give me something to eat or drink. He knew I was scared. Later it was OK.

> I remember the first time I went to see the patient very, very well. When I got home I threw all my clothes in the wash. I knew it wasn't rational, but I couldn't help it.

> One day the patient's housemate gave me a little box of candy he had made. I know it's silly, but I couldn't eat it. I threw it away when I got home . . . and you know I've never told anybody about that; it seems so silly.

> The first time I went to see the patient I tried to be cool. I brought us some lunch. I thought he'd think I wasn't afraid if we, oh you know, if

> we "broke bread together," so to speak. While we were eating he started
> to cough real bad, and I jumped up to help him. There I was with a
> sandwich in one hand and my other hand on this patient, and I was
> thinking, "Oh, boy, what do I do now?"

Some administrators found it impossible to recognize or acknowledge
staff fears. Such acknowledgment was viewed as a potentially damaging
reflection on administrative competence. It was also viewed as a threat to
the hospice's image and credibility in the community.

An erosion of public confidence could pose a threat to funding and, to
a lesser extent, to job security. Anyone who spoke openly about fear or the
inadequacy of the medical protocol was therefore viewed as a threat,
sometimes even as a traitor, to the cause of the hospice movement.

Selected responses by administrators to the question, What impact has
this patient care experience had on staff relationships? were:

> Well, I certainly hope it hasn't had any impact. I'll admit there were a
> few problems, but on any staff you have a few people who keep raising
> questions when there really isn't anything to be worried about.

> We did have one staff person who seemed really upset about how this
> case was handled, but fortunately he isn't with us anymore.

Another way for staff members to negotiate the conflict with administrators is to assume that the problem was their own personal problem
rather than an institutional problem (Mills 1959).

When asked, Did your feelings about the hospice change because of
this experience?, two direct care providers answered:

> I hate to say this. But yes. I was really scared, and when I tried to talk
> about it to any of the supervisors they just told me I was being unprofes-
> sional. I guess I was.

> I think I was too idealistic. I used to think hospice people helped each
> other, but when I'd try to tell somebody that I didn't feel like we knew
> enough about procedures and I was scared they'd tell me to be quiet or
> I'd upset everybody else. I suppose that's right, we had to take care of
> the patient.

When asked, How did you handle your own feelings?, another direct-
care provider answered:

> I had a hard time about that. I never, ever talked to people on the out-
> side about my patients before. But nobody at the hospice would talk to

me about being afraid. So I have this friend I really trust, and I'd talk to her a lot. Sometimes I'd just call and cry. But don't misunderstand me, there are some wonderful people at the hospice. This was just a very hard situation.

Coping with Conflicting Values

Some feelings of discomfort felt by staff members were created by conflicts between their professional values and their personal or family values. Professional values dictate that health care workers are obligated to care for all patients regardless of the circumstances (Fuller 1985). At the same time, family and personal values require that a health care worker, who may also be a spouse and a parent, has an obligation to protect herself or himself from serious health risks. The perceived risk is to both the individual's health and life and to the health and lives of the individual's family.

Examples of comments made by staff members in conversation during observations within hospice settings are:

I might have taken that case if it weren't for my family. My husband said I had no right to take that chance with our family.

I'm no hero. I certainly wouldn't have taken the case if I were pregnant.

I figured that since I'm single and gay I should probably take it, instead of making somebody with kids do it.

In our limited sample, such values took priority over professional values.

DISCUSSION

The acceptance of people with AIDS, a potentially fatal, contagious disease, presented hospice personnel with value conflicts that they thought had been resolved years earlier. The intensity and pain of these ethical dilemmas were especially difficult for hospice personnel who, by their very commitment to hospice work, felt that they had clarified their values by their commitment to, and experience in, hospice work. Now they had to reexamine their earlier choices.

In order to understand the hospice personnel responses to the AIDS care experience we turned to human behavior theorists. From Sigmund Freud (1953) and Anna Freud (1966) came an explanation of ways in which the mind protects itself against the distress of intense feelings. For example, the staff worker who threw all her clothes in the wash after visiting the person with AIDS described the irresistible but "irrational" need to *do* something that would decrease her anxiety. She and others like her should be reassured that their actions are normal.

We sought an explanation for the many interviewees who reported that they "went through the motions" of care giving, but that they were so overwhelmed by their own fear that they could hardly perform necessary tasks (e.g., the nurse who held her sandwich in one hand but had to help the coughing patient and thought, "Oh boy, what do I do now?"). We drew upon Weber's (1957) concept of *Verstehen,* his suggestion that behavior has subjective meaning that includes not only what people do but also how they *feel* and what they think about what they do.

The mutual influence of the environment on the individual and the individual on the environment were described by Hartmann (1958) and add insight into the AIDS care dilemma. The hospice environment demanded that the nurse perform "professionally," but her fear influenced both her performance and the environment within which patient care took place. As she said, "the patient knew I was scared."

Supervisors of AIDS caregivers need to be aware of both the phenomenon described here and the psychosocial explanations for it. When staff members are almost overwhelmed by feelings and fears, they need psychological support as badly as they need instructions about following the medical protocol.

Other theoretical insights helped explain the reasons for which hospice personnel were embarrassed by their fears and irrational thoughts. Sumner (1940), and, later, Vidich and Bensman (1968), observed that a "strain toward consistency" exists among members of a group who are playing by the same rules. Sometimes the rules are not easy to follow because they contradict one another. In AIDS care, a number of socially accepted rules contradicted each other. For example, one unspoken but important rule states that hospice staff are to help one another. On the other hand, hospice staff are supposed to keep their personal fears to themselves and not upset other staff members, patients, or patients' families. People caught in that contradiction usually ended their description of their distress with phrases like, "I guess I was being unprofessional," or, "I guess I was silly."

In fact, they were neither unprofessional nor silly. They were trying to integrate severely dissonant dimensions of the work atmosphere. We believe it unfortunate that they found it necessary to accept personal blame for their inability to "make sense" out of their actions and their feelings.

Mills (1959) described the tendency of society to encourage people to treat difficult public conflicts as if they were personal problems. In spite of the fact that AIDS is a growing health problem, society as a whole does not want to deal with AIDS. It tends to isolate both the patients and their caregivers. Isolation only adds to the difficulty of coping with fear; it does not solve problems for either the staff or the patients.

CONCLUSION

Some hospices will not admit people with AIDS, and others have difficulty finding staff who will care for AIDS patients.[1] The four hospices involved in this study were similar in that they all admitted AIDS patients. The care was not identical in all facilities. Each hospice had some problems that were met with varying degrees of success.

The facilities that participated in this study have on-going support programs, usually in the form of interdisciplinary team meetings, that allow time for discussion of issues affecting caregivers as well as discussion of patient/family needs. Staff support has always been an issue of concern in the administration of hospices. However, AIDS presents problems that require additional attention to the needs of caregivers. Astute and supportive supervision is essential when caregivers are faced with situations that raise fears and value conflicts.

REFERENCES

Benoliel, Jeanne Quint. 1982. *Death Education for the Health Professional.* New York: Hemisphere Publishing Co.

Centers for Disease Control (CDC). 1984. *Acquired Immunodeficiency Syndrome Weekly Surveillance Report–United States.* Atlanta: CDC. June 4.

Conte, John E. et al. 1983. Infection Control Guidelines for Patients with the Acquired Immunodeficiency Syndrome (AIDS). *New England Journal of Medicine* 309 (12):740–744.

Corr, Charles and Donna Corr (eds.). 1983. *Hospice Care: Principles and Practices.* New York: Springer.

Freud, Anna. 1966. The Ego and the Mechanisms of Defense. In *The Writings of Anna Freud,* Vol. 2. New York: International Universities Press.

Freud, Sigmund. 1953. *The Complete Psychological Works of Sigmund Freud* (James Strachey, ed.). London: Hogarth Press.

Fuller, Ruth L. 1985. The Participants in the Doctor-Patient Relationship. In *Understanding Human Behavior in Health and Illness,* 3rd ed., Simons, Richard C. and Pardes, Herbert, eds. Baltimore: Williams & Wilkins.

---

[1]These comments were made after a presentation by Geis, Luke, and Holbrook at a National Hospice Organization workshop.

Gottlieb, Michael S. et al. 1983. The Acquired Immunodeficiency Syndrome: UCLA Conference Proceedings. *Annals of Internal Medicine* 99: 208–220.

Hamilton, Michael and Helen Reid (eds.). 1980. *A Hospice Handbook: a New Way to Care for the Dying.* Grand Rapids, Mich.: William Eerdmans Publishing Co.

Hartmann, Heinz. 1958. *Ego Psychology and the Problems of Adaptation.* New York: International Universities Press.

McNulty, Elizabeth and Robert Holderby. 1983. *Hospice: A Caring Challenge.* Springfield, Ill.: C. C. Thomas.

Mills, C. Wright. 1959. *The Sociological Imagination.* New York: Oxford University Press.

Rossman, Parker. 1977. *Hospice: Creating New Models of Care for the Terminally Ill.* New York: Association Press.

Saunders, Cicely and Mary Barnes. 1983. *Living with Dying, the Management of Terminal Disease.* New York: Oxford University Press.

Solomon, Steven L. 1984. AIDS, Risk of Transmission to Medical Care Workers. *Journal of the American Medical Association* 251 (3): 397.

Sumner, William Graham. 1940. *Folkways.* Boston: Binn & Co. (originally published in 1906).

Vidich, Arthur J. and Joseph Bensman. 1968. *Small Town in Mass Society.* Princeton: Princeton University Press.

Weber, Max. 1957. *The Theory of Social and Economic Organization* (translated by A. A. Henderson and Talcott Parsons). New York: The Free Press (originally published in 1925).

Wentzel, Kenneth B. 1981. *To Those Who Need It Most Hospice Means Hope.* Boston: Charles Riber Books.

Chapter Fifteen

Ideology and Politics in the Control of Contagion:
The Social Organization of AIDS Care

Roberta Lessor and Katarin Jurich

Acquired immunodeficiency syndrome (AIDS) is a contagious disease currently of epidemic proportions in several major cities of the United States. Although AIDS presents a public health risk primarily to circumscribed groups, principally sexually active homosexual (gay) men and intravenous-drug users, the precise risk to medical personnel caring for people with AIDS at this time (January 1985) remains unknown. In instances for which medicine becomes interlinked with a social problem, as in the case of AIDS, clinicians and researchers are reminded that biomedical information is being redefined in the larger world. The need to grapple with the social problem as part of medical reality opens the way for redefinitions of contagion risk that override traditional biomedical conceptions. Thus, risk definition and risk management in the work organization may conform more to ideological and political realities than to biomedical possibilities.

MEDICAL UNIT FOR PEOPLE WITH AIDS
AT A LARGE HOSPITAL

In July 1983, an AIDS Unit was initiated at a large hospital in the western United States. The question immediately arose, How were the people who had chosen to do AIDS work handling the problem of risk? These persons' health risk was apparently enmeshed in what was considered a public health threat by most citizens (*USA Today* 1983). The news media frequently reported that people with AIDS had been evicted from their homes, thrown out of jury boxes, and fired from their jobs as fear of the spread of

245

the fatal disease grew (Gallup 1983; *San Francisco Examiner* 1983; Wood 1983). The public felt at risk, and so did apparently many health professionals. In the city where the hospital is located, fire fighters expressed reluctance to make routine inspections in apartment buildings of persons alleged to have AIDS, and several nurses and physicians refused to care for people with AIDS.[1] But three groups definitely wanted to be involved in AIDS work: research physicians, a group of nurses at the hospital, and many persons in the gay community.

Medical researchers at first did little to discourage the public's concern over AIDS. They admittedly used public sentiment to garner support for research funding. Few citizens could object to money being spent to find the cause and cure of the disease that seemed to spread so quickly. Furthermore, researchers had a stake in the formation of a unit, because drug treatment in confirmed cases of AIDS could more reliably be conducted in a setting solely devoted to AIDS care.

The gay community was anxious to see care provided to patients who had been made pariahs in many hospitals; many patients could no longer pay for care due to job and health insurance loss. To gays, AIDS was an issue of personal concern that demanded practical attention. Providing funding for AIDS care in the city where the hospital is located offered the city government a chance to gain popular support from the gay community. Gay men employed at the hospital, physicians, nurses, and social workers, many of whom had never been politically active, were coming face to face with the devastation of AIDS and lobbied for establishing an AIDS unit within the hospital.

A third group was the hospital nurses who saw the opportunity to establish a nurse-run unit that could emphasize counseling, health teaching, and preparation for self-care after discharge. Nurses saw the AIDS unit as an opportunity to test such a nursing model because their attempts to establish a unit elsewhere in the hospital had been frustrated. Like many city hospitals across the country, the hospital was short staffed and morale had been poor since the fiscal austerity imposed by "New Federalism." A unit staffed exclusively by registered nurses (RNs), with a high nurse:patient ratio, that would become the hub of an envisioned network of community

---

[1]From May through July 1983, Lessor collected data in interviews with civil service and hospital workers in a pilot study for the investigation reported here. However, we first became aware of "AIDS anxiety" during an earlier study of employee conceptions of occupational health (conducted from October 1982 to April 1983). When questioned as to their greatest on-the-job health concerns, hospital workers frequently listed exposure to hepatitis B and to AIDS as a "new worry." Nurses explained that they had previously worried most about psychological burnout or back injury, or in many instances chemical exposure, but not contagion. We thank Barbara Burgel for her comprehensive field notes on this subject.

care seemed ideal. Thirty-six nurses volunteered for the 12 available positions.

The medical researchers, the nurses, and the gay community advanced their proposed solutions to the problem of AIDS by realizing the wish of the public and the hospital administration to isolate and confine the problem. The twelve-bed unit opened and rapidly filled with very sick patients.

THE FIELD-STUDY METHOD

During the first nine months of its existence, we observed the specialized AIDS ward and conducted on-site interviews with staff. Our aim, which was to discern the *social* aspects of risk management apart from the biomedical or even the psychological aspects, dictated an anthropological fieldwork design. We attended weekly interdisciplinary staff conferences in which medical, nursing, and social care of patients was reviewed and planned, listened to change-of-shift reports, interviewed staff members in groups, and held numerous informal discussions with nurses, physicians, counselors, hospice workers, hospice visitors and with patients and their loved ones. In conducting formal interviews, the twelve full-time registered nurses working on the unit were interviewed in depth. The interviews were open-ended and each nurse was encouraged to talk freely about his or her experience. Several areas of questioning were consistently included: previous work history, factors involved in the choice to work on the AIDS unit, nature of discussions with friends and family during the choice process, personal assessment of health risks on the AIDS unit, sources of information consulted, and assessment of public opinion and of the opinion of professionals in non-AIDS work. We inquired about their work on the unit and elicited descriptions of interactions with colleagues and with patients. A number of questions were asked regarding self-care and personal health. Topics raised by the interviewees were explored, as were aspects of daily ward activity that arose during the course of the study.

We also observed the evolving patterns of practice of the research physicians. Contrary to the norm in academic medical research, physicians specializing in the investigation of AIDS treatment become actively engaged in clinical practice. Thus, when we began to hear a great deal about collaborative practice in our interviews with nurses, we turned to the physicians with more specific inquiries regarding the work they did with nurses. Similarly, as the AIDS ward (and the field study) matured, other interactants came to the forefront; we found we needed to talk with hospice workers and volunteer counselors and with the public health nurses associated with the ward in order for us to put together a coherent picture of the work effort. We concurrently observed two other hospitals in which people with AIDS were cared for in a general medical ward and in an oncology ward. In these other settings, providers were as isolated as their patients and we wanted to compare their work to that done as part of an organized effort at the hospital. These techniques are aspects of the grounded-theory methodology known as theoretical sampling (Glaser 1978; Glaser and Strauss 1967): that is, "paying special attention to selected data-yielding events, chosen on the basis of an emerging theory—a theory which evolves from the outset of the research project and is modified continually throughout its entire course" (Strauss et al. 1982).

In discussions with individuals, our emphasis was on discerning the work done in this unique situation: the type of work, the division of labor, the ways in which the workers dealt with the ever-present public and institutional scrutiny of their efforts, and the demands presented by the unfolding situation. Our reasons for this were both sociological and ethical. In the first place, despite the public interest in who "would want to work in a ward full of dying gay men" (Shilts 1984), motivational inquiry is not particularly fruitful. The fact of the matter is that we discerned no common "psychological" pattern that brought nurses or others to the AIDS ward. The personal reasons encompass everything from obtaining particular working conditions (or even getting work at all in the current hospital nursing cutbacks), to learning new skills, to actualizing a personal philosophy, to building a career. Moreover, the individual reasons changed over time in the setting. For nurses, physicians, and other active workers, their careers, like those of people in other occupations, unfolded with the contingencies presented by the situation (Faulkner 1974; Lessor 1984).

The second reason for keeping our sociological eye on the organizational process concerned protecting the privacy of our subjects. To investigate and report the evolution of the first AIDS ward by definition violates anonymity, and we are grateful to our respondents for revealing their experiences so freely to us. We have attempted in this analysis to tie those experiences to generalizable concepts in the study of work; that is, the social psychology, structure, and ideology of work (Berger 1964a; Berger 1964b). Ideology is the particular emphasis in this chapter. In respect to this emphasis, Dingwall and McIntosh have commented that the word "ideology" is in no way pejorative, but rather,

> For the social scientist . . . "ideology" retains its neutrality as a description of a historically and socially situated set of ideas and beliefs which is regarded by those who hold it as a true and adequate explanation of some set of phenomena and as furnishing sufficient grounds for them to plan and execute courses of social action (1978:36).

This was not a *verification* study of "ideological positions" on an AIDS ward. Our method was much more existential in nature, and so our notions of the importance of ideology emerged in the analysis. What we did know at the outset was that the risk of contagion was being addressed in the medical literature with mild reassurances and little certainty (Centers for Disease Control 1983; Department of Health and Human Services 1983), that public perception of health risk was high (Collier and Horowitz 1983), and that homophobia related to AIDS was recognizable (Clavreul 1983).

Finally, in this inquiry by participant observation, we treated our own assumptions about risk as "problematic." A methodological error easily made in the fieldwork is the treating of the frame of reference of one's study as if it were the organizing frame of reference of the participants in the setting. We therefore asked the generic questions, What is the nature of AIDS work? Does it include risk work, and if so, what is its nature? Where does risk fit into the scheme of things?

SOCIOPOLITICAL AND MEDICAL CONTEXTS

The widespread perception of AIDS as not only physical but also social contamination became quickly apparent. Among the public, many people were concerned and could not imagine any reason that health workers would put themselves at risk by working with people with AIDS. Citizens telephoned the nursing staff to ask just that or to say that they thought the nurses were "crazy." The nurses who assumed risk were presumed to be gay. During a network television interview, "non-homosexual nurse" was noted on the screen, underscoring what was presumed to be one nurse's atypical status. If one is already contaminated, one may be presumed to be at lower risk. Thus, the public assumed that primarily gay nurses and physicians would be the ones to work with people with AIDS. Although gay male professionals have been influential, they are by no means the only professionals working with people with AIDS.

The public handed a risky problem to the health professionals who were laying claim to it. Although they felt that the price was high, the public was willing to pay it, because the risk seemed intolerably high. The city allocated $900,000 for the AIDS ward and other public health services. The presence of AIDS influenced distribution of funds within hospitals as well. For example, at the hospital and in several other hospitals, infection control nurses had unsuccessfully tried to obtain disposable syringe and needle units that eliminate broken needles. After the AIDS news stories, the money for the units became available. If the perception of risk had continued to escalate unabated, however, it would have interfered with recruiting, organizing, and getting the work done. This was observed in other departments at the hospital and in two other major hospitals. Although the AIDS experts became "risk administrators" primarily concerned with minimizing the presence of risk, at times they alternatively inflated it. When AIDS slipped from prominence in the news in the fall of 1983, some AIDS workers worried that funding would be lost. (The concern with media coverage was perhaps quite realistic. Feldman [1984] has monitored the frequency of high-risk sexual practices among gay men in New York in relationship to the amount of media coverage of AIDS and has found a significant, positive relationship). Too much risk may be unwieldly for the entire community. When the AIDS epidemic threatened plans for the July 1984 Democratic National Convention or the San Francisco tourist industry, public health officials were obliged to de-escalate the problem. The definition of risk appeared to shift with prevailing political winds.

On a more practical level, this political frame of reference and the periodically rising perception of public risk had implications for the private lives of health care providers. One physician related to us his having to explain to his children that he was not in danger but that people outside the hospital were afraid of contracting the disease because their knowledge of it was limited. Nurses reported having discussed their decision to work in the unit with their families and friends. All had relied primarily on their interpretation of available epidemiological data and anecdotal data from care of people with AIDS in New York for the previous three years.[2] The epidemiological findings used by AIDS workers were predominantly: 1) that AIDS is mainly transmitted through sexual contact involving the contact of semen and blood among males; 2) that it is associated with sexual activity with numerous partners; and 3) that it most often occurs in persons with a history of sexually transmitted diseases and hepatitis. Thus, the gay men working with AIDS patients were able to discount risk by thinking of themselves as not being in the same "high-risk group" that the public perceives. In AIDS care, internal status distinctions exist between healthy, gay male nurses and gay men with AIDS. Nurses, although sympathetic and politically active on behalf of patients, nonetheless characterize patients as "guys who've lived in the fast lane." Gay health providers clearly distinguish between being a gay man and being "actually" at high risk. On the ward, one hears most often in response to questions about risk that "not one health worker who was in a high-risk group has contracted AIDS." This information frequently serves in negotiating with family and friends over acceptable risk levels.

Under certain circumstances, AIDS work can involve social risk such as ostracism by former colleagues. Before the opening of the AIDS ward, a

---

[2]Although AIDS was not reported in the medical literature until 1981, nurses at the hospital were reassured to learn that nurses on the East Coast had safely cared for people with AIDS for periods of time longer than the presumed incubation period of the disease. Nurses shared information informally and in conferences such as those sponsored by the Department of Nursing, National Institutes of Health, Clinical Center, in 1983.

nursing administrator told a story about a nurse on a general medical unit who was walking past a room in which a young man had just had a cardiopulmonary arrest. The arrest was totally unexpected and the ward staff were trying to decide what to do. The nurse, described as very self-assured, went in and began mouth-to-mouth resuscitation. The man had AIDS. Others joined in the "code" (resuscitation) but she was the only one performing mouth-to-mouth. Afterward, other staff told her she should never have done it, and asked her how she could risk herself and her family. Reportedly, their reaction was so upsetting that the nurse took a leave from work, and after she returned, normal relations with her colleagues resumed slowly. In comparative observations in other hospitals, we saw the reluctance of some staff to give physical care to AIDS patients, such as feeding or mouth care. Clavreul (1983) noted similar behaviors among nursing staff in several hospitals.

As the AIDS program began, debate in medical circles centered on the extent to which health care providers may be at physical risk while caring for people with AIDS. The Centers for Disease Control (CDC) in Atlanta issued guidelines for AIDS work similar to those that exist for handling hepatitis B (Centers for Disease Control 1982). Some hospital workers felt that these guidelines provided insufficient protection. At the hospital, pharmacists would not accept return of unused unit dose packages from the AIDS ward; interns reported to the AIDS ward in full protective gear of spacesuit proportions; and phlebotomists refused to draw blood of people who may have had AIDS. The nurses who had elected to work on the ward and the internal medicine physicians who had begun to treat AIDS asserted that the recommended precautions of handwashing and gloving when handling secretions were adequate. These emerging AIDS specialists determined that they were not at risk, and they begun teaching others about the extent of physical risk. Nurses and physicians teamed up to speak to groups in their own hospital and in other hospitals throughout the state. Risk management soon turned into an information and persuasion process.

The health professionals accepted all the help they could get as the number of AIDS patients grew daily. Within a few weeks of opening, the unit rarely had an empty bed. People who had acute infections that their compromised immune systems had not been able to resist were admitted as patients. The medical treatment consists of a three week trial of one of the randomly assigned antibiotics being tested. Early in the patient's illness such treatment is often effective and the patient is able to return to out-patient treatment and self-care until the next episode of infection. Most patients have four or five admissions during the course of their disease, and with each admission the infections are more severe and the patient's response increasingly weak. Although treatment has extended survival time by a few months past the recorded national average, chemotherapy itself creates side effects. As a physician sadly commented in speaking of a patient, "I think we've toxified him with our pentamidine." The reality on the AIDS ward is very harsh: in the first year, nearly 100 of its patients, most of them in their twenties and thirties, died.

SENTIMENTAL WORK AND THE "DISAPPEARANCE" OF CONTAGION

In observing the type of work that claims the preponderance of staff time and attention and the beliefs that support the work, an explanation can be found for what *appears* to be a seeming disregard for contagion risk. The findings of Strauss and associates on sentimental work (1982) and Roth on the social organization of contagion control (1957) provide a theoretical framework for understanding the work of the AIDS unit. Strauss et al. in examining contemporary high technology medical care, defines the task of medical work in social terms. They describe types of interactions that hospital staff members must carry out in addition to the necessary technical tasks, and the ways in which, in many instances, such "sentimental work" is essential to gaining the patient's participation in treatment. They note the roots of the concept of sentimental work in the old notion of the physician's "bedside manner" or the nurse's "tender loving care," but demonstrate that the complexity of developing medical technology necessitates a correspondingly complex range of sentimental work.

If work is often as interactional as it is technical, as Strauss and his colleagues demonstrate, Roth (1957) had earlier shown that getting work done in the hospital may conform more to organizational demands than to biological laws, particularly when such "laws" are not yet completely understood. In his descriptions of contagion control measures in the tuberculosis (TB) hospital, Roth showed that staff employed measures such as gowning and masking when it was convenient to do so and dropped them when the measures presented a barrier to friendly social intercourse with patients (1957:314). He asserted that even if general rules were formulated, major problems would exist in putting them into place if the social context were ignored.

Currently, the humanistic sentimental work (Strauss et al. 1982) and comfort care that staff perform are likely to be more effective than the drug treatment. No cure is known for AIDS. The social stigma already mentioned is combined with physical suffering and severe wasting and disfigurement of young men who prided themselves on their attractive bodies. The treatment itself is arduous. All of these factors complicate the provision of care. For everyone concerned, exposure to the patients' suffering is great. Nurses work full-time, 12 hour shifts. Volunteer support counselors see the patients daily in and out of the hospital. All research physicians see patients clinically.

Because of the patients' length of stay, the amount of visits by families and friends, and the time commitment of the staff, all see a great deal of one another. The ward is a home away from home, cleaner than any other in the hospital and decorated with donated artwork. "Normalizing" has been made a cornerstone of treatment. Patient rooms are filled with personal mementos; some even with coffee tables and rugs. The centrally located conference room, that on other wards is for "staff only," is the hub of the ward. A large table covered with a fresh cloth dominates the scene. The refrigerator is stocked with snacks, and coffee and tea are available. At one end of the room are stacked cases of soft drinks, a television set, and a videocassette recorder donated by the police department.

The room is shared by staff and patients except during two change-of-shift reports each day and the nurses' twice weekly support group meeting led by the ward psychiatrist. Physicians, nurses, and counselors review and write on charts, and patients and visitors sit and talk. New interns do their chartwork at the ward desks initially. Sooner or later, however, everyone uses the conference room, checking there first on entering the ward to learn the newest information or to give it. Patients frequently visit between admissions and tell how they are caring for themselves at home or the results of their latest laboratory tests. More often than not, food is on the table for all, leading to the impression that the distance created by gowning and gloving for some procedures is counterbalanced by the staff's willingness to break bread with the patient.

The devastating consequences of AIDS diseases have forced people to reconceptualize the boundaries of nursing and medical care. Many new tasks have been thrust upon AIDS workers: public relations, speaking to the press, talking to morticians, consulting with other health institutions, helping families cope with a son's coming out as gay *and* with his dying. Some tasks are even more difficult: talking with a patient about designating power-of-attorney and making a living will to ensure that he will not be "coded" (resuscitated) if he becomes terminal. The staff feels that their sensitive interactions can only take place in a hospital and community atmosphere of warmth and caring. The prevailing ethic is that staff members reveal themselves and their emotions to patients and to each other. Everyone is expected to tell one's own diagnosis and plan, and one's reactions and feelings. Few taboos are found. One taboo is not being open to giving and receiving emotional support. The notion that to "come out" with one's feelings provides personal health and well-being stems from the gay participants' desire to normalize AIDS care and from the therapeutic-community approach pervading the nurses' orientation.

All staff have adopted "normalizing," sharing "feelings," and the notion of a therapeutic community. One physician gave a weekly running commentary during the formal care conferences regarding the trials and tribulations of a neighbor's struggles with AIDS, his family, his lover, and their negotiating with the health care delivery system. Such a case account was informative for all the assembled colleagues and served as an implicit reminder of the human needs of the patients and of the emotional needs of the staff in their care of dying patients, patients who had become friends. The following comments of a number of nurses who talked to us about their experiences with the patients illustrate the social-psychological nature of the work:

> We have taken a totally different approach because we get involved with our patients and still maintain our professional relationships. To have a patient like _____ [a man who had just visited] come in and visit everybody on the ward brings a lot of cheer and brings me a lot of humor. It's a reward, you look forward to it . . . . I think they really know that we care, that we want to know what is going on with them . . . . We touch them, we hug and kiss them, and sit down and listen to their woes since they've seen us last: "Guess what's happening in my life, my landlord is trying to kick me out, my family is having fits, my friends won't talk to me" . . . . We counsel them, we hook them up with other people who can help, we listen . . . . We get to know them very intimately. We really know them. And it's a wonderful feeling being known that way by someone.

Quite clearly, the staff finds rewards and the patients derive satisfactions for such care. A physician, self-described as one who always "avoided the psychiatric business at all costs," allowed that while the drug therapy investigation was exciting, the unexpected satisfaction had been becoming involved in holistic care in collaboration with nurses, counselors, and others sharing an equal level of interest. For all concerned, the social closeness demanded by the work mitigates the physical distance demanded by anti-contamination procedures.

The Ideology of Sentimental Work in AIDS Care

"Success" in AIDS care relies more on the application of sentiment than of technology. Strauss and associates (1982) have described seven types of sentimental work done by health professionals in the technologized hospital; some of this work is done on the AIDS ward. Interaction that promotes *personal identity* and *awareness* of the patient's cues regarding his readiness to discuss dying (Strauss et al. 1982:263–265) are two types of sentimental work prominent on the AIDS ward. Strauss and associates touch on another type of sentimental work in the hospital: interaction concerning the breaking of moral rules. Their theoretical concern is the violation of the small, almost implicit everyday moral rules that govern interaction. Violation of these moral rules frequently occurs in hospitals (for instance, health professionals being brusque, leaving without warning, or interrupting another's conversation). They point out that this situation necessitates that staff orient the patient to the hospital culture and give warnings and explanations, a type of sentimental work (1982:258–259).

The question of violating moral rules surfaces in AIDS care not only in a person-to-person way, for people with AIDS are subject to the potential insensitivities of hospital culture and routine much like any other patient, but in terms of the perceived influence of the larger moral order of society. The presence of AIDS is a reminder of stigmatized status that in some quarters of heterosexual (straight) society is seen as a violation of the moral order. Our data are replete with examples of the continuing presence of this moral context. An infection control nurse, who telephoned from another hospital for advice that she could give to reluctant hospital plumbers, relayed the plumbers' comment, "It's not really being afraid of getting AIDS, but if you got it everybody would know you were gay." Such responses reflect public concern over *social* contamination in much the same way as do debates over whether gay persons shall be allowed to be scout troop leaders or school teachers (cf., Bancroft and Shilts 1984; Grieg 1983).[3] This powerful social context is quite simply ever pervasive and presents a barrier that must be symbolically broken by AIDS workers if care is to be seen as "humanistic" and "holistic." The patient's personal identity can only be protected and preserved if that identity is seen as legitimate, and one significant aspect of identity is the patient's gayness. Thus, AIDS workers must either suspend the ordinary moral rules or actively assert that those rules are wrong. Under either condition, carrying out sentimental work becomes possible. In the case of the former, the staff member is apt to make a comment such as the following: "I'm not here to judge . . . . It is a privilege working here. The work is personal and you can get involved with the patient and family." In the case of the latter, the comments of one gay, male worker are illustrative: "I want to take care of these men. They are friends and brothers . . . . Any fear I have doesn't come from working here, it comes from being a gay male in our society. There is a great deal of fear in doctors and nurses [elsewhere]. I worked [in other places] before the unit was set up and I saw some awful things." Thus, whether staff suspend the moral rules, or, attempt to rewrite the meaning system, an ideological

---

[3]We are indebted to Robert Dingwall for pointing out this feature of social contamination.

position is taken. Furthermore, whether or not persons were recruited into the work with this point of view matters little; in order to carry out sentimental work, they become converted.

To meet psychosocial needs, to do identity work, family work, or any type of sentimental work, the patients (and their milieu) must be socially *decontaminated*. In the social decontamination process, the putative AIDS agent is believed by the outside world to disappear in the face of warm and caring social interaction. Roth found that when staff in the TB hospital socialized with patients they never wore masks or assumed other protection against contagion, leading Roth to comment that there seemed to be a widespread belief that the tubercle bacillus works during business hours (1957:314).[4] The comments of an infection control nurse working with AIDS illustrate our intuitive human appreciation of the increasing psychological distance that elaborative protective clothing creates. She noted that she discourages nurses throughout the hospital from wearing masks while caring for AIDS patients on their wards: "They don't need them because it's not an airborne infection, but they really shouldn't wear them because covering the mouth cuts off communication and makes the patient feel isolated and even more alone."

Staff in the TB hospital sometimes dropped contagion control measures in order to get the work done (Roth 1957: 310). This is also the situation in the AIDS ward: barriers are dropped in order to get the work done. The work, however, is expressly "sentimental," as Strauss et al. described in the "technologized hospital" (1982). A third explanatory concept, *ideology*, surfaces from the AIDS data. Without a belief system, one means by which practitioners explain to each other and to outsiders the importance of the object of their work, and therefore their work, could not be effectively communicated.

DISCUSSION AND CONCLUSION

Knowledge about AIDS has grown substantially in the past year, and the professionals at the hospital have made a major contribution. But much, including the risk of contagion in AIDS care, remains unexplained. The passage of time offers reassurance. As of August 1984, the Centers for

---

[4]Further illustrating the relationship between physical and social barriers, Lessor found in a field study of the tuberculosis hospital that when hospital staff wished to emphasize their social distance from nonwhite, poor, and otherwise "deviant" patients, they took great pains to establish physical barriers; furthermore, wearing masks (or more often, making the patient wear a mask) bore no relationship to the patient's established degree of contagion (whether or not he or she had a positive sputum for tubercle bacillus) (Lessor 1969).

Disease Control (CDC) in Atlanta report that "so far there have been no known cases of acquired immunodeficiency syndrome (AIDS) being transmitted to health care workers who are involved in the care of AIDS patients" (*American Nurse* 1984:23). The statistics are encouraging to workers, in spite of the lack of medical certainty. As one medical researcher heavily involved in clinical work with people with AIDS remarked, "Let's face it, we really don't know how much at risk we are . . . . you don't really start out by thinking about it in those terms. You see a couple of patients, your involvement grows, the patient load goes up, and before you know what happened, you're into it . . . . you didn't really plan it. Now you've probably been as exposed as you possibly can be anyway." Similarly, the nurses who staff the AIDS ward, in spite of all their advance planning, were at times surprised in the early months to find themselves in the midst of so much physical disease and patients needing so much bodily care, the reminder of potential contagion. Our individual interviews confirm that at times staff think about risks and may become briefly fearful for reasons they cannot always articulate. Their responses are not unlike those of other workers exposed to risk. Flight attendants reported in answer to questions about fear of crashing, "Well, sometimes you just have a 'squirrelly' [uneasy] day, but you're on the ride, you just see it through" (Lessor 1982). Similarly, these professionals working with people with AIDS have chosen their path of work, and the work is sufficiently exciting and rewarding for them to "see it through." Occasionally, specific instances may elicit staff fear, such as an accidental puncture from a needle used on a patient. Nurses and doctors have reported that they did what they could—"made it bleed," "prayed," "had faith"—but also relied on their knowledge that getting stuck with needles has always been an occupational hazard and therefore one that other AIDS workers throughout the country must have been exposed to for some time.

The point we want to emphasize is that AIDS workers certainly think about personal risk on occasion; they do so to the same extent that anyone whose job presents risk thinks of it. For the most part, people are too busy doing the job to be absorbed in much else, and the job here is providing care to people with AIDS. Although, as we have seen, effort is directed toward research and testing, "success" with patients is measured in terms of creating a network of care—teaching self-care, providing home care, training a variety of community workers and volunteers to help, bolstering the patient's social network of friends and mending family ties to provide support, and making the way for the patient's dignified death. Politics and ideology are essential ingredients in creating conditions that make the work possible. Politically, AIDS workers have leveraged power, often that of their professional expertise, in order to get what they needed to carry out their work. Moreover, an ideological position that asserts the patient's humanness relies on the removal of ascriptions of stigma or "social contamination." In the course of expunging social contamination, staff have likely disregarded all concern for contagion.

Roth observed that seemingly irrational procedures in TB care grew out of "man's" uncertainties regarding the laws of nature. The ritual and magic were "man's laws." We are no more certain of nature's laws with respect to AIDS, and, in addition, we experience conflict and doubt over society's norms regarding homosexuality. In the context of these uncertainties, "man's laws," to use Roth's term, may be ideological and political as well as ritualistic and magical.

ACKNOWLEDGMENTS

This study was partially funded by a Biomedical Research Support Grant to Roberta Lessor, principal investigator. We wish to thank the staff and volunteers associated with the AIDS ward at the hospital for their invaluable assistance in making the study possible.

REFERENCES

The American Nurse. 1984. No Known Cases of AIDS Transmitted to Health Care Workers. *American Nurse*. July/August: 23.

Bancroft, Ann and Randy Shilts. 1984. Gay Job Rights Bill Vetoed: Law Not Needed, Governor Says. *San Francisco Chronicle*, March 14, p. 1.

Berger, Peter L. 1964a. Some General Observations on the Problem of Work. In *The Human Shape of Work: Studies in the Sociology of Occupations*, Peter Berger, ed. South Bend, Ind.: Gateway Editions, Ltd.

———. 1964b. *The Human Shape of Work*. New York: Macmillan.

Centers for Disease Control. 1982. Acquired Immunodeficiency Syndrome: Precautions for Clinical and Laboratory Staffs. *Morbidity and Mortality Weekly Reports* 31: 577–579.

———. 1983. Nosocomial Transmission of AIDS. *Morbidity and Mortality Weekly Reports*, July 15.

Clavreul, Genevieve. 1983. An Evaluation of "AIDS Apprehension" Among Nursing Personnel and its Observed Effects on Level of Patient Care. Unpublished paper presented at the National Clinical Nursing Conference on Acquired Immune Deficiency Syndrome (A.I.D.S.). Bethesda, Maryland, October 7.

Collier, Peter, and David Horowitz. 1983. Whitewash. *California Magazine*, pp. 52–57, July.

Department of Health and Human Services. 1983. *Facts About AIDS*. Washington, D.C.: United States Public Health Service, September.

Dingwall, Robert, and Jean McIntosh. 1978. *Readings in the Sociology of Nursing*. Edinburgh: Churchill Livingstone.

Faulkner, Robert T. 1974. Coming of Age in Organizations: A Comparative Study of Contingencies and Adult Socialization. *Sociology of Work and Occupations* I: 131–173.

Feldman, Douglas A. 1984. Social Change and the AIDS Epidemic. Unpublished paper presented at the Society for Applied Anthropology, Toronto, Canada, March.

Gallup, George. 1983. Americans Fear Spread of AIDS. *San Francisco Chronicle,* July 7.

Glaser, Barney G. 1978. *Theoretical Sensitivity: Advances in the Methodology of Grounded Theory.* Mill Valley, Cal.: The Sociology Press.

Glaser, Barney G. and Anselm L. Strauss. 1967. *The Discovery of Grounded Theory: Strategies for Qualitative Research.* Chicago: Aldine Publishing Company.

Grieg, Michael. 1983. Big Vote for Gay Rights: 2-to-1 Backing from Callers. *San Francisco Chronicle,* February 23.

Lessor, Roberta. 1969. Deviant Behavior and Personal Identity in the Tuberculosis Hospital. Master's thesis, School of Nursing, University of California, Los Angeles.

————. 1982. Unanticipated Longevity in Women's Work: The Career Development of Airline Flight Attendants. Doctoral dissertation, Sociology Program, University of California, San Francisco.

————. 1984. Social Movements, the Occupational Arena and Changes in Career Consciousness: The Case of Women Flight Attendants. *Journal of Occupational Behavior* 5:37–51.

Roth, Julius. 1957. Ritual and Magic in the Control of Contagion. *American Sociological Review* 22:310–314.

Shilts, Randy. 1984. Life on Ward 5B. *San Francisco Chronicle,* "This World" section, p. 9, January 15.

Strauss, Anselm, Shizuko Fagerhaugh, Barbara Suczek, and Carolyn Wiener. 1982. Sentimental Work in the Technologized Hospital. *Sociology of Health and Illness* 4(3):254–278.

USA Today. 1983. AIDS Threat. *USA Today,* p. 10A, April 4.

Wood, Jim. 1983. Outcast in the Jury Box: An AIDS Victim's Ordeal of Prejudice, Ignorance and Panic. *San Francisco Examiner,* June 26.

Conclusion

Douglas A. Feldman and Thomas M. Johnson

Gay men and anxiety about AIDS. Haitian voodoo. New needles for IV-drug users. Media-induced panic over AIDS. Hospice care for advanced AIDS patients. AIDS health education. Clearly, one message prevails in this volume: it is that AIDS is by no means just a medical problem. The inquiry into a search for its origins, an understanding of the cultural and psychosocial determinants and effects of the disease, and possibly even a search for a cure require a truly interdisciplinary approach. Biomedical researchers must work with medical sociologists, medical anthropologists, psychologists, social workers, and other social scientists and public health researchers to facilitate a comprehensive understanding of AIDS epidemiology, prevention, and health care.

A major problem in AIDS research has been inadequate or misallocated funding. Before television, newspapers, and radio informed and frightened the U.S. public in May 1983 with the possibility that AIDS could be contracted by heterosexuals, little public funding for AIDS research was available, with virtually nothing available for sociomedical research. After the publicity about AIDS, the federal government funded AIDS biomedical research by moving budget allocations out of existing health programs, such as herpes surveillance and childhood immunization, and into AIDS (Westmoreland 1984). Indeed, in fiscal year 1985, federal spending for psychological and social factors of AIDS amounted to a meager 2.1% of the $92.8 million actually spent (*New York Times* 1985). Certainly, many more dollars need to be allocated for cultural and psychosocial AIDS research.

AIDS is perhaps the most complex and intriguing medical mystery of the century. As more pieces of this giant jigsaw puzzle are found, we see more clearly the enormity of the puzzle. AIDS has given medicine the opportunity to learn more about immunity and retroviruses in a few short years than it otherwise would have in decades. If isoprinosine proves successful as a treatment for immunosuppression, when used in conjunction with interferon or perhaps another immunomodulator, then the lowered T-cell ratios of ARC and possibly less advanced AIDS could be returned to normal.

AIDS has also given the social and behavioral scientist the opportunity to learn more about the gay community (a population that has had a major impact upon social relations in the United States and other developed nations, especially within the past two decades), IV-drug users, stigmatized illness, Haitian-American health and Haitian religious and medicinal practices, traditional medicine in Central Africa, hospital health care, hospice care, sexual behavior, social change, and psychological counseling for at-risk individuals and seriously ill patients.

Regrettably, AIDS is unlikely to be eradicated very soon. Quite simply, lives are at stake. The ways in which we respond to the challenge of AIDS in the late 1980s will be crucial in shaping the direction of the disease and in forming the foundation for all other future interdisciplinary, health-related research.

REFERENCES

New York Times. 1985. Where the Money Goes. *New York Times*, June 2, p.6E.
Westmoreland, Tim. 1984. Can Research Be Mobilized in Response to a Health Crisis? Unpublished paper presented at American Association for the Advancement of Sciences meeting, New York, May 26.

Index

263

About the Editors and Contributors

THE EDITORS

Douglas A. Feldman received his Ph.D. in Anthropology from the State University of New York at Stony Brook. He is currently teaching Anthropology in the Department of Degree Studies of New York University and is a Research Associate at the Human Relations Area Files of Yale University. He has taught Anthropology and Medical Anthropology courses since 1974 at John Jay College of Criminal Justice, Marymount Manhattan College, and other colleges and universities in the New York area. Dr. Feldman conducted a study evaluating sexually transmitted disease health care on Long Island, NY in the late 1970s. Beginning in 1982, he conducted a study on behavioral change within the gay community of New York City as a response to the growing AIDS epidemic. He has frequently lectured on AIDS during the mid-1980s. He recently returned from a study of AIDS and traditional healers in central Africa.

Thomas M. Johnson, is Assistant Professor of Anthropology at Southern Methodist University and Clinical Assistant Professor of Psychiatry at the University of Texas Health Sciences Center – Dallas. As an applied medical anthropologist who has worked for the past ten years in community mental health and medical school settings, he has emphasized teaching in clinical settings, including supervision of medical students in obstetrics and gynecology, internal medicine, and psychiatry. Dr. Johnson has conducted research on strategies to reduce pain in burn care, the process of medical education, physician-patient interaction, and high-risk obstetrics. He has been a member of the Education Committee of the Association for the Behavioral Sciences and Medical Education and is the editor of the *Medical Anthropology Quarterly*, the official publication of the Society for Medical Anthropology.

THE CONTRIBUTORS

Edward Albert is an Assistant Professor in the Department of Sociology at Hofstra University. He specializes in the area of health and medicine and in the sociology of sport. He received his doctorate from York University, Toronto in 1978. His publications include articles in the areas of the social construction of medical emergencies, ethnomethodology and content analysis, and the construction of sport realities.

Andrea Baker is currently teaching sociology at Ohio University–Lancaster. Among her course offerings are social problems, sex roles, deviance, and social movements. Her interest in AIDS grew out of research into lesbian-feminist and gay liberation movements. As a field researcher, she has also studied agency responses to domestic violence. Dr. Baker continues to explore the images of social movements and social problems in the mass media, to understand the nature of media's role in the promotion or slowing of social change. An ongoing focus on the processes of leadership, recruitment and commitment in change-oriented organizations led to the 1982 publication of "The Problem of Authority in Radical Movement Groups: A Case Study of Lesbian-Feminist Organization" in the *Journal of Applied Behavioral Science*.

David V. Baker earned an M. A. in sociology from California State University, Northridge. He is currently a graduate student in the Department of Sociology at the University of California, Riverside, and is researching social psychological determinants of public attitudes toward the death penalty.

Laurie J. Bauman, Ph.D., is a medical sociologist whose work focuses on the relationship between stress, illness, coping and social support. She is a Senior Research Associate at Memorial Sloan-Kettering Cancer Center and holds an appointment as Research Staff Associate at the Graduate School of Business, Columbia University.

Diane Bolognone is a doctoral candidate in Medical Anthropology at Southern Methodist University and received her B.A. in Anthropology from the University of Texas at San Antonio. She is also a registered nurse and has experience in public health education in both the United States and South America. In addition, she has administered public health care in Colombia, South America. Since 1977, she has been involved with obstetrical care in Texas. She presently works as the editorial assistant of the *Medical Anthropology Quarterly*, a publication of the Society for Medical Anthropology.

Peter L. Callero is Assistant Professor of Sociology at the University of California, Riverside. He received his Ph.D. in sociology from the University of Wisconsin and is currently investigating the process of role commitment as it applies to the act of voluntary blood donation.

Jeannette Carpenter is a graduate student in the Department of Sociology at the University of California, Riverside where her current interest is the sociology of the deaf.

Virginia Casper is currently completing her doctoral training in developmental psychology at the Albert Einstein College of Medicine Campus/Ferkauf Graduate School of Yeshiva University. She specializes in infancy research at Babies Hospital/Columbia Presbyterian Medical Center in New York City.

William W. Darrow, Ph.D., was awarded his doctoral degree in sociology by Emory University in 1973. He has been a member of the CDC Task Force on AIDS since its inception, and now is Research Sociologist, AIDS Branch, Division of Viral Diseases, Center for Infectious Diseases, Centers for Disease Control, Atlanta, Georgia.

Don C. Des Jarlais, Ph.D., is the Assistant Deputy Director for Research of the New York State Division of Substance Abuse Services, and principal investigator for the Risk Factors for AIDS among Intravenous Drug Users study. His training is in social psychology and epidemiology. He has conducted a wide range of studies in drug abuse, including program evaluation, ethnographic and historical research.

Robin Flam, MPH; Affiliate of the G. H. Sergievsky Center at Columbia University, Epidemiologist at the Westchester County Health Department. Most of her work has been in reproductive epidemiology, and on severe childhood disability. She is presently a doctoral candidate at the Columbia University School of Public Health in Epidemiology.

Samuel R. Friedman, Ph.D., is a sociologist who has written a number of articles on the epidemiology of AIDS among drug users. He is currently Project Director and co-principal investigator of a study of AIDS among IV drug users being conducted at Narcotic and Drug Research, Inc. His previous work includes a book on labor activism and articles on economic sociology and political sociology.

Ruth Fuller, M.D., F. A. P. A., is an assistant professor of psychiatry at the University of Colorado Health Sciences Center where she practices psychiatry, child psychiatry and psychoanalysis. She is also a consultant in psychiatric education to the National Institutes of Mental Health. She is a member of numerous professional organizations including the American Psychiatric Association, American Psychoanalytic Association, Black Psychiatrists of America and the American Academy of Child Psychiatry. In the past, Dr. Fuller served as psychiatric director of the James Weldon Johnson Family and Children's Counselling Center (East Harlem, NY), as adjunct visiting lecturer at the School of Social Work of Columbia University, and as clinical instructor in psychiatry at the Downstate Medical Center, State University of New York.

Sally Geis, Ph.D., is a clinical associate professor of psychiatry at the University of Colorado Health Sciences Center where she is involved in sociological research. She is also an adjunct professor at the University of Colorado Denver Center and at the San Francisco Theological Seminary in California. She serves as a consultant to the Hospice of Metro Denver and to the Federation of Patients and Friends of Lesbians and Gays, Inc. Dr. Geis received her Ph.D. from the University of Denver, holds numerous civic and governmental appointments, has coauthored a book and written a number of articles. She has served as chair of the Sociology/Anthropology Department at Colorado Women's College.

Brad P. Glick, M.P.H., entered the Master's of Public Health Program, Emory University School of Medicine, after completing his undergraduate studies at Emory. His thesis was on the social correlates of AIDS.

E. Michael Gorman, Ph.D., M.P.H., received his doctoral degree in anthropology from the University of Chicago in 1979, and his master's degree in public health from the University of California, Berkeley, in 1982. After completing a post-doctoral fellowship in the Department of Epidemiology at the University of California, San Francisco, he joined the Center of Health Promotion and Education, Centers for Disease Control, as an Epidemic Intelligence Service Officer in 1983.

Katarin Jurich received her master's degree in public health from the University of California, Berkeley in 1980 and is currently a doctoral candidate in sociology at the University of California, San Francisco. Her major research interests include medical sociology and health policy. She has conducted research in the field of energy conservation and has done extensive fieldwork on American Indian reservations in the Midwest.

Joseph A. Kotarba is associate professor and director of graduate studies in sociology at the University of Houston—University Park. He received his Ph.D. from the University of California at San Diego. In addition to his interest in the social psychology of the AIDS phenomenon, he is conducting research on the corporate wellness movement and the social organization of aerospace medicine. His most recent book is *The Existential Self in Society* (University of Chicago Press).

Norris G. Lang is assistant professor and director of graduate studies in anthropology at the University of Houston—University Park. He received his Ph.D. from the University of Illinois at Urbana. In addition to his interest in the anthropology of the AIDS phenomenon, he is currently conducting research on homophobia and sexual compulsivity in the gay community. His previous work dealt largely with the economic anthropology of plantation systems in Ecuador.

Ronald D. Le Baron holds the DDS and an MS in cellular and molecular biology from the University of Southern California, where he is Clinical Assistant Professor of Microbiology and Immunology in the School of Dentistry. He practices dentistry in Hollywood, and is a member of the Scientific Advisory Committee of the L.A. City/County AIDS Task Force.

Roberta Lessor teaches in the Department of Sociology at Chapman College (Orange, CA). She received her Ph.D. in sociology from the University of California, San Francisco in 1982 and has directed research on occupations and work organizations, occupational health and medical sociology. She has published on women's work and women's health in the workplace. She also holds a master's degree in nursing from UCLA and serves as a consultant to nursing organizations.

Jane Magarigal is a graduate student in the Department of Sociology at the University of California, Riverside where her current interest is political sociology.

Alexander Moore, Ph.D., a social anthropologist, was educated at Harvard and Columbia. He has done field work in highland Guatemala and in the San Blas islands of Panama. He has taught at Emory, University of Florida, and the University of Southern California, where he is currently chairman of the Anthropology Department. He is the author of three books and numerous articles.

Karolynn Siegel, Ph.D., is Director of Research in the Department of Social Work at Memorial Sloan-Kettering Cancer Center. A clinical sociologist, Dr. Siegel is also Associate Research Professor in Psychiatry at New York Medical College and Assistant Professor of Sociology in Public Health at Cornell University Medical College. She is also in private practice in psychoanalytic psychotherapy.

Zena Stein, MA, MB: Director of the Epidemiology of Brain Disorders Research Department at the New York State Psychiatric Institute, and Professor of Public Health (Epidemiology) at the Columbia University School of Public Health. She has had extensive work in reproductive and cross-cultural epidemiology.

David Strug, Ph.D., M.P.H., is an anthropologist and an alcohol and drug researcher. He is currently carrying out a study of alcohol use among New York City Hispanics. He is a Research Associate at the Hispanic Research Center of Fordham University in the Bronx.

Lydia Temoshok, Ph.D. is Assistant Professor in the Department of Psychiatry and the Langley Porter Psychiatric Institute at the University of California, San Francisco. She received her Ph.D. in both clinical and social psychology from the University of Michigan in Ann Arbor, where she held a National Science Foundation Fellowship. She is Coordinator of the Clinical Health Psychology Cluster in the Clinical Psychology Training Program, and is a faculty member in the Consultation–Liaison Psychiatry Service, the Behavioral Medicine Unit of the Division of General Program. She is coeditor of the UCSF Mind and Medicine Series, published by Grune & Stratton, and senior editor of the first volume in that series. Dr. Temoshok has published in the areas of psychosocial oncology, somatoform disorders, and emotion. Her most recent research interests include the psychoimmunological aspects of malignant melanoma and of AIDS.

Jane Zich, Ph.D. is currently completing an Individual National Research Service Award fellowship at the University of California, San Francisco with an emphasis on clinical services research. She received her Ph.D. in Clinical Psychology from Arizona State University. Dr. Zich has published in the areas of depression and the treatment of suicidal patients. Her current research and clinical interests include depression among medical patients, adjustments to illness and major life events, and the psychoimmunologic aspects of AIDS.